Anonymous

The Postage Stamps, Envelopes, Wrappers, Post Cards, and

Telegraph Stamps

of the British colonies in the West Indies together with British Honduras and the

colonies in South America

Anonymous

The Postage Stamps, Envelopes, Wrappers, Post Cards, and Telegraph Stamps
of the British colonies in the West Indies together with British Honduras and the colonies in South America

ISBN/EAN: 9783337317515

Printed in Europe, USA, Canada, Australia, Japan

Cover: Foto ©Andreas Hilbeck / pixelio.de

More available books at **www.hansebooks.com**

THE

POSTAGE STAMPS,

Enbelopes, Wrappers, Post Cards, and Telegraph Stamps,

OF

THE BRITISH COLONIES IN THE WEST INDIES,

TOGETHER WITH

BRITISH HONDURAS

AND

THE COLONIES IN SOUTH AMERICA.

With Thirty-two Sheets of Autotype Illustrations.

COMPILED AND PUBLISHED

BY

THE PHILATELIC SOCIETY, LONDON.

LONDON, 1891.

PREFACE

THE Reference Lists of the Stamps of the various West Indian and other Colonies comprised in the present work were revised and completed (so far as was possible at that time) by the Philatelic Society of London more than twelve months ago. Various circumstances have combined to induce the Committee appointed to superintend their publication to postpone the actual production of the work. The Society had recently received from Mr. Basset Hull, the manuscript of his elaborate treatise upon the stamps of Tasmania, and it was thought best to at once revise and publish his catalogue in priority to the West Indies lists, although the latter were immediately in hand at the time. The labour and expense necessary to the production of the "autotype" illustrations of the one Catalogue, would alone have occasioned delay in proceeding with the other, but this was not the only reason which has compelled the Committee to ask for some indulgence at the hands of the Society and the Philatelic public.

None but those who have worked, and been in constant intercourse, with the late Vice-President of the Society, Mr. Thomas K. Tapling, can at all appreciate how severe was the blow dealt, how essential the prop displaced, by his untimely death in the zenith of his career of useful labour in the pursuit of Philately. Within comparatively but a few days of his death he was actively engaged in the final revision of the British Guiana reference list, and in elucidating the details and difficulties attaching to that Colony, which, even after the careful work of the Society, still presented themselves to the Committee. It was natural, and the Committee feel that but little apology is due for such a result, that the loss of so valuable a coadjutor, whose hand had been a master hand in this as in previous works of the Society, should delay the production of so important a treatise.

The invaluable assistance rendered under the critical circumstances above referred to by the late Secretary to the Society, Mr. E. D. Bacon, deserves grateful acknowledgment by his colleagues on the Committee. His careful and untiring labours cannot be too highly appreciated, and the short "Preliminary Notes" from his pen, introductory to the reference list of each Colony, together with the unique example of elaborate research displayed in his Paper on the Stamps of British Guiana, must alone tend to render the present work acceptable and noteworthy amongst Philatelic publications.

The method of illustration by the "autotype" process has again been adopted, and it is hoped to some extent with satisfactory results. It is obviously not equally suitable in all cases, but it must be acknowledged that the method of reproduction, by what is practically a system of photography, of the actual stamp, is preferable to the very best illustration by engraving, which can only purport to depict a copy, however exact, of the original design. The majority of the stamps so reproduced in illustration of these lists have been, as on former occasions, lent for the purpose by the late Mr. Tapling.

It may be observed, that in all cases where, throughout the following pages, dates are assigned to any issues of stamps at variance with those long recognised and accepted in former Catalogues or Philatelic literature, the grounds and authorities, on which the Society base their present information, will invariably be found in Mr. E. D. Bacon's "Preliminary Notes."

When describing postcards, it should be noted that the term *light buff* is employed when the card is of a brownish hue, but the word *straw* is used in contradistinction when the card is of a lighter shade.

There remains only to add that the lists will be found completed down to the end of 1890.

DOUGLAS GARTH,
Secretary, Phil. Soc., London.

LIST OF ABBREVIATIONS.

T.	Top.
B.	Bottom.
R.	Right.
L.	Left.
C.	Cent or cents.
d.	Penny or pence.
s.	Shilling or shillings.
$	Dollar or dollars.
£	Pound.
Perf,	Perforated.
in.	Inches.
Mm.	Millimètres.

ANTIGUA.

PRELIMINARY NOTES.

By E. D. BACON.

BEFORE making a few remarks upon the stamps of Antigua, I wish to say how much I am indebted to Messrs. Perkins Bacon and Co., Limited, for the information they have furnished me with, not only concerning the stamps of this Colony, but also respecting those of all the other islands of the British West Indies printed by their company. I feel under a special obligation to Mr. James D. Heath, the Managing Director, and Mr. Alfred Bacon, the Secretary, for the trouble they have constantly taken, searching through old account books, letters, &c., in order to procure me as full and complete replies as possible, to the various lists of questions I have handed them at different times. I tender these gentlemen my sincere thanks for their kindness, and I acknowledge with gratitude the invariable courtesy I have met with from all the other officers of the company I have come in contact with.

Antigua has never possessed an *Official Gazette*, but Government notices are now published in *The Gazette of the Leeward Islands*, together with those relating to the other five Colonies composing that group. As the latter publication gives no postal information peculiar to the various islands, I am unable to give any particulars of the stamps of Antigua from that source.

The plates of the one penny and six pence, constructed by Messrs. Perkins Bacon and Co., were of steel, and each contained 120 stamps, arranged in ten horizontal rows of twelve. These plates were handed over to the Crown Agents on the 23rd November, 1871, and afterwards given to Messrs. De la Rue and Co., who have since printed all further stamps required by the Colony. Proof impressions in black upon white card, struck from the engraved dies of the one penny and six pence are known. It is most probable that the six pence was issued some months earlier than the one penny, as the first supply of the former value was forwarded on July 1st, 1862, while the first consignment of the latter was only despatched on December 12th of that year. A note in one of Messrs. Perkins Bacon and Co.'s books states, that the first supply of the six pence printed in June, 1862, was upon *plain* paper, that with *star watermark* being used for the first time on November 7th in the same year.

REFERENCE LIST OF THE PHILATELIC SOCIETY, LONDON.

Issue I. 1862.

One value. Printed in *taille-douce*, by Messrs. Perkins Bacon and Co., of London. Coloured impression on medium white wove unwatermarked paper. Yellowish gum. machine perforated 15. Design: Diademed profile of Queen Victoria, to left. Above and below are straight labels of solid colour, which do not reach to the sides of the stamp, inscribed with the name of the Colony and the value in words, in white block letters. The background of the stamp is composed of nine vertical bands of reticulations in which two patterns alternate. Two plain coloured lines compose the border and complete the design. Shape, upright rectangular. *(Illustration 1.)*

T. "ANTIGUA." B. "SIX PENCE."
6d., deep green.

Issue II.   January (?), 1863.

Two values. Printed in *taille douce*, by Messrs. Perkins Bacon and Co., of London. Coloured impression on white wove paper varying much in substance, watermarked with a six-rayed star. Yellowish gum. Both values are of the same design, which is that of issue I. *(Illustration 1.)*

T. "ANTIGUA." B. "ONE PENNY." "SIX PENCE."

A.—*Imperforate.*
1d., lilac-rose.
6d., yellow-green.

B.—*Machine perforated* 14, 14½, 15, 15½ *compound.*
1d., lilac-rose, rose, orange-vermilion (shades of each).
6d., deep green, yellow-green (shades of each).

C.—*Imperforate vertically.*
1d., orange-vermilion.

Remarks.—Unsevered pairs of the one penny and six pence imperforate, are known.

In 1874 some correspondence took place in the columns of the *Stamp Collector's Magazine*, pages 63, 95, and 110, as to certain varieties of watermark that had been noticed in the early issues of Antigua. It appears that the first watermarked stamps had the "star" with one point up, and that during the issue of the one penny in orange-vermilion, the paper was watermarked with a star with two points up. Except for enabling a collector to determine the approximate date of a particular specimen, the fact appears to be of small importance. The theory of "A London Collector," that there were two *plates* used for watermarking the paper, or that the "stars" were turned when the plates were cleaned, was conclusively disproved by "A Parisian Collector," who showed (page 111) that *plates* are never used for watermarking paper. He remarks, "the presence of a watermark in the paper is simply due to a design worked into the web of the wire network over which the pulp passes, or on which it spreads itself when in a liquid state." It is possible that there may have been two such wire frames employed, but, in any case, those varieties, while deserving perhaps of passing mention, do not appear to the Society to be more worth cataloguing than the numerous varieties of inverted watermarks, etc., which may be found in many other countries.

Issue III. 1873.

Two values. Printed by Messrs. De la Rue and Co., of London, on slightly surfaced white wove paper of stoutish substance, watermarked Crown C.C. White gum. The stamps are the same in design as those of Issue II., and were printed from the same plates. (*Illustration* 1.)

A.—*Perforated* 12½.

1d., red-lake, orange-vermilion (shades of each).
6d., light and dark green (shades).

B.—*Perforated* 14.

1d., red-lake, orange-vermilion (shades of each).
6d., deep green (shades) very dark green.

Varieties. *a.* The six pence exists without watermark, perforated 11½ top and bottom, and 14 at the sides. The date when this variety was in use has not been ascertained. *b.* In 1883 the one penny was divided in half either vertically or diagonally for use as a halfpenny value.

½d., (right half 1d.) red-lake.
½d., (left   ,,   ,,)   ,,

Issue IV. 1879.

Two values. Designed and surface printed by Messrs. De la Rue and Co., of London. Coloured impression on surfaced white wove paper, watermarked Crown C.C. White gum, machine perforated 14. Design : Diademed profile of Queen Victoria to left, on ground of horizontal lines within a single lined octagon. Straight white labels above and below inscribed with name of Colony and value in coloured block numerals and letters. Side labels of colour with a vertical row of sixteen small white lozenges down the centre. In the spandrels, triangular coloured blocks with white floriate ornaments. Border composed of a single coloured line. Shape upright rectangular. (*Illustrations* 2, 3.)

A. "ANTIGUA."   B. "2½ PENNY."   "FOUR PENCE."

2½d., red-brown (shades).
4d., blue   (,,   )

Issue V. 1882.

Three values. Precisely the same in design as the preceding issue, printed upon the same paper, but with the watermark changed to Crown C.A. The perforation remains 14. (*Illustrations* 2, 3.)

½d., pale green (shades).
2½d., red-brown (,,   )
4d., blue   (,,   )

Issue VI. 1884.

One value. The one penny of issue III., with the watermark changed to Crown C.A. Machine perforated. (*Illustration* 1.)

A.—*Perforated* 12.
1d., bright red.
B.—*Perforated* 14.
1d., rose red.

Issue VII. 1885.

One value. The six pence of Issue III., with the watermark changed to Crown C.A. Perforated 14. (*Illustration* 1.)

6d., deep green.

Issue VIII. 1886.

Three values. Similar in design to Issue IV., but the colours are changed and a new value, one shilling, is added. The watermark is Crown C.A. and the perforation 14. (*Illustrations* 2, 3.)

2½d., ultramarine (shades).
4d., red-brown   („)
1s., lilac   („)

FISCALS USED FOR POSTAGE.

M. Moens catalogues the one penny "Stamp Duty" adhesive, as having been employed in 1885 for postal use, but no satisfactory postmarked specimen is known to the Society. The same stamp may be found with the lower label surcharged in two straight lines, POSTAGE and REVENUE in thin black block letters, and the words STAMP DUTY at the bottom of the stamp, struck through with a thin black bar. (*Illustration* 4.) The surcharge was applied in Europe and the stamp sold as a *soi-disant* provisional issued in 1885. No variety of this kind was ever in use in Antigua.

POSTCARDS.

Issue I. End of 1879.

One value. Designed and printed by Messrs. De la Rue and Co. upon medium light buff card. Size 121×87 mm. or 4⅘×3¾ inches. The inscription, which is at the top of the card, is in four straight lines as follows :—1st, UNION POSTALE UNIVERSELLE ; 2nd, ANTIGUA (ANTIGOA) ; 3rd, POST CARD, the two words being separated by the arms and supporters of Great Britain ; 4th, THE ADDRESS ONLY TO BE WRITTEN ON THIS SIDE. The first and fourth lines are in small block letters, the second in Roman capitals, and the third in large fancy capitals. The stamp, which is similar in design to the adhesives issued at the same date, occupies the right upper corner. The card is without frame. (*Illustration* 5.)

1¼d. light brown (shades).

Issue II. 1886.

Two values. Designed and printed by Messrs. De la Rue and Co. upon stout straw card. Size 139×88 mm, or 5½×3½ inches. The inscription is similarly disposed to that on the preceding issue, and the type employed is the same. The stamp is in the right upper corner. Design : Diademed head of Queen Victoria to left upon ground of solid colour, enclosed within a circle. Straight labels of solid colour above and below the circle, the upper inscribed with the name of the colony, and the lower with the value in words in block letters. The spandrels contain conventional ornaments, and a thick outer line of colour completes the stamp. The cards have no frame. (*Illustration* 6.)

1d., carmine   (slight shades).
1¼d., dark brown („   „)

REPLY PAID CARDS.

Issue I. 1886.

Two values. Similar in every way to the single cards of Issue II., but the first half has the following additional inscription in four lines, in the left lower corner, in small block letters: THE ANNEXED CARD IS INTENDED—FOR THE ANSWER.—(LA CARTE CI-JOINTE EST DESTINÉE—À LA RÉPONSE.) The second half has the word REPLY, in Roman capitals, beneath THE ADDRESS ONLY, &c. The cards are joined along the top, perforated 4½, and the design is impressed upon the first and third pages. *(Illustration 7.)*

1d.+1d., carmine   (slight shades).
1½d.+1½d., red-brown (,,   ,,   )

Remarks.—The adhesives and cards of Antigua were withdrawn from circulation at the end of October, 1890, when a new set, inscribed "Leeward Islands," intended for use in the six Colonies composing this group, were issued in their place.

BAHAMAS.

PRELIMINARY NOTES.

By E. D. BACON.

As in the case of Antigua, I have very little new information I can add to the Reference List of the stamps of these Islands, compiled by the Society. The Colony has never possessed an *Official Gazette*, so I am unable to furnish copies of any notices giving dates of issue of the various values. Messrs. Perkins Bacon and Co. inform me they forwarded the first consignment of one penny stamps to the Islands on the 3rd May, 1859; so the date given by M. Moens, in his *Catalogue*, as June 10th of that year, is, no doubt, the correct one. The plates of the one penny, four pence, and six pence, constructed by Messrs. Perkins Bacon and Co., were of steel, and each contained 60 specimens in six horizontal rows of ten. The plates of the two higher values were each finished in October, 1861, and the first supply of these two stamps was sent out on November 27th of that year. It seems probable, therefore, that the issue took place either at the end of December, 1861, or early in January, 1862. M. Moens gives the issue as December 16th, 1861, but, taking into consideration the date at which the stamps were despatched, this barely allows, I think, sufficient time for their delivery in the Colony.

Proof impressions of all three values in black, taken from the plates, upon stout white card are known, and the one penny is also found upon India paper, and the four pence upon plain white paper. Proof impressions of each value in black, struck from the dies, upon stout white card, also exist.

The plates were handed over to the Crown agents on 28th January, 1862, and afterwards by them to Messrs. De la Rue and Co., who have since printed all further supplies of stamps required by the Colony.

REFERENCE LIST OF THE PHILATELIC SOCIETY, LONDON.

Issue I. June 10th, 1859.

One value. Engraved in *taille-douce*, and printed by Messrs. Perkins Bacon and Co., of London. Coloured impression on thin white transparent wove paper, or on thicker paper less transparent, yellowish gum, imperforate. Design: Diademed full face portrait of Queen Victoria, looking to left, on ground of horizontal and vertical crossed lines within a narrow double lined oval. At the top of the stamp is the name of the Colony, and at the bottom the value, in white block letters. Over the head is a white scroll inscribed in coloured block letters "INTERINSULAR POSTAGE."

On either side of the portrait medallion, just over the value, are white ovals, that on the left containing a pine-apple, and that on the right a conch shell. The remainder of the stamp is filled in with reticulations. Shape, upright rectangular. *(Illustration 8).*

T. "BAHAMAS." B. "ONE PENNY."

A.—*On thin transparent paper.*
    1d., rose-red (shades).

B.—*On thicker paper, less transparent.*
    1d., rose-red (shades).

Remarks.—This stamp, like some of the Ceylon and sundry other adhesives, varies in size from that upon the watermarked paper. The stamps were all printed from the same plate, and the difference in size is due to the various textures of paper employed.

Issue II. December, 1861.

Three values. Engraved in *taille-douce*, and printed by Messrs. Perkins Bacon and Co. Coloured impression on white wove paper varying in substance. Yellowish gum, perforated. Designs:—ONE PENNY, same as the preceding. FOUR PENCE and SIX PENCE, the portrait is the same as in the one penny value but for the addition of a necklace, and the oval frame is rather larger. Straight coloured labels at top and bottom inscribed with the name of the Colony, and the value in white block letters. White blocks in the four corners with coloured eight-rayed star with white centre. Narrow white scroll between the portrait medallion and the label of value, inscribed in coloured block letters POSTAGE. The background of the stamp is formed of twelve vertical bands of two alternating reticulated patterns. Shape upright rectangular. *(Illustrations 8, 9, 10.)*

T. "BAHAMAS." B. "ONE PENNY." "FOUR PENCE." "SIX PENCE."

A.—*Perf.* 14 to 16 compound.
    1d., rose-red, brownish-red (shades).
    4d., rose (shades).
    6d., dull lilac (shades).

B.—*Perf.* 12.
    1d., bright rose-red (shades).
    4d., pale and bright rose (shades).
    6d., lilac, grey-lilac (shades).

C.—*Perf.* 13.
    1d., rose-red, bright red, brownish-rose (shades).
    4d., pale and bright rose (shades).
    6d., lilac, grey-lilac (shades).

Variety. Perforated 11 top and bottom, 12 at the sides (signalled by Mr. C. B. Corwin.)
    1d., bright carmine.

Issue III. 1862-1875.

Four values. ONE PENNY, FOUR PENCE, SIX PENCE, and ONE SHILLING. The first three values were printed by Messrs. De la Rue and Co. on slightly surfaced medium white wove paper, watermarked Crown C.C., from the plates originally engraved by Messrs. Perkins Bacon and Co. Yellowish and white gum. The ONE SHILLING was designed and surface printed by Messrs. De la Rue and Co., on the same paper.

Designs : ONE PENNY, FOUR PENCE, and SIX PENCE, same as the preceding. ONE SHILLING, Diademed portrait of Queen Victoria to left on ground of horizontal lines within a key-patterned oval, with a small circular ornament at top, curved label above with the name of the Colony in white block letters on ground of horizontal lines. Straight label of solid colour at bottom with value in white block letters. Between the label with value and the portrait medallion is a narrow band of key-patterned ornamentation, at each end of which is a broken white oval, that on the left containing a pine-apple, and that on the right a conch shell. The angles above the upper label are filled in with solid colour, and the remainder of the stamp with arabesques. The outer border is composed of two coloured lines. Shape upright rectangular. (*Illustrations* 8, 9, 10, 11.)

A.—Perf. 12½.

1d., rose-red, red, brownish and lake-red, blood-red, crimson-lake, orange-vermilion (shades).
4d., dull rose, bright rose (shades).
6d., grey-lilac, lilac, bright, dull and deep lilac (shades).
(1863) 1s., green.

Remarks.—The shades of the one penny are very numerous.

(1875) B.—Perf. 14.

1d., bright orange-red (shades).
4d., dull rose, bright rose (shades).
1s., green, pale green (shades).

Varieties. All four values are known imperforate.

Issue IV. March, 1882.

Three values. Engraved and printed as before, but on paper watermarked Crown C.A. White gum. (*Illustrations* 8, 9, 11.)

A.—Perf. 14.

1d., bright orange-red.
4d., pale and bright rose.
1s., green.

B.—Perf. 12.

1d., bright orange-red.
4d., bright rose.

Issue V. May, 1883.

One value. This stamp is the SIX PENCE of Issue III., surcharged FOUR PENCE in one line in black Roman capitals. Length of surcharge 19 millimètres, height 2 millimètres. Watermark Crown C.C., perf. 12½. (*Illustration* 12.)

4d., black surcharge, on 6d. mauve.

Variety. Surcharge inverted.

4d., black surcharge, on 6d. mauve.

Remarks.—The surcharge is also found placed diagonally, and in various other positions.

Issue VI. August, 1884.

Four values. Designed and surface printed by Messrs. De la Rue and Co. on medium white surfaced paper, watermarked Crown C.A. White gum, perforated 14.

Design : Diademed portrait of Queen Victoria to left on ground of horizontal lines within a double lined circle. Curved white label at top with the name of the Colony in coloured block letters. Straight white label at bottom with the value in coloured block letters. In each of the lower spandrels, above the label of value, is a broken white oval, that on the left containing a pine-apple, and that on the right a conch shell. The remainder of the design is filled in with white floreate ornaments on a solid ground, and the design is completed by a single outer coloured line. Shape upright rectangular. (*Illustration* 13.)

T. "BAHAMAS." B. "ONE PENNY." "FOUR PENCE." "FIVE SHILLINGS." "ONE POUND."

1d., bright rose (slight shades).
4d., orange-yellow („ .,)
5s., sage-green („ „)
£1, maroon (.. „)

Issue VII. 1888-1890.

Two values. Design : Engraving, printing, &c., as the last issue. Watermark Crown C.A. Perforated 14. White gum (*Illustrations* 13, 14.)

(May, 1888), 2½d., blue.
(Oct., 1890), 6d., mauve.

ENVELOPE.

Issue I. March, 1881.

One value. Designed and embossed by Messrs. De la Rue and Co. upon white laid paper, with the upper flap pointed, 5½×3¼ inches (140×82 mm.) The stamp is embossed in colour in the right upper corner. Design : Diademed profile of Queen Victoria to left in plain relief, on a scallopped oval ground of solid colour, surrounded by an oval frame, with inner and outer white line, bearing inscriptions in coloured block letters on a ground of reticulations, the whole enclosed in an outer oval border of white beads on a coloured ground. (*Illustration* 15.)

T. "BAHAMAS POSTAGE." B. "FOUR PENCE."
4d., violet.

POSTCARD.

Issue I. March, 1881.

One value. Designed and printed by Messrs. De la Rue and Co., upon stout, light buff surfaced card. Size, 127×89 mm., or 5×3½ inches. The inscription is in three straight lines at the upper part of the card as follows :—1st, UNION POSTALE UNIVERSELLE; 2nd, BAHAMAS ; 3rd, THE ADDRESS ONLY TO BE WRITTEN on THIS SIDE. The first line is in thin, the second in thick, and the third in small block letters, and between the first and second lines are the arms and supporters of Great Britain. The stamp is in the right upper corner, and except for the change of the name of the Colony, is similar in design to that on the first issue card of Antigua. The frame of the card is composed of a Greek pattern, running between two straight lines, and measures 117×79 mm. or 4⅗×3¹⁄₁₀ inches. (*Illustration* 16.)

1½d. rose (shades).

c

REPLY PAID CARD.

Issue I.　September, 1883.

One value. Designed and printed by Messrs. De la Rue and Co. on stout straw card. Size 140×89 mm. or 5½×3½ inches. The disposition of the inscription, and the type employed, is the same as that on the single card. The first half has in the left lower corner four lines of additional inscription in small block letters as follows :— THE ANNEXED CARD IS INTENDED—FOR THE ANSWER—(LA CARTE CI-JOINTE EST DESTINÉE—À LA RÉPONSE), and the second half has the word REPLY beneath THE ADDRESS ONLY, &c. The stamp on each half is in the right upper corner. Design : Diademed head of Queen Victoria to left, on ground of solid colour, enclosed within a narrow upright oval. Surrounding the oval is a broad plain band inscribed with the name of the Colony above and the value in words below in coloured block letters, a period at either side separating the two inscriptions. The band is surrounded by a festooned border, and a single outer coloured line completes the design. The cards are joined along the top, perforated 4, and the design is impressed upon the first and third pages. Both halves are without frame. (*Illustration* 17.)

1½d. + 1½d. carmine (slight shades).

BARBADOS.

PRELIMINARY NOTES.

By E. D. BACON.

I HAVE been unable to find any copy of the *Official Gazette* of this colony, prior to 1871. No notice of the threepenny and five shillings adhesives, issued in 1873; or the provisional one penny adhesive, surcharged on half of the five shillings, issued early in 1878, appeared in *The Gazette*, so far as I have been able to discover.

The stamps up to the 17th November, 1874, were printed by Messrs. Perkins Bacon and Co., on which day the plates were handed over to the Crown Agents, and by them to Messrs. De la Rue and Co. The latter firm made use of these plates until 1882, when they constructed fresh ones from a new design, in which the figure of Britannia was replaced by the Queen's head.

The plate of the stamps first issued, "without expressed value," and those of the six pence and one shilling issued in 1859, each contained 110 specimens, arranged in eleven horizontal rows of ten; the plates of the halfpenny, one penny, three pence, and four pence, each contained 120 stamps in ten horizontal rows of twelve, while the plate of the five shillings only comprised 48 stamps in four horizontal rows of twelve. All these plates were of steel, and were constructed by Messrs. Perkins Bacon and Co., the figure of Britannia being common to all the values. The plates of the halfpenny, one penny, three pence, four pence, and five shillings were all finished in April, 1873, that of the six pence in September, 1858, and that of the one shilling in October, 1858. The plate "without expressed value" had been constructed several years previously. Proof impressions in black, taken from the plates, upon plain white paper, of all the above values are known, as well as proofs in black, struck from the engraved dies upon white card. I have also seen a proof of the five shillings printed in brownish lake upon plain white paper, of course imperforate.

I am indebted to Messrs. Perkins Bacon and Co., Limited, for the following list of the consignments of stamps sent out by them to Barbados, down to the end of 1858.

30th December,	1851	10,000 Labels.
" " "		50,000 Blue (1d.)
16th January,	1852	50,000 Blue (1d.)
		10,000 Purple.
18th February,	1852	30,000 Green ($\frac{1}{2}$d.)
15th June,	1852	50,000 Blue (1d.)
15th January,	1853	50,000 Blue (1d.)
27th August,	1853	50,000 Blue (1d.)
12th August,	1854	50,000 Blue (1d.)

13th September, 1851	50,000 Blue (1d.)
,, ,, ,,	50,000 Green (½d.)
28th September, 1851	50,000 Blue (1d.)
,, ,, ,,	50,000 Green (½d.)
28th December, 1854	50,000 Red (4d.)
25th May, 1855	100,000 Blue (1d.)
,, ,, ,,	50,000 Green (½d.)
21st May, 1856	100,000 Blue (1d.)
15th April, 1857	100,000 Blue (1d.)
11th September, 1857	100,000 Blue (1d.)
,, ,, ,,	100,000 Green (½d.)
14th October, 1858	100,000 Blue (1d.)
,, ,, ,,	55,000 One shilling, Brown.
,, ,, ,,	82,500 Sixpence, Red.
24th November, 1858	100,000 Green (½d.)

The first consignment of stamps shipped to Barbados was lost at sea, during the voyage out in the *Amazon*, which accounts for a second supply following so quickly after that sent in December, 1851. It will be noticed that the colour of the 10,000 stamps despatched on the 16th January, 1852, is entered in Messrs. Perkins Bacon and Co.'s books as *purple*. This is undoubtedly a mistake for *red*, similar to that made over the one shilling sent out in October, 1858, the colour of which is stated as *brown* instead of *black*. Besides the other particulars given, the table is interesting for the values it assigns to the different coloured stamps without expressed value, as it confirms those found in the Catalogues. It is quite possible that the one penny and four pence came into use before the halfpenny, but if the date of the first issue —17th April, 1852 - as given by M. Moens is correct, all three values would have arrived in the Island by that time, and consequently would be issued together.

The six pence and one shilling values were probably first issued early in 1859, for the prepayment of postage to the United Kingdom, which corresponds with the date at which the four pence, six pence, and one shilling of Trinidad first came into use. I have previously stated the plates were constructed in the autumn of 1858, and we see from Messrs. Perkins Bacon and Co.'s list of stamps sent out, that the first supply of these two values was not despatched to the Colony until October 14th of that year.

Mr. J. Graham Taylor, of Trinidad, has shown me a curiosity in the shape of part of a letter-sheet, postmarked "Barbadoes, Aug. 21st, 1854," which bears half of a blue stamp, without expressed value, on "blued" paper, of the first issue. The stamp had been divided vertically down the centre, and the fragment on the letter-sheet is the right-hand portion of the stamp. The half-stamp apparently franked the letter-sheet, and probably did duty as a halfpenny during a temporary exhaustion of that value. If we refer once more to the list of stamps forwarded by Messrs. Perkins Bacon and Co., we find that the first consignment of the green stamps, which consisted of only 30,000, was sent out on February 18th, 1852, so it is not at all surprising if by August, 1854, the stock was exhausted. This is borne out by the fact that at this time a further lot had been ordered from England ; as we see by the table, the next consignment was shipped on September 13th of that year. At any rate, the date at which the variety was used proves it is perfectly genuine, and not like some of the half-stamps of recent years, merely obtained for the benefit of collectors. Barbados was admitted into the Universal Postal Union on September 1st, 1881, when the issue of three halfpenny postcards became necessary, and as there was no probability of the cards arriving from England by the requisite date, a provisional supply had to be obtained in the Colony. With this object the following notice was published in *The Official Gazette* of August 4th, 1881.

POST CARDS.

" Sealed Tenders, in duplicate, will be received by the Clerk of the Executive Council up to 12 o'clock noon on Tuesday, 9th instant, for the supply to the Government of two thousand post cards. A pattern of the card, and of the quality of material to be used, may be seen on application to the Clerk of the Executive Council.

"The cards to be delivered to the Clerk of the Executive Council not later than Tuesday, 23rd August, 1881, at 12 o'clock noon.

"(Signed) E. LYTE STOKES,
Clerk Executive Council.

"*4th August*, 1881."

The notice gives the number of the first supply of these provisional cards, and as no varieties are found in the lettering, it seems probable the 2,000 were sufficient to meet all demands until the arrival of the cards ordered from England.

In December, 1881, the rates to certain adjacent islands were reduced, as appears from the following taken from *The Gazette* of Dec. 5, 1881.

POST OFFICE NOTICE.

" THE British Islands of St. Vincent, Grenada, Trinidad, Tobago, St. Lucia, and Dominica, and the French Islands of Martinique and Guadeloupe being 300 nautical miles of this Island, the postage on Correspondence and Mail matter addressed to those Islands will in accordance with the Postal Union Convention be as under : —

Letters ...	...	...	...	2½d. per ½ oz.
Post Cards ...	...	...	...	1d. each.
Newspapers	...	...	...	½d. „

Books and other printed matter, ½d. per 2 ozs. increasing by ½d. for every additional 2 ozs. Commercial documents 2½d. per 10 ozs., increasing by ½d. for every additional 2 ozs. Samples and Patterns 1d. per 4 ozs., increasing by ½d. for every additional 2 ozs.

"(Signed) WM. P. TRIMINGHAM, *Acting Col. Postmaster.*

" GENERAL POST OFFICE, *2nd December*, 1881."

As no one penny card was available, recourse had to be once more made to the Colonial Printers for a temporary supply, until a card of the requisite value could be obtained from England. Some delay seems to have occurred before the receipt of the latter card, as it was not ready for issue until October 6th, 1882. More than one supply of the provisional cards were therefore required, and it appears from the three varieties found in the lettering, that at least three separate printings took place at different periods. Newspaper wrappers and stamped envelopes were first issued on October 2nd, 1882, according to the terms of the following notices extracted from *The Gazette* of October 5th of that year.

POST OFFICE NOTICE.

STAMPED NEWSPAPERS WRAPPERS of the value of ½d. and 1d. each will now be sold to the public as under : —

At the General Post Office.

½d. wrappers in parcels of 1 doz. for 7d.
1d. „ in parcels of 1 doz. for 1s. 2d.

At the Treasury.

½d. wrappers in parcels of 200 doz., 5 per cent. off, £5 15s. 6d.
1d.   „   in parcels of 100 doz., 5 per cent. off, £5 15s. 6d.

N.B.—In England like wrappers are sold as under :—

½d. wrappers 1 doz. for 7d.
„   „   10   „   „ £1 2s. 10d.
1d.   „   1   „   „ £0 1s. 1d.
„   „   20   „   „ £1 1s. 3d.

At the Treasury the wrappers will be sold under 5 per cent. discount in quantities of 40 dozen halfpenny and 20 dozen penny if mixed with other stamps to the value of £5 and upwards. These wrappers may be used —

Of the value of ½d. each
{ For each Newspaper sent by Inland Mail. For Book Packets or Prices Current not exceeding 2 oz. in weight addressed only to St. Vincent, Grenada, Trinidad, Tobago, St. Lucia, Dominica, Martinique, and Guadeloupe.

Of the value of 1d. each
{ For each Newspaper addressed to the United Kingdom and to other British Colonies and Foreign Countries comprised in the Postal Union (except those to the eastward of Suez). Book Packets or Prices Current not exceeding 2 oz. in weight, addressed to the United Kingdom and to other British Colonies and Foreign Countries comprised in the Postal Union (except those to the eastward of Suez).

"(Signed)   WM. P. TRIMINGHAM, *Colonial Postmaster.*
"GENERAL POST OFFICE, *2nd October*, 1882."

POST OFFICE NOTICE.

STAMPED ENVELOPES as described below can be obtained at the General Post Office at the prices named :—

Embossed Penny Stamped Envelopes, 5¼in. × 3in. } For local use, 1s. 2d. per doz.

Registered Letter Envelopes bearing a penny stamp embossed on the flap, 5in. × 3in. } For local use, 1½d. each.

Registered Letter Envelopes bearing a fourpenny stamp embossed on the flap, 5in. × 3in. } For foreign use, 4½d. each.

Registered Letter Envelopes bearing a fourpenny stamp embossed on the flap, 10 × 7 and 11 × 6 } For foreign use, 5½d. each.

" (Signed)   WM. P. TRIMINGHAM, *Col. Postmaster.*
"GENERAL POST OFFICE, *2nd October*, 1882."

Mr. Wm. P. Trimingham was appointed Colonial Postmaster on September 8th, 1882, in the place of Mr. B. Lawrence, deceased.

At the same date as the one penny card of Messrs. De la Rue and Co.'s make came into use, a halfpenny card for local service was issued. This latter value was also printed by the same firm, and the notice of the issue is given in *The Gazette* of October 9th, 1882.

GENERAL POST OFFICE.

" LOCAL POST CARDS will in future will be sold at this Office as under :—
1 for 1d.
4 for 3d.
12 for 9d.

And at the Treasury in quantities to the value of £5 and upwards, or mixed with other stamps to that value with a discount of 5 per cent.

" (Signed)   WM. P. TRIMINGHAM, *Col. Postmaster.*"
" GENERAL POST OFFICE, *6th October*, 1882."

On May 5th, 1883, another size (5in. × 5in.) was added to the registration envelopes. The notice of the issue is found in *The Gazette* of May 10th of that year.

POST OFFICE NOTICE.

" ENVELOPES for Registered Letters can be obtained at the General Post Office, Bridgetown, of the undermentioned sizes :—

INCHES.

5¼ × 3¼ for Local Letters, including fee at 1¼d. each.

5¼ × 3¼ for Foreign Letters   ,,   ,,   4½d.   ,,

8 × 5 for   ,,   ,,   ,,   5d.   ,,

11 × 6 for   ,,   ,,   ,,   5½d.   ,,

10 × 7 for   ,,   ,,   ,,   5 d.   ,,

       " (Signed)   WM. P. TRIMINGHAM, *Colonial Postmaster.*

" GENERAL POST OFFICE, *5th May,* 1883."

The next notice gives the date of issue of the reply paid three halfpenny card. It is taken from *The Gazette* of May 21st, 1883:—

POST OFFICE NOTICE.

" FROM and after the 1st of June next reply cards of the value of 3d. can be obtained at the General Post Office, Bridgetown.

       " (Signed)   WM. P. TRIMINGHAM, *Colonial Postmaster.*

" GENERAL POST OFFICE, *18th May,* 1883."

In August, 1884, the one penny envelope and the one penny wrapper were slightly reduced in price, in accordance with the terms of the notice published in *The Gazette* of August 14th of that year.

POST OFFICE NOTICE.

" THE price of penny envelopes and of penny and halfpenny wrappers have been reduced, and will now be sold as under :—

At the Colonial Treasury.

Envelopes, 2 sizes (1d. duty), including postage, at £4 13s. 4d. per 1000, with 5 per cent. off.

Do. superior quality (do.) £4 15s. 10d.   do.

Wrappers (do.) £4 10s. 10d.   do.

Do. (½d. duty) £2 8s. 7d.   do.

The above will be sold in quantities to the value of £5, or mixed with stamps to that value. No denomination must be of less than £1 in value.

At the Post Office.

" Envelopes two sizes (1d. duty) including postage 1s. 1½d. per doz.

Do. superior quality (,,   )   ,,   ,,   1s. 2d.   ,,

Wrappers   (,,   )   ,,   ,,   1s. 1½d.   ,,

       ,,   (½d. duty)   ,,   ,,   7d.   ,,

Besides being used for local letters, the Envelopes can be used for prices current and printed papers, and also for letters sent to places abroad, by adding the additional postage required in postage stamps.

       " (Signed)   WM. P. TRIMINGHAM, *Colonial Postmaster.*

" GENERAL POST OFFICE, BARBADOS, *8th Aug.,* 1884."

On the 1st January, 1875, the Registration fee for foreign postage was reduced from four pence to two pence, the reduction being notified in *The Official Gazette (Extraordinary)* of November 20th, 1884, as follows :—

NOTICE.

"The following Supplemental Rules relating to the registration of letters, and other articles at the General Post Office, and by the District Postmasters, are published for general information.

" By order of the Executive Committee,

" (Signed)   GARNETT T. TAYLOR, *Acting Clerk.*

" PUBLIC BUILDINGS, *13th November,* 1884."

SUPPLEMENTAL RULES

relating to the Registration of Letters and other articles at the General Post Office, and by the District Postmasters :—

Letters, &c., addressed to places abroad.

" 1. On and after the 1st January next, the fee for Registration shall be 2d. under the conditions mentioned in Rule 2.

" 2. From the above date every letter tendered for Registration (except as mentioned in Rule 4) shall be enclosed in a special envelope to be obtained at all District Post Offices, and at the General Post Office.

" 3. The envelopes for Registered Letters are of the sizes and will be sold to the public at the prices following, inclusive of the fee for Registration impressed on the flap of the envelope.

5¼in. × 3¼in. for 2½d.
8in. × 5in. for 3d.
11½in. × 6in. for 3¼d.
10½in. × 7in. for 3¼d.

" 4. From the 1st January next, Deputy Post Masters are not to accept Foreign Letters for Registration except they are enclosed as stated in Rule 2, but the Colonial Postmaster may authorise a letter not so enclosed, to be registered, should it appear to him that the writer or sender is ignorant of the Regulation, and that, consequently, inconvenience might arise from delay by a refusal to Register.

" 5. On Letters allowed to be registered, as mentioned in the preceding rule, the fee shall be 2½d.

" 6. Book Packets, Commercial Documents, and patterns and samples, when registered need not be enclosed in the special envelope, but they must be securely fastened to the satisfaction of the Registering Officer. The fee on these articles will be 2d. each packet.

Inland Letters, &c.

" 7. On and after the 1st January next, all Inland Letters tendered for Registration at the General Post Office or at any District Post Office shall be enclosed in a special envelope except as mentioned in Rule 9.

" 8. These envelopes are 5¼in. × 3¼in. in size, and will be sold to the Public at 1¼d. each, inclusive of the fee for Registration, at the General Post Office and all District Post Offices.

" 9. Should an Inland Letter be too large for enclosure in the special envelope provided, Deputy Postmasters and Registering Officers may accept such letters, provided they are put up in strong covers, securely fastened, and if containing coin, such coin must not be put in loose, but must be packed and enclosed in such a way as to move about as little as possible.

" 10. These Rules are supplemental to those passed by the Governor-in-Council on the 8th December, 1880.

" Laid before his Excellency the Governor in Executive Committee, and approved this 13th day of November, 1884.

" (Signed) GARNETT T. TAYLOR,

" *Acting Clerk Executive Committee.*"

The 11½in.×6in. envelope mentioned in the above notice, appears never to have been issued, as it has not been catalogued in the magazines with the other sizes ; and although I have made inquiries, I can find no copy in any collection in this country.

At the end of November, 1885, a new size was added to the two penny registration envelopes, according to the following notice which appeared in *The Gazette* of November 30th of that year.

POST OFFICE NOTICE.

" From this date a new Registered Letter Envelope, 6in. × 3¾in. will be issued at this Office. Price, including Registration fee, 2½d. each.

" (Signed) WM. P. TRIMINGHAM, *Colonial Postmaster.*

" GENERAL POST OFFICE, *28th November*, 1885."

The one penny embossed envelopes do not appear to have been a success, and were, it seems, little used. We have seen that the price of these envelopes was reduced on the 8th August, 1884, probably with the view of clearing off the surplus stock. If so, the reduction in price, apparently, did not have the desired effect, as we find from a notice in *The Gazette* of November 7th, 1887, the price was still further lowered.

POST OFFICE NOTICE.

" In future the envelopes bearing embossed Stamps of one penny each, will be sold at this Office at the rate of 1s. 1d. per dozen ; that is :—

For the value of the embossed stamps thereon	...	...	1s.	0d.
Dozen envelopes ...	...	...	...	0s.	1d.
Total	...	...	...	1s.	1d.

" These envelopes will also be sold at the Treasury to the Public at the rate of 7s. per thousand, in addition to the face value of the stamps, that is, £4 10s. 4d. per thousand stamped envelopes, with a discount of 5 per cent., provided they are purchased to the value of £5, either by themselves or mixed with adhesive stamps making up that value. These envelopes are of two sizes (4¾in.×3½⅛in. and 5¾in.×3½in.), and of good paper, and may be used for Foreign Letters provided the proper postage is made up by the addition of adhesive stamps.

" (Signed) WM. P. TRIMINGHAM, *Colonial Postmaster.*

" GENERAL POST OFFICE, *4th November*, 1887."

REFERENCE LIST OF THE PHILATELIC SOCIETY, LONDON.

Issue I. April 17th, 1852.

Three values. Engraved in *taille-douce*, and printed by Messrs. Perkins Bacon and Co., of London. Coloured impression on different wove papers, varying in substance: imperforate. Design : Figure of Britannia seated on bales of merchandise, her right hand holding a spear, and her left arm resting on a shield charged with the

D

Union Jack. In the background to the right is a three-masted ship in full sail. Straight coloured label at bottom with name of colony in white block letters. White blocks in the four corners with coloured eight rayed stars with white centres. White reticulated borders at the top and sides, and engine-turned background. The stamps have no expressed value. Shape, upright rectangular. (*Illustration* 19.)

B. BARBADOS.

A.—*Paper blued by chemical action of the ink.*

(½d.) green (shades).

(1d.) blue, Indigo (shades).

(4d.) brick (shades).

Variety. Aug., 1854 (½d.) half (1d.) blue.

B.— *White paper.*

½d.) yellow-green (shades).

(1d.) very deep to pale blue (shades).

(4d.) brick (?).

Remarks.—It is doubtful whether the four pence on white paper exists imperforate. No satisfactory copy is, at any rate, known to the Society. Specimens are occasionally found in collections, but these are believed to either belong to the perforated series or to have been originally on blued paper from which the colour has been discharged. The shade of the few known copies is different to that of the stamps on the blued paper : being a kind of dull rose-red in place of brick.

Issue II. January, 1859.

Two values. Engraved in *taille-douce*, and printed by Messrs. Perkins Bacon and Co. Coloured impression on white wove paper, imperforate. The design is the same as in the previous issue, except that the value is printed in the lower label, and the name of the Colony in a curve above the head of Britannia, all in white letters. The six pence has the value in block type and the name of the Colony in Roman capitals, while in the one shilling exactly the reverse is the case. Shape, upright rectangular. (*Illustrations* 20, 21.)

T. "BARBADOS." B. "SIX PENCE." "ONE SHILLING."

6d., dull rose (shades).

1s., black, grey-black (shades).

Issue III. 1860-1861.

Five values. Of the preceding designs printed upon white wove paper varying in substance. Perforated 11½, 12½ to 16 compound. (*Illustrations* 19, 20, 21.)

(½d.) yellow-green to dark green (shades).

(1d.) very dark to pale blue.

(4d.) red-brown, dull rose, orange-vermilion (shades).

6d., rose, lake-red, orange (shades).

1s., brown-black to grey-black (shades).

Varieties. Imperforate.

(4d.) dull orange-red.

6d., orange.

Remarks.—The gauge and nature of the perforations of this and the succeeding issue vary greatly, and it is almost impossible to make up complete sets of the different sizes. Two distinct sets may, however, be made, one of which shows the holes merely "punctured" without any part of the paper being removed, while the other is a true machine perforation,

Issue IV. 1871-1872.

Five values. Similar in design to the stamps of the last issue, but printed upon white wove paper, watermarked with a six-rayed star. Perforated 12½ to 15½ compound. *(Illustrations* 19, 20, 21.)

(½d.) green (shades).
(1d.) blue („)
(4d.) dull rose, brick-red, orange-vermilion (shades).
6d., vermilion (shades).
1s., black („)

Variety. The (1d.) cut in half diagonally and used as a ½d. stamp.

½d. half (1d.), blue.

Remarks.—This issue is usually divided into two separate sets by the difference in size "large" or "small" of the star watermark. The size of the watermark varies considerably, and many other sets might be made up with a little trouble. It seems possible that all the varieties are found upon the same sheet and constitute only one issue. The differences in size are therefore of no special significance, though two perfectly distinct sets may easily be distinguished.

Issue V. 1873.

Two values. Engraved in *taille-douce* by Messrs. Perkins Bacon and Co., and printed upon yellowish wove paper watermarked with a six-rayed star, yellowish gum, machine perforated, 14 for the three pence and 15½ for the five shillings. Designs: That of the three pence is similar to the one shilling of the former issues, but both inscriptions are in block letters. The five shillings has the figure of Britannia on engine-turned background as in the previous values, within a pearled circle. Straight white labels at top and bottom with name of Colony and value in coloured block numeral and letters. Square white blocks in the four corners with coloured ornaments formed by placing a St. Andrews over an ordinary cross. Conventional ornaments in spandrels. Border formed of plain outer line. Shapes, small upright rectangular for the three pence, large upright rectangular for the five shillings. *(Illustrations* 18, 22.)

T. "BARBADOS." B. "THREE PENCE." "FIVE SHILLINGS."

3d., violet-brown (shades).
5s., dull rose („)

Issue VI. 1874.

Two values. Printed by Messrs. Perkins Bacon and Co. upon white wove paper, watermarked with a six-rayed star. Yellowish gum. Machine perforated 14. The design is the same as that for the three pence of the last issue. *(Illustration* 22.)

T. "BARBADOS." B. "HALF PENNY." "ONE PENNY."

½d., dark green (shades).
1d., dark blue („)

Issue VII. 1875-78.

Six values. Printed by Messrs. De la Rue and Co. upon white wove paper watermarked Crown C.C. White gum. The designs are unchanged, and remain the same as those of the same values of the preceding issues. A new value of four pence is added. The inscriptions on this are in block letters like the three lower values. *(Illustrations* 20, 21, 22.)

r. "BARBADOS.   B. "HALF PENNY."   "ONE PENNY."   "THREE PENCE."   "FOUR PENCE.
"SIX PENCE."   "ONE SHILLING."

     A.—*Perforated* 12½.
        ½d., emerald green.
        4d., deep vermilion.
        6d., orange-yellow.
        1s., deep mauve.

      B.—*Perforated* 14.
        ½d., emerald green (shades).
        1d., ultramarine   („)
(April, 1878)   3d., pale mauve   („)
        4d., carmine-red   („)
        6d., orange-yellow   („)
        1s., mauve, reddish-mauve, deep mauve (shades).

Variety. The 1d. cut in half diagonally for use as a ½d. stamp.

        ½d. (half 1d.) ultramarine.

Remarks.—The one penny perforated 14 is sometimes met with quite grey and even grey-black in colour, but these varieties are believed to be due to changes in the colour of the ultramarine stamp, probably from accidental causes.

Issue VIII. March 1878.

One value. Owing to a temporary dearth of the ordinary one penny stamps, the authorities were driven to extemporise a provisional, which they effected by cutting the label of value from the five shillings stamp and perforating it 12, vertically down the centre. Each half of the stamp was surcharged horizontally 1D. in black, the numeral measuring 7 mm. in height, each five shillings stamp being thus divided into two one penny ones. There are two prominent varieties of the surcharge. In one the numeral has a curved serif, while in the other it is straight. The letter D also varies in size, and there is sometimes a comma after it, in place of the more usual period. (*Illustration* 23.)

     A.—*Surcharged on the right half of the five shillings stamp.*
       1d., black surcharge, on half 5s., dull rose.
Variety. Surcharge inverted.
       1d., black surcharge, on half 5s., dull rose.
     B.—*Surcharged on the left half of the five shillings stamp.*
       1d., black surcharge, on half 5s., dull rose.
Variety. Surcharge inverted.
       1d., black surcharge, on half 5s., dull rose.

Issue IX. August 28th, 1882.

Four values. Engraved and surface printed by Messrs. De la Rue and Co. upon medium white wove slightly surfaced paper, watermarked Crown C.A. White gum. Machine perforated 14. Design: Diademed head of Queen Victoria to left upon background of horizontal lines, enclosed within a circle framed by a coloured line. Straight white labels of the width of the stamp, above and below the circle, inscribed with the name of the Colony and value in words in block letters. The two pence halfpenny has the value in figures before the word "PENNY." The spandrels contain small white conventional ornaments and the design is completed by a single outer coloured line. Shape, upright rectangular. (*Illustrations* 24, 25.)

T. "BARBADOS." B. "HALF PENNY." "ONE PENNY." "2½ PENNY." "FOUR PENCE."

½d., green   (shades).
1d.. carmine   („   )
2½d., ultramarine („   )
4d., grey   („   )

Remarks.—The same die did duty for all the stamps, the bottom label with the value being added afterwards, and printed separately.

Issue X. 1885 to 1887.

Five values. Same type, watermark, and perforation, &c., as in the preceding issue. (*Illustration 25.*)

T. "BARBADOS." B. "THREE PENCE." "FOUR PENCE." "SIX PENCE." "ONE SHILLING."
"FIVE SHILLINGS."

3d., lilac   (shades).
4d., brown   („   )
6d., grey-black („   )
1s., brown-red („   )
5s., bistre   („   )

ENVELOPES.

Issue I. October 2nd, 1882.

One value. Designed and embossed by Messrs. De la Rue and Co. upon white laid paper, two sizes. The stamp is embossed in colour in the right upper corner. Design : Diademed profile of Queen Victoria to left in plain relief on a plain oval ground of solid colour, enclosed by a single white line; surrounding this is an oval frame with inscriptions in coloured block letters on a ground of reticulations, contained by a border of a single white and a single coloured line. (*Illustration 26.*)

T. "BARBADOS POSTAGE." B. "ONE PENNY."
1d., rose, 4¾ × 3⅝ inches (121 × 92 mm.)
1d.,   „   5¾ × 3½   „   (146 × 90 „)

Remarks.—The smaller size of this envelope was not issued until sometime after the larger.

REGISTRATION ENVELOPES.

Issue I. October 2nd, 1882.

Two values. Bag-shaped envelopes of white wove linen-lined paper, with the flap on the left. There are crossed lines on the back and front of the envelopes, and on the address side an inscription in three lines along the upper margin : 1. "REGIS-TERED LETTER," in large block letters. 2. "THIS LETTER MUST BE GIVEN TO AN OFFICER OF THE POST OFFICE." 3. "TO BE REGISTERED, AND A RECEIPT OBTAINED FOR IT," in small block letters, with full capital initials. In the left upper corner is a large block letter " R," and in the right upper corner is a single-lined rectangle, enclosing the inscription, in five lines, "THE STAMP—TO PAY THE—POSTAGE—MUST BE—PLACED HERE." These inscriptions, &c., are all in *blue*. The stamps were designed and embossed by Messrs. De la Rue and Co. on the flap, in different colours. Designs : Diademed profile of Queen Victoria to left in plain relief on a solid ground of colour, surrounded by a circular frame bearing inscriptions, in coloured block letters, on a ground of reticulations. In the ONE PENNY the central disc is enclosed by a plain white line, and the outer border is formed of a white and a coloured line with eight scallops; while in the FOUR PENCE the central disc has a white outline of eight scallops, and the outer border is formed of a plain white and a plain coloured circle. (*Illustrations* 27, 29, 30.)

T. "BARBADOS REGISTRATION FEE." B. "ONE PENNY." "FOUR PENCE."

1d., rose	$5\frac{1}{4}\times3\frac{1}{4}$	inches	(133×83 mm.)
4d., olive-grey	$5\frac{1}{4}\times3\frac{1}{4}$	,,	(133×83 ,,)
4d., ,,	10×7	,,	(253×178 ,,)
4d., ,,	$11\frac{1}{2}\times6$	,,	(292×153 ,,)

Variety. With a small circle printed in black, on the face, in the left lower corner.

4d. olive-grey $5\frac{1}{4}\times3\frac{1}{4}$ inches (133×83 mm.)

Remarks. The sizes are those known in the British post offices as F, I, and K, respectively. A fourth size of the four pence (200×127 mm.) is catalogued by M. Moens, but is unknown to the Society. On referring to the notice of the issue in Mr. E. D. Bacon's paper, it will be seen that only the three sizes given in the above list were obtainable. There are some varieties in the manufacturers' inscriptions, in small block letters, to be found at the upper margin under the flaps of these envelopes, which are perhaps worthy of note. Of the copies examined, the one penny envelope and the two large sizes of the four pence, are inscribed, in *black*—

"McCORQUODALE & Co., LIMITED. PATENT REGISTERED ENVELOPE."

The four pence, small size, is inscribed in *blue*—

"McCORQUODALE & Co. LIMITED. CONTRACTORS,"

Issue II. May 5th, 1883.

Two values. The same as in Issue I., but with the envelopes differently constructed; the flap is now on the right, and the large letter "R" in the left upper corner is enclosed in an upright oval frame. The inscriptions, &c., are in *blue*, as before. (*Illustrations* 28, 29, 30.)

1d., rose,	$5\frac{1}{4}\times3\frac{1}{4}$	inches	(133×83 mm.)
4d., olive-grey,	$5\frac{1}{4}\times3\frac{1}{4}$	,,	(133×83 ,,)
4d., ,,	8×5	,,	(202×127 ,,)

Remarks.—The larger size of the four pence is catalogued by M. Moens *without* the word "To." The inscription under the flaps of these envelopes is the first described in the previous note, printed in *blue* on the one penny, and four pence (Size F), and in *black* on the four pence size 8×5 inches, (Size H.)

Issue III. January 1st, 1885–1889.

One value. The envelopes are similar to those of Issue II., but the inscriptions, &c., are in *red*. A fresh size was introduced later in the year, G, $6\times3\frac{3}{4}$ inches (152×96 mm.) The design of the stamp resembles that of the one penny, but it has a plain white outer circle, with a number of small coloured scallops beyond it, each containing a white dot. (*Illustrations* 28, 31.)

T. "BARBADOS REGISTRATION FEE." B. "TWO PENCE."

A.—The inscription under the flap printed in *red*, is —
" McCorquodale & Co.   Contractors,"
    Limited.

(January 1st, 1885,)   2d., ultramarine, size F.
(,,   ,,   )   2d.,   ,,   ,,   H.
(,,   ,,   )   2d.,   ,,   ,,   I.
(November 28th, 1885,) 2d.,   ,,   ,,   G.

B.—The inscription under the flap also in *red*, is –
" Thos. De la Rue & Co. Patent,"
(1889) 2d., ultramarine, size F.

Remarks.—Size K is chronicled by M. Moens, but the Society does not believe in the existence of this envelope.

WRAPPERS.

Issue I.   October 2nd, 1882.

Two values. Designed and printed by Messrs. De la Rue and Co. upon buff wove paper, 12×5 inches (305×127 mm.) gummed and tapered at the upper end; the stamp is typographed near the right-hand side, and about two-and-a-half inches from the top; across the wrapper, a little above the stamp, is an instruction in five lines, as on the wrappers of Great Britain issued in November, 1875. The stamp and the instruction are printed in the same colour. Designs. For the HALFPENNY value: Diademed profile of Queen Victoria to left on a solid ground of colour; surrounding this is a plain circular band bearing inscriptions in coloured block capitals, and the design is completed by a single-lined rectangular frame, which touches the circular band at top and bottom and cuts off a portion of it at each side; there is a trefoil ornament in each spandrel. For the ONE PENNY, the same profile, but the solid disc has a fancy border of festoons; the surrounding band is larger, and the inscriptions in larger letters; there is a double-lined frame, formed at top and bottom by the outline of the circular band, while the sides are straight and touch the festooned border of the central disc. (*Illustrations* 32, 33.)

T. " BARBADOS." B. " HALFPENNY." " ONE PENNY."
½d., red-brown.
1d., carmine.

POSTCARDS.

Issue I.   September 1st, 1881.

One value. Designed and printed in the Colony as a provisional issue, upon stout white card. Size, 124×89 mm., or $4\frac{9}{10}\times3\frac{1}{2}$ inches, varying somewhat in dimensions. The inscription is in three lines at the upper part of the card: 1. UNION POSTALE UNIVERSELLE in small, thick Roman capitals; 2, BARBADOS—(BARBADE) the first word in large, the second in smaller Roman capitals; 3, THE ADDRESS ONLY TO BE WRITTEN ON THIS SIDE, in small Roman capitals, with period at end, and with a plain straight line directly underneath, broken under the T of TO. The card has no frame. (*Illustration* 34.)

Without expressed value (1½d.). Black impression, franked with 1d. light blue, and ½d. light green, adhesives, " Britannia" type.

Issue II.   November 28th, 1881.

One value.   Designed and printed by Messrs. De la Rue and Co. upon medium light buff card.   Size, 140×89 mm., or 5½×3½ inches.   The design is similar to that of the first issue card of Antigua, except that the second line of the inscription is altered to BARBADOS (BARBADE) and the name of the Colony at the top of the stamp is changed.   (*Illustration* 35.)

1½d., light brown (shades).

Issue III.   December 8th, 1881.

One value.   Designed and printed in the Colony as a provisional issue, upon stout white card.   Size 114×78 mm., or 4½×3¼₆ inches.   The design of the card is the same as that of Issue I., but the straight line underneath, THE ADDRESS ONLY, &c., is much thicker, and the punctuation after the words is different.   This card was only available for the following places: St. Vincent, Grenada, Trinidad, Tobago, St. Lucia, Dominica, Martinique, and Guadeloupe.   (*Illustrations* 36, 37, 38.)

Variety A.   Comma after UNIVERSELLE, period after BARBADOS. (BARBADE.) no period after SIDE

Without expressed value (1d.)   Black impression, franked with a 1d., light blue, adhesive, " Britannia " type.

Variety B.   Period after UNIVERSELLE. BARBADE. and SIDE. none after BARBADOS [BARBADE.] is enclosed between parenthesis with square, instead of curved ends.

Without expressed value (1d.)   Black impression, franked with a 1d., light blue, adhesive, " Britannia " type.

Variety C.   Period after UNIVERSELLE. and BARBADOS. none after BARBADE or SIDE (BARBADE) between curved parenthesis.   The W of WRITTEN and S of SIDE are larger than the other letters of these words, and correspond in height to the T of THE and the A of ADDRESS.

Without expressed value (1d.)   Black impression, franked with a 1d., rose, adhesive, type with Queen's head.

Issue IV.   October 6th, 1882.

Two values.   Designed and printed by Messrs. De la Rue and Co. upon thick white card.   The halfpenny measures 121×74mm., or 4½×2⁹₁₀ inches: and the one penny 140×89 mm., or 5½×3½ inches.   The inscription on the halfpenny is in three lines at the upper part of the card: 1, POST CARD, in large fancy capitals, with the arms and supporters of Great Britain between the two words; 2, BARBADOS, in Roman capitals; 3, THE ADDRESS ONLY TO BE WRITTEN ON THIS SIDE in small block letters.   The stamp is in the right upper corner.   Design: Diademed head of Queen Victoria to left upon ground of solid colour enclosed within a plain broad band inscribed BARBADOS above, HALFPENNY below, in coloured block letters.   Conventional ornaments in the four corners and a plain outer line of colour, which impinges upon the inscribed band at either side, completes the stamp.   The inscription on the one penny is the same as that on the card of Issue II.   The stamp is placed in the right upper corner.   Design: The same head of Her Majesty as on the halfpenny value, but enclosed within a festooned circle.   Following the curve of the circle is BARBADOS above, and ONE PENNY below, in large coloured block letters. Two plain outer lines, straight at the sides, and curved at the top and bottom complete the stamp. *(Illustrations 39, 40.)*

½d., light brown (shades).
1d., carmine (,,)

Issue V. September (?), 1886.

One value. The card of Issue II. changed in colour, and printed upon stout yellowish card. Size, 139×88 mm., or 5½×3½ inches. *(Illustration 35.)*

1½d., mauve (slight shades).

REPLY PAID CARD.

Issue I. June 1st, 1883.

One value. Precisely similar to the single card of Issue V., but printed upon a paler card, and each half has the usual additional inscription like the reply cards of Antigua. The cards are joined along the top, perforated 4, and the design is impressed upon the first and third pages. *(Illustration 35.)*

1½d.+1½d., mauve (slight shades).

BERMUDA.

PRELIMINARY NOTES.

By EDWARD B. EVANS.

THE following notes are founded upon Official Records, which I had an opportunity of examining while in Bermuda. The accounts in the Receiver General's office show that the ONE PENNY, SIX PENCE, and ONE SHILLING stamps were first supplied to the Colonial Postmaster on the 13th September, 1865; they were probably issued to the public on the same date, but I was unable to obtain any official notice of their issue. The TWO PENCE passed into the Postmaster's hands just six months later, on the 14th March, 1866.

In 1873 the THREE PENCE was issued for payment of the single rate of postage between Bermuda and British North America; a supply of 9,800 of this value reached the Colony on the 10th March of that year. This supply seems to have been exhausted by the following February, and a temporary substitute of some kind became necessary. I could find no official correspondence upon the subject, but, as all the Government Offices are close together, it is quite possible that the Colonial Postmaster may have applied personally to the Council, who authorised the conversion of one shilling stamps into threepenny, as shown by the following extract from the Minutes of their proceedings : —

> "1874, 21st February. The Council approve of the issue of a portion of the redundant *One shilling* postage stamps in store as *Threepenny* stamps, with a distinct crossing of 'three' or '3d.' if possible of a different coloured ink."

The Receiver General's books show 4,500 *One Shilling* stamps converted to *Threepence*, March 12, 1874; the same number on the 20th of the month; and the same again on the 9th May, 1874. These numbers seem to indicate that the one shilling stamps were sent out in quarter sheets of 60, not in entire sheets of 240. Of the stamps thus converted 4,000 are shown as issued to the Postmaster on the 12th March, 2,400 on the 31st March, and 2,400 on the 19th May, 1874. A second supply of threepenny stamps was received from England on the 2nd July of the same year, so that no further overprinting was necessary. I found no special record of the actual printing of the surcharge, and I could obtain no information from the Government Printers, who probably did the work, though there was a tradition that some work of this kind was done by the Royal Engineers, who had a small press in their office; there was no means, however, of verifying this. There was, of course, no notice taken in the official books of the fact that there are two varieties of type of the surcharge, and there was no record whatever of any other values besides the one shilling having been converted to three pence, at this or at any other period. We get no information, therefore, from official sources as to which variety of the surcharge was issued first, but I think the following extract from *The American Journal of Philately* for May 20, 1874, tends to prove that it was the one in fancy italics, unless both came out together :—

"BERMUDA.—The latest thing from this colony, the notice of which was inadvertently left out of our last number" (April 20, 1874), "is the shilling green, with surcharge (in black) *THREE PENCE* in line-shaded italic capitals, running diagonally across the stamp."

Specimens of the *One Penny* and of the *Two Pence* are known with the same surcharge in both the varieties of type and of these some copies are apparently *used*, or at all events obliterated; it is, of course, very easy to imitate an overprint of this kind, but there is no doubt that specimens exist with a perfectly genuine surcharge ; still in the absence of all official record of their issue, and in view of the statement which follows, I am inclined to consider them proofs, or essays only.

A few years ago about half of a quarter-sheet of one penny stamps, bearing the surcharge in italic capitals, was found in the Receiver-General's office, and was given by him to a collector in Bermuda. The Receiver-General was of opinion that these stamps had been purchased by his predecessor, during whose period of office the surcharges were printed, and left inadvertently in the drawer in which they were found ; but it appears to me that the fact of these specimens being found where they were is rather a proof that they formed a portion of a trial sheet, struck to show the appearance of the surcharge ; in like manner the other type of the surcharge may have been tried on the one penny, and both types on the two pence also. These varieties were first chronicled in 1875, or some twelve months after the three pence on one shilling was brought into use.

The provisional " One Penny " stamps were made in this latter year, 1875, and it was noted at the time in Philatelic magazines as a curious circumstance that the one penny on three pence, and the three pence on one penny should have appeared at the same time. The accounts show that 14,400 *One Shilling* stamps were converted to *One Penny* on the 11th March, 1875 ; 6,720 of the same value, and 4,800 *Two Pence* similarly treated on the 31st of the same month ; and 2,380 *One Shilling* on the 16th April, 1875 ; also that fifty sheets (12,000) *Three Pence* stamps were converted to one penny about the same time, though the exact date of this is not given.

The subsequent issues appear to call for no special remark.

REFERENCE LIST OF THE PHILATELIC SOCIETY, LONDON.

Issue I. September 13th, 1865.

Four values. Engraved and surface-printed by Messrs. De la Rue and Co., of London, upon medium white wove surfaced paper, watermarked Crown C.C. White gum, machine perforated 14. Designs, ONE PENNY: Diademed profile of Queen Victoria to left on ground of horizontal lines enclosed within a circle. Straight coloured labels above and below, contain the name of the Colony and value respectively in white block letters. The spandrels are filled in with arabesques and a single

outer line of colour completes the design.   Two PENCE, similar to the design of the
One Penny, but the lower label containing the value is curved instead of being straight.
The label is white and is inscribed in coloured block letters.   The arabesques in the
spandrels are also of a different pattern.   SIX PENCE, similar in design to the One
Penny, except that the labels above and below the Queen's head are curved, with
arabesques at either side of the two inscriptions.   The arabesques in the spandrels
also differ from those on the other values.   ONE SHILLING, similar in design to the
One Penny, but with curved label above, like the Six Pence.   The arabesques in the
spandrels differ in pattern to those on the other values.   Shape, upright rectangular.
(*Illustrations* 42, 43, 44, 45.)

T. " BERMUDA."   B. "ONE PENNY."   "TWO PENCE."   " SIX PENCE."   "ONE SHILLING."

1d., deep to pale rose-red (shades).

(March 14th, 1866,) 2d., blue (shades).

6d., dark to pale lilac (shades).

1s., green (shades).

Variety.   Imperforate.

1d., rose-red.

Issue II.   March 10th, 1873.

One value.   Engraved and surface-printed by Messrs. De la Rue and Co. upon
medium white wove surfaced paper, watermarked Crown C.C.   White gum, machine
perforated.   Design : The design is similar to the One Penny of Issue I., but the
circle enclosing the Queen's head is surrounded by an octagonal frame.   Straight
white labels above and below the octagon are inscribed in coloured Roman capitals,
the upper one having a star-like ornament at either end.   Arabesques in the four
corners and an outer line of colour complete the design.   Shape, upright rectangular.
(*Illustration* 46.)

T. " BERMUDA."   B. "THREE PENCE."

A.—*Perforated* 14.

3d., yellow-ochre, buff (shades).

B. —*Perforated* 14 *horizontally,* 12½ *vertically.*

3d., buff.

Issue III.   March 12th, 1874.

One value.   In consequence of a dearth of threepenny stamps, provisional ones
of this value were formed in the Colony by surcharging the One Penny, Two Pence
and One Shilling of Issue I., with the words THREE PENCE in various types.

A.—Surcharged obliquely (from the left bottom to the right top corner), with
the words *THREE PENCE* in fancy italic capitals, 1½ mm. in height, 23 mm. in
length.   (*Illustration* 47.)

3d., black surcharge, on 1d. rose-red (shades).

3d., „   „   „ 2d. blue   („   )

3d., „   „   „ 1s. green   („   )

Variety.   With plain instead of fancy letter P to the surcharged word PENCE.
(*Illustration* 48.)

3d., black surcharge, on 1d. rose-red.

3d., „   „   „ 2d. blue.

3d., „   „   „ 1s. green.

B.—Surcharged obliquely (from the left bottom to the right top corner), with the words THREE PENCE in Roman capitals 2 mm. in height and 24 mm. in length. (*Illustration* 49.)

>   (May 19th, 1874,) 3d., black surcharge, on 1d. rose-red (?)
>   („   „   ) 3d.,   „   „   „ 2d. blue (?)
>   („   „   ) 3d.,   „   „   „ 1s. green.

Remarks.—The surcharges on these stamps have been extensively forged, and it is most difficult to discriminate the good from the bad. There is some doubt whether the one penny and two pence, with surcharge type A, were ever issued for use : and it is still more doubtful whether these two values were over-printed with surcharge type B. All the copies of the two latter stamps examined by the Society have the surcharge differing from that found on the one shilling value.

Issue IV. March and April, 1875.

One value. The supply of one penny labels being exhausted, provisional stamps of this value were formed in the Colony by surcharging the two pence, three pence, and one shilling of Issues I. and II. The surcharge consists of the words "One Penny" in two lines, in the centre of the stamp, in ordinary lower case Roman type, each word having a capital initial letter. The words measure 6½ and 10 mm. in length respectively. (*Illustration* 50.)

>   (March 11th, 1875,) 1d., black surcharge, on 2d. blue.
>   (April, 1875,   ) 1d.,   „   „   „ 3d. buff.
>   („   „   ) 1d.,   „   „   „ 1s. green.

Varieties. a. All three values are found without period after the word "Penny."
           b. Surcharge inverted.

>   1d., black surcharge, on 1s. green.

Issue V. March 25th, 1880.

Two values. Engraved and surface-printed by Messrs. De la Rue and Co., on medium white wove surfaced paper, watermarked Crown C. C. White gum, machine perforated 14. Designs, HALFPENNY : Diademed profile of Queen Victoria to left on ground of horizontal lines, enframed by an oval band of solid colour, which touches the four sides of the stamp. The band is inscribed with the name of the Colony above, and the value in words below, in white block letters, the two inscriptions being separated at either side by a key pattern ornament. Small square blocks in the four corners contain a white cross on ground of solid colour surrounded by a white line. A fancy border, and a plain outer line of colour complete the design. FOUR PENCE, same head of Her Majesty as on the halfpenny value, but enclosed within a beaded circle. Curved labels of solid colour above and below, following the shape of the circle, the upper inscribed with the name of the Colony, and the lower with the value in words, in white block letters. The corners contain conventional ornaments, and a single outer line of colour rounded at the four corners completes the design. Shape, upright rectangular. (*Illustrations* 51, 52.)

>   T. "BERMUDA." B. "HALFPENNY." "FOUR PENCE."
>   ½d., stone-brown (shades).
>   4d., orange („)

Issue VI. 1884.

Two values. Engraved and surface-printed by Messrs. De la Rue and Co., upon medium white wove paper, watermarked Crown C.A. White gum, machine perforated 14. Designs: That of the ONE PENNY is the same as Issue I. The TWO PENCE HALFPENNY has the same head of Her Majesty, but enclosed within a smaller circle. Labels of solid colour above and below, shaped so as to form, with the sides of the stamp, an hexagonal frame to the circle. The upper label is inscribed with the name of the Colony, and the lower with the value in words, all in white block letters. Conventional ornaments in the four corners, and two plain outer lines of colour complete the design. Shape, upright rectangular. (*Illustrations* 42, 53.)

T. "BERMUDA." B. "ONE PENNY." "TWO PENCE HALFPENNY."
(May (?) 1884.) 1d., rose-red.
(November 10th, 1884.) 2½d., ultramarine.

Issue VII. 1886.

Three values. Printed by Messrs. De la Rue and Co., upon medium white wove paper, watermarked Crown C.A. White gum, machine perforated 14. The designs are the same as those of the corresponding values of Issues I. and II. (*Illustrations* 42, 43, 46.)

(December, 1886,) 1d., carmine.
(,, ,,) 2d., blue.
(January. ,,) 3d., grey.

POSTCARDS.

Issue I. September, 1880.

Two values. Designed and printed in the Colony, as a provisional issue, by Mr. Donald M'Phee Lee, the Government printer, and publisher of *The Bermuda Royal Gazette*, at Hamilton. The impression is in carmine, on stout light blue card for the halfpenny, and on stout light buff card for the three halfpenny. Size 139×88 mm., or 5½×3½ inches. The design is evidently copied from the first issue card of British Guiana, and is the same for both values. At the top in a straight line is UNIVERSAL POSTAL UNION, in small block letters. Beneath this is a transverse oval band, inscribed BERMUDA in the upper, and POST OFFICE in the lower curves, in thick block letters, with a Maltese cross at either side separating the two inscriptions. The centre of the oval contains a royal crown. At the left of the oval is BERMUDA, and at the right in two lines, LES ISLES—BERMUDES, in tall Roman capitals. Beneath the oval is POST CARD, in early English type, with a capital initial letter for each word. Below this, in a straight line, is, *Only the address to be written on this side*, in italics, with a thick straight line underneath, extending quite across the card. The halfpenny has a plain single-lined upright rectangle in the right upper corner for the stamp, inscribed HALF—PENNY, in two lines in small block letters. The three halfpenny has two rectangles for stamps joined together. The left inscribed HALF—PENNY, and the right ONE—PENNY, both in two lines, in small block letters. (*Illustrations* 41, 54.)

A. The word " Bermudes " measures 25mm.

½d., carmine impression on light blue card (shades) franked by a ½d. adhesive (Issue, March 25th, 1880).

1½d., carmine impression on light buff card (shades) franked by a 1d. adhesive (Issue, September 13th, 1865) and a ½d. adhesive (Issue, March 25th, 1880).

B. Same as variety A., but the letter P of Post Card is partly over the space between the words *Only the*, instead of being directly above the word *the*.

1½d., carmine impression on light buff card (shades) franked with 1d. and ½d. adhesives as above.

C. Same as variety B., but the word " Bermudes " measures 23mm.

1½d., rose impression on light buff card (shades), franked with 1d. and ½d. adhesives as above.

Issue II. February 25th, 1885.

One value. Variety C., of the three halfpenny card of Issue I., used as a provisional halfpenny, with a stamp in the right hand rectangle; the left hand rectangle being vacant and showing the inscription HALF—PENNY. (*Illustration* 41.)

½d., rose impression on light buff card (shades) franked by a ½d. adhesive (Issue, March 25th, 1880).

Issue III. March 25th, 1885-1886.

Two values. Designed and printed by Messrs. De la Rue and Co. upon stout straw card. Size, 139×88 mm., or 5½×3½ inches. The inscription on the halfpenny is in three straight lines : 1, POST CARD in fancy capitals, the two words being separated by the arms and supporters of Great Britain; 2, BERMUDA in Roman capitals ; 3, THE ADDRESS ONLY TO BE WRITTEN ON THIS SIDE in small block letters. The inscription on the three halfpenny, and the stamps on both values are the same as the second issue cards of Antigua, except for the modification of the name of the Colony, and the change of value at the bottom of the stamp on the halfpenny. (*Illustration* 55.)

½d., blue (shades).
(1886) 1½d., carmine („)

BRITISH GUIANA.

PRELIMINARY NOTES.

By E. D. BACON.

SOME NEW FACTS CONNECTED WITH THE HISTORY OF THE POSTAGE STAMPS OF THIS COLONY.

(A Paper read before the Philatelic Society, London, May 3rd, 1889, and reprinted from " The Philatelic Record " of May and June, 1889, with sundry alterations and many additions.)

THE particulars concerning the history of these stamps given in the following paper consist mainly of Post Office notices extracted from *The Royal Gazette of British Guiana*, the title of which, after May 10th, 1851, was changed to *The Official Gazette of British Guiana*, to distinguish it from the newspaper which bore the same name. I have been fortunate enough to come across a file of *The Gazette*, which, although not by any means a complete one, yet enables me to give some particulars that I hope may prove interesting. For other information I am indebted to Mr. E. C. Luard, a gentleman residing in the colony, with whom I have been in communication. Mr. Luard, until recently, possessed a fine collection of all the early stamps, and has taken a great deal of trouble to hunt up the history of their production with the view of clearing up the various points that still require elucidation. I also desire to acknowledge the valuable assistance I have received from Mr. J. B. Rapkin, the gentleman at the head of the engraving department of Messrs. Waterlow and Sons, Limited, who has been kind enough to give me full details as regards the printing of the stamps manufactured by his firm.

Issue I. July 1st, 1850.

The following notice appeared in *The Royal Gazette* of Saturday, June 15th, 1850 :

NOTICE.

"THE public is informed, that on and after the 1st proximo, Daily Mails (Sundays excepted) will be made up at the Post Office, Georgetown, at 3 p.m. for the following places, to be forwarded by the 4 o'clock train :—

Name of Place.	Receiving Office.	Rate of Postage.
Plaisance	Mr. J. F. Cuming's	4 Cents per oz.
Beterverwagting	Mrs. Van Grovenstein's	,, ,,
Buxton	Mr. J. T. Glover's	,, ,,

" Return Mails will be made up daily at the above places, at half-past 8 o'clock a.m., to be forwarded by the 9 o'clock train.

" At 10 o'clock a.m. every week-day there will be a delivery of Letters from the Post Office for all persons residing or having offices in Water Street or Main Street.

" Every Tuesday and Friday, at 3 p.m., additional Mails will be made up for :—

Name of Place.	Receiving Office.	Rate of Postage.	
Victoria	Mr. E. Glover's	4 Cents per oz.	
Mahaica	Mr. J. Smellie's	,,	,,
De Kinderen	Police Station	8 ,,	,,
Mahaicony	Ditto	,,	,,
Belladrum	Ditto	,,	,,
Fort Wellington.	Ditto	,,	,,
Ferry	Ditto	,,	,,
New-Amsterdam	Ditto	12 ,,	,,

" Return Mails will be made up in New-Amsterdam every Monday and Thursday at noon, to arrive in Georgetown by the 9 o'clock train, in time for the town delivery.

" On Tuesdays and Fridays, at 4 p.m., Mails will be made up for :—

Name of Place.	Receiving Office.	Rate of Postage.	
'Pln. Hague	Police Station	4 Cents per oz.	
Boeraserie	Messrs. J. & C. Harrison's	,,	,,
Vergenoegen	Police Station	,,	,,
Leguan	Ditto	8 ,,	,,
Wakenaam	Ditto	,,	,,
Spring Garden	Ditto	12 ,,	,,
Zorg	Mr. Tilbury's	,,	,,
William's Town	Police Station	,,	,,
Henrietta	Ditto	,,	,,

* Plantation.

" The Return Mail for Georgetown and the intermediate places will leave Henrietta every Monday and Thursday at 8 a.m.

" Newspapers will be forwarded free of charge.

" Prepayment of Letters will be necessary in all cases, to facilitate which, Postage Stamps of the respective values of 4, 8, and 12 Cents are being printed, and will be ready for Sale on or before the 24th instant, at the Post Offices in Georgetown and New Amsterdam, and at the different Receiving Offices.　　　(Signed)　　　E. T. E. DALTON, D.P.M.G.

" POST OFFICE, GEORGETOWN, 15th June, 1850."

The Royal Gazette, July 17th, 1850, contains this supplementary notice :—

NOTICE.

" On and after Friday, the 19th instant, the Mails for Essequibo will be made up at 2 o'clock p.m., instead of 4 p.m. as at present. An Extra Bag will also be made up for Pln. Edinburgh, West Coast. Receiving Officer, Mr. J. Williams. Postage, 4 cents per ounce.

　　　　　" (Signed)　　　E. T. E. DALTON.

" POST OFFICE, 16th July, 1850."

F

From the above notices we learn, first, the date of issue to be July 1st, 1850; and, secondly, the rates of postage paid by the three stamps of four, eight, and twelve cents. No mention is made of a two cents stamp, nor of any postal rate of that value. In my former paper I was unable to give any official information touching the history of this value, but I am pleased to say I am now (April, 1891) in a position to furnish full particulars concerning its use. I can, therefore, replace the suggestions I put forward in my previous paper to account for its existence by facts which have come to my knowledge in the following manner :—Some short time since I wrote again to Mr. Luard telling him the West Indian catalogue was almost ready for publication, and I asked him if he had any fresh information upon the stamps of British Guiana he could send me. He replied that a paper entitled *The Post Office in British Guiana before 1860*, by Mr. James Rodway, F.L.S., had recently appeared in the December number of *Timehri*, the journal of the Royal Agricultural and Commercial Society of British Guiana, and he kindly sent me a copy of the number referred to. The Paper by Mr. Rodway is replete with information of the most interesting description, but by far the most important paragraph as regards Philatelists is that which speaks of the " circular " two cents stamp. Mr. Rodway states that " this stamp appears to have been issued in accordance with a notice dated February 22nd, 1851." I have consulted *The Royal Gazette* for this date, and I am now able to give an exact copy of the notice Mr. Rodway draws attention to. I must have overlooked this notice when I searched *The Gazette* some two years ago.

NOTICE.

"By order of His Excellency the Governor, and upon the request of several of the merchants of Georgetown, it is proposed to establish a delivery of Letters twice each day through the principal streets of this city, viz., Water-street, Main-street, their intermediate streets, and the Brick-Dam, as far as the Roman Catholic Chapel.

" The following gentlemen have consented to receive Letters for delivery at their respective Stores, that is to say —Mr. CARPENTER and Mr. RICHARDSON in Water-street; Mr. B. L. WATSON and Mr. F. H. STEWART in Main-street ; Mr. TORRES on the Brick-Dam.

" Each letter must bear a stamp, for which Two Cents will be charged, or it will not be delivered, and when called for will be subject to the usual postage of Eight Cents.

" The deliveries will take place at 10 a.m. and 2 p.m. every lawful day.

" Stamps may be obtained at the Post Office or at any of the receiving offices.

" This delivery to commence on the 1st of March.

"(Signed)   E. T. E. DALTON.

" POST OFFICE, GEORGETOWN, *22nd February*, 1851."

Mr. Rodway states that this delivery of letters was discontinued soon after it was started, which accounts for the rarity of the stamp. After the suppression of this local delivery, the supply of two cents stamps left on hand was no doubt later on sold off to prepay the higher rates of postage, as copies are known postmarked in October, 1851.

Since the publication of my paper in *The Philatelic Record*, I have had an opportunity of seeing a good many more specimens of the stamps of this issue, among others the fine collection of Herr P. von Ferrary, to whom I now tender my sincere thanks for the kindness and courtesy shown me during my visit to Paris

One of the results of these new investigations is that I am quite in accord with Mr. F. A. Philbrick, in the opinion he has expressed, that the dies used for printing these stamps were set up from ordinary printer's type, instead of being engraved with movable centres, as I once thought might have been the case. The reason for changing my opinion will be seen later on.

The same dies were used for printing all the values, the numeral in the centre only being altered. One type occurs much more frequently in my experience than the others, and I have never seen but this one for the two cents. The only hypothesis I can put forward to account for this is, that all the stamps may have been printed at first from this one type, and that afterwards, when larger quantities were required, other dies were set up with this original one, and used together for printing later supplies. We know, at any rate, that at some period during their use the latter was the case, as unsevered pairs of the twelve cents are known, showing two distinct varieties of type.

Since writing the last two or three sentences in 1889, I have examined a pair of the two cents (*Illustration* 57) now in the possession of Herr P. von Ferrary, and I find the two stamps are printed from the same die, which also corresponds with the type of the four other known copies of this value. On the right hand one of the pair, between the frame and letters AN of GUIANA and on the small piece of margin opposite the letter N, there is an extra circular line, reversed as regards the direction of the frame. This must, I think, have formed part of the next stamp, which would consequently have slightly overlapped its neighbour. It is clear from the above facts, that the two cents was printed from only one die, and it is therefore quite possible that at some time or other during their employment the other values were also.

I have carefully compared every stamp of this issue I have seen during the last few years, and I am now able to establish eight varieties of type in all. Of these I have seen one (*Illustration* 61) common to all four values, a further three (*Illustrations* 62, 63, 64) common to the four, eight and twelve cents, while I have found three other varieties (*Illustrations* 65, 66, 67) peculiar to the eight cents, and another (*Illustration* 60) peculiar to the twelve cents. My reason for now thinking the blocks used for producing the stamps were formed of ordinary printers' type, and were not engraved, is, that I believe some of the varieties noted above were printed from the same blocks, but that in changing the numeral of value, a few of the letters of the inscription sometimes got shifted. Take for instance, *Illustrations* 63 and 65. Both these stamps have the fine outer line, which is more oval than circular, with the break in it opposite the period after GUIANA. The only difference between the varieties is in the position of the letters I s of BRITISH. Again, *Illustrations* 64 and 67 are very much alike. Both have the break in the frame over the first I of BRITISH, the I of GUIANA below the other letters, and the period after the word *Cents* in a line with the top of the letter *s* instead of occupying the more usual position. The difference is, that in *Illustration* 64 the line is much closer to the first letter I of BRITISH, than it is in *Illustration* 67. Both stamps, numbers 65 and 67, are dated January, 1851, and therefore probably belong to a later printing, and I have no doubt whatever in my own mind that they are printed respectively from types 63 and 64, which have become to a certain extent reset. The twelve cents *Illustration* 60 is printed from type *Illustration* 63, but the numeral 2 of 12 is larger, and has a straight instead of a curved foot. It is only found, so far as my experience goes, upon the pale blue paper. This variety (*Illustration* 63) of the twelve cents is also found with the numeral 12 in the more usual type, like that found on *Illustration* 62. These alterations in the setting up of the dies I have just called attention to, add yet a further difficulty to the means of determining the number of varieties to the sheet, and I very much fear the solution of this question will ever remain unsolved.

I have altogether seen five horizontal pairs of the twelve cents, four of the medium shade of blue, and one of the pale blue. In these pairs the types of the *Illustrations* are placed as follows :—

			Left Stamp.		Right Stamp.	Collection.
1st pair,	blue	...	61	...	64	Herr P. von Ferrary.
2nd ,,	,,	...	63	...	64	,, ,, ,, ,,
3rd ,,	,,	...	61	...	63	Mr. Douglas Garth.
4th ,,	,,	...	61	...	64	The late Mr. T. K. Tapling.
5th ,,	pale blue	...	61	...	64	Herr P. von Ferrary.

It is clear from the above, that in different printings the arrangement of the types was altered. At first sight, it would appear from the second and third pairs, that types 61, 63, and 64, followed in a line, but on the other hand, it is possible type 64 was not used in all the printings. These pairs of stamps, therefore, do not help us in the arrangement of the sheet, but only show what two types are found together. Allowing for some of the blocks being reset, I am of opinion the sheet of each printing did not contain more than three or four varieties repeated a certain number of times. In this unsatisfactory state, I must leave the question of the number of types to the sheet.

Mr. Luard tells me these stamps were printed by Mr. Henry Mackay, at the *Demerara and Essequibo Gazette* office. He says they were not printed so as to be easily cut square, as, although they were arranged in horizontal rows upon the sheet, they were not placed in a direct line vertically, but the stamps in the second row came beneath the spaces between those of the first row, and so on. The horizontal rows were also placed close together. This explains why pairs of these stamps are so rare, and it also accounts for the stamps being so frequently found cut round.

The stamps, before being sold, were initialed in black, red, blue, or violet ink, or occasionally in black pencil, by hand, to guard against fraud. The following is a list of the initials that are met with and the names they represent :—

E. T. E. D. = E. T. E. Dalton, Deputy Postmaster-General.
E. D. W. = E. D. Wight, Clerk Colonial Department of Post Office.
J. B. S. = J. B. Smith, Clerk Imperial Department of Post Office.
H. A. K. = H. A. Killikelly, Clerk Post Office, Georgetown.
W. H. L. = Unknown.

In my former paper, I was unable to give the signification of the initials H.A.K. This has since been furnished by Mr. F. A. Philbrick, in a paper published in *The Philatelic Record* for June, 1889, but Mr. Luard informs me the name should be spelt as above, and not as Mr. Philbrick wrote it, " Kilkelly." Mr. Philbrick remarks in his paper that he thinks I am inaccurate in describing Mr. Wight and Mr. Smith as clerks in the Colonial and Imperial Departments of the Post Office respectively. Mr. Luard tells me he derived the information from the *British Guiana Directory* for 1851, and he has again referred to that work and finds he copied correctly. We must remember that at that date the management of the Post Office, except as regards the purely Inland service, was still under the control of the Postmaster-General of Great Britain, which, to my mind, is sufficient to account for the two departments in the Post Office of the Colony.

Copies may occasionally be found without any initials. These were evidently the result of an oversight. The stamps of this and all the following issues down to the year 1860, were tor use solely for inland postage, and were not available for foreign letters. As we shall find when we come to the "Notice" of the second issue, these stamps were in use until the end of the year 1851; that is, for just a year and a half, a somewhat longer period than has hitherto been thought probable.

Mr. Luard says : " Mr. Wight is still alive and living in the colony, but he is in his dotage, and either cannot or will not remember anything about these old stamps, except that he initialed them. He has been so pestered on the subject that the mention of old stamps to him is like a red rag to a bull."

Issue II.   January 1st, 1852.

The Inland Postal system of charging letters by distance not meeting with approval, an alteration was made during the year 1851, and a uniform rate of four cents for half-ounce letters, and one cent for newspapers, throughout the colony, was fixed. The new rates came into operation on January 1st, 1852, as the following notice, published in *The Official Gazette*, of December 27th, 1851, shows: —

NOTICE.

" Post Office, Colonial Department,
" *Demerara, 25th December*, 1851.

" PURSUANT to the Resolution of the Combined Court, the following Reduced Rates of Postage will be charged on and after the First of January, 1852, on Letters and Newspapers forwarded by the Inland Mail to all parts of the Colony :—

On Letters under ½ an ounce, 4 cents.

     ,,   ,,   exceeding ½ an ounce and under 1 ounce, 8 cents.

     ,,   ,,   ,,   1 ounce and under 2 ounces, 12 cents.

     ,,   ,,   ,,   2   ,,   and   ,,   3   ,,   16   ,,

and so on, 4 cents for every additional ounce.

" Each Newspaper will be charged 1 cent.

" Prepayment by stamps necessary both for Letters and Newspapers.

         " (Signed)   E. T. E. DALTON, C.P.

" N.B.—Stamps may be obtained at the Post Offices in Georgetown and New Amsterdam, and at all the branch offices."

The stamps mentioned in the above are, of course, the large upright rectangular 1 cent, black on magenta, and 4 cents, black on blue, designed and manufactured by Messrs. Waterlow and Sons, of London. Since writing my former paper I have had one or two interviews with Mr. J. B. Rapkin, of Messrs. Waterlow and Sons, Limited, and he assures me that these stamps, like all the other British Guiana issues manufactured by his firm, were printed by lithography, and not from engraved plates as Philatelists have previously thought. Mr. Rapkin believes that *all* the British Guiana dies used by them were engraved on copper, but he is quite at a loss to explain how it was that *two* impressions of the design were engraved for each of these two stamps. He tells me that this is such an unusual course to pursue that he could not credit a man, knowing anything of his business, resorting to such a method, and until I showed him the two varieties in the design he could hardly believe such was the case. A friend of mine, Mr. F. de Coppet, of New York, has sent me a block of four of the one cent value, which he thinks all differ in type, and he has had them photographed upon an enlarged scale to accentuate what he considers the points of difference. I submitted this photograph to Mr. Rapkin, who told me that the small variations are merely caused in the process of transferring impressions of the dies on to the stone. The system of transferring is as follows :—A certain number of impressions are taken from the engraved dies on to transfer paper. These specimens are cut out and pasted on a sheet of paper, leaving a regular space between each pair of stamps. After the requisite number of rows are completed, the whole sheet is transferred to a lithographic stone at one operation. Mr. Rapkin says that some of the stamps on the sheet are almost certain to present slight differences in the shape of the lettering, &c., when printed by lithography. The variations in the two types of each value are chiefly noticeable in the drawing of the small forts in the background, and the wavy lines representing the sea. Mr. Luard tells me that, for a short time after these stamps first came into use, the envelopes or newspapers were initialed " e. d. w." by Mr. Wight in passing through the post. He also says: "A large unused stock of both values existed in the Government Secretary's office in the Guiana Public Buildings up to 1878. In that year the late Governor of the Gold Coast (Mr. A. G. Young) was Government Secretary of British Guiana, and annoyed by the persistent applications he received from Government clerks and others for these stamps, he deliberately had them all *burnt.* Three specimens of each colour were handed over to the local post office previous to the cremation, and these ultimately ' disappeared ' from the post office collection. Our post office boasts a stamp collection, but has none of this colony's stamps in it! It consists mainly of ' specimen ' stamps from the post offices of other colonies, &c."

We see from the official notice of this issue that the 1 cent stamp was intended to prepay newspapers, which, it will be remembered, were allowed to pass without charge at the time the "circular" stamps came into use, according to the notice then published. We find by the following notice in *The Official Gazette,* April 3rd, 1852, that local newspapers were once more allowed to pass free for a short time.

NOTICE.

" PURSUANT to the Resolution of the Combined Court of the 17th ult., Notice is hereby given that, pending the passing of the Inter-colonial Postage Ordinance, Local NEWSPAPERS, posted within one week after publication, will be forwarded Free of Postage.

　　　　　　　　　　　　　" (Signed)　　　　　　　E. T. E. DALTON, C.P.
" POST OFFICE, 3rd April, 1852."

Issue III. 1853.

The Gazette contains no notice, so far as I have been able to discover, of the date of issue of these two stamps. This is no doubt accounted for by the fact that the values of the stamps and the postal rates were unchanged. We know, from the date on the stamps and from the obliterations of certain copies, that the issue took place in this year, but I am afraid we shall not now discover the exact day they first came into use. The earliest postmarked specimen I have seen is a four cents, dated November 18th, 1853. This series, like the last, was manufactured by Messrs. Waterlow and Sons. Mr. Rapkin tells me that like the other British Guiana stamps printed by his firm, all those dated 1853 are lithographs. Both values were printed from a single engraved die, the bottom labels of the stamps containing the value, being separately engraved. The lithographic stone was prepared as follows:—A number of specimens were taken from the die, as described for the last issue, and a similar number of impressions of the label containing the value required. The latter were then carefully cut out with a pair of scissors and pasted on the sheet of paper at the bottom of each of the stamps, and the whole was then transferred to the lithographic stone at one operation. The white line sometimes found along the top of the value upon some of the stamps is accounted for by the workman not pasting the label quite high enough up so as to touch the upper portion of the design. The dot after the letter s of Postage found on some of the four cents, and other slight differences of this kind, are due to defects in the transferring process. Several supplies of these stamps were sent out to the colony, and a fresh transfer was taken for each consignment. Mr. Rapkin was unable to account for the three varieties in the bottom label of the one cent value I showed him (*Illustrations* 70, 72, 73), but he said the stamps must have been printed from three separately engraved labels. He thinks that when fresh supplies of the stamps were ordered the engraved label of value used for the previous lot was lost, and that a new one had to be engraved in its place. It is singular that this should apparently have happened twice in the case of the same value. He assigns a like reason for the use of the new die of the four cents, "with the figures of the date in a frame." He suggested that possibly after each printing the engraved dies were handed to the Crown Agents of the Colony, and that perhaps they mislaid them, so that Messrs. Waterlows were obliged to engrave new ones when orders for fresh supplies were received. He told me that this new die of the four cents had the value engraved upon it. If we may draw a conclusion from the earliest known dates of postmarked copies, this variety of the four cents was not issued until about May, 1860.

Issue IV. Early in 1856.

These stamps were issued provisionally, pending the arrival of a fresh supply from England of the stamps of the preceding issue. The January to July volume of *The Gazette* for 1856 is missing from the file I have consulted, but Mr. Luard informs me he has searched the volume most carefully without finding any reference whatever to these provisionals. We know, however, from postmarked specimens that the issue took place near the beginning of the year. The earliest date on those in the late Mr. T. K. Tapling's collection is March 25th, 1856; but Herr P. von Ferrary possesses a copy of the four cents magenta, postmarked February 12th of that year.

Mr. Luard informs me these stamps were printed by Messrs. Joseph Baum and William Dallas, the printers and publishers of *The Official Gazette*, the office of which was at No. 23, High Street and Church Street, Cumingsburg, Georgetown. The little ship in the centre is the same as that employed for heading ordinary shipping advertisements in the daily papers. The stamps were type-set, and there are as many varieties as there were stamps to the sheet. As in the case of the first issue, I have seen a great many more copies of these stamps than I had at the time of writing my previous paper, and I have now altogether noted eight distinct types: which will be found given as *Illustration* 82. The order the stamps are placed in for illustrative purposes is entirely arbitrary, as nothing definite is at present known as regards the number of types to the sheet, how they were arranged, or whether the types were set up more than once. All the information I can furnish at the time of writing, I regret to say, is to notify the number of varieties I have so far been able to determine.

While in Paris, I had a long-wished-for opportunity of examining the only known copy of the one cent of this issue, of which Herr P. von Ferrary is the fortunate possessor. Doubts have more than once been expressed about the "face" value of this stamp, but after a most careful inspection I have no hesitation whatever in pronouncing it a thoroughly genuine one cent specimen. The copy is a poor one, dark magenta in colour, but somewhat rubbed. It is initialed E. D. W., and dated April 1st, the year not being distinct enough to read.

The stamps of this issue, like those first employed, were initialed by the Post-office clerks previous to being used. Besides some of the initials found on the "circulars," those of C. A. W. are sometimes met with. Mr. Luard tells me they stand for the name of a letter-carrier—C. A. Watson.

I have already mentioned that the stamps of all the early issues were only used to prepay Inland letters. Letters to England were forwarded, either prepaid by coin or altogether unpaid, until early in the year 1858, when the following "Notice" appeared in *The Gazette*, February 13th, making it compulsory for senders to pay the postage in advance.

NOTICE.

" Post Office, Demerara, 11*th February*, 1858.
"On and after the *First of April next* all Letters for the *United Kingdom* must be paid in advance. Letters posted *unpaid* after that date will be returned to the writers.
" (Signed)   E. T. E. Dalton, d.p.m."

It will be seen from the next "Notice," extracted from *The Gazette*, May 12th, 1858, that the postage on the above letters was paid by Great Britain stamps.

NOTICE.

"Postage Stamps of the respective values of 6d., 4d., and 1d. having been received from England by the Steamer that arrived on the 9th instant, are for Sale at the Stationery Establishments of Messrs. Richardson and Co. and Mr. Short, as well as at the Post-Office.
" (Signed)   E. T. E. Dalton, d.p.m.g.
" Post Office, 11*th May*, 1858."

Letters posted unpaid were not returned to the writers according to the terms of the notice of the 11th February, but the addresses were advertised in *The Official Gazette* from time to time, stating the letters were detained until the requisite postage was paid. I am unable to say how long this arrangement of paying postage with the stamps of the mother country lasted. It certainly, however, did not extend much beyond the following year, 1859, as we find the British Guiana stamps of the 1860 Issue on letters sent to England in that year.

The volumes of *The Gazette* for 1860, and from June, 1861, to the end of the year 1870, are, unfortunately, wanting in the series I have had access to, but from the latter date to the present day the file is complete.

Mr. Rapkin tells me the die used for printing the set issued in 1860 had the whole design engraved upon it, with the exception of the value, the small space between the numerals in the two bottom corners being left vacant for it. The values were all engraved separately, and the lithographic stones from which the stamps were printed, were made in the same way as I have described for those of the 1853 issue. New engravings of the values were afterwards made for the one, two, eight, and twelve cents, with the value closer to the word "cents." Mr. Rapkin can assign no reason why this was done, beyond the supposition that the earlier engravings of these values were missing when a fresh supply was ordered. He believes that all the stamps of the 1860 set were printed in sheets of one hundred, arranged in ten rows of ten.

The twelve cents of the 1860 Issue is sometimes found with a large numeral "5" and a small letter "d" struck upon it in red ink. That this was not a surcharge made upon the stamp before use, is clear from specimens found upon letters showing a portion of the figure " 5 " or letter "d" on the stamp, the remainder being on the letter the stamp was used upon, and, as a rule, these specimens show no other obliteration. I have also seen letter-sheets with the " 5d." struck upon them without any part touching the stamp. Although it is obvious, from the details I have given, this " 5d." cannot be considered as a surcharge, altering the value of the 12 cents stamp, it has always been a moot point with collectors what purpose the "mark" was intended to serve. I have given a good deal of thought to this old enigma, and I have at length solved the riddle, at any rate to my own satisfaction. It has always struck me as curious, that the " 5d." is only found on stamps or letters sent from the Colony to England, and I at once surmised the " mark" must have something to do with the postal rate between the two countries. The following is, in my opinion, the explanation of its use. On the 1st May, 1860, according to the " Report" of the Postmaster-General of Great Britain for that year, British Guiana, along with most of the West Indian Colonies, took over the control of its own postal affairs from the Home Government. From information, kindly obtained for me by Mr. Pearson Hill, from the General Post Office, London, it appears the arrangement at that period with the Colonies as regards the cost of conveyance of mails to and from Great Britain was as follows. The postal rate on a quarter ounce letter was sixpence, which was thus divided, fourpence for the sea postage and one penny each for the inland rates at both ends. On any letter forwarded to British Guiana or the West Indies from this country, the British Post Office received, of course, the whole of the money for the postage stamp (6d.) employed in prepayment, and of this sum five pence was retained by the Post Office and one penny was credited to the Colony for its inland service. In like manner, any West Indian Colony received 6d. on each quarter ounce letter it despatched to this country, and gave the British Post Office credit for fivepence, the whole cost of the Packet service up to the establishment of the Postal Union (about 1878-79), being paid by Great Britain. On the establishment of the Postal Union, a different system was adopted. The British Post Office still makes the contract with the Royal Mail Steam Packet Company, and hands over to that Company the annual sum due to it under the contract, but the Post Office obtains from the West Indian Colonies in the aggregate one half of the subsidy (contributed by the several Colonies in fixed amounts, which are roughly in proportion to the amount of correspondence sent to and received by each), and in order to avoid the trouble of separate accounts with every mail, the arrangement has been adopted that Great Britain keeps all the postage on the outward mails, and the Colonies keep all the postage on the homeward mails. The annual loss on the service is thus divided between Great Britain and the Colonies, instead of being wholly borne by the former as was the case in time past. This being so, I conclude the " mark" of " 5d." on the twelve cent stamp was applied at the date we find it used, to show the amount the British Guiana Post Office had to credit Great Britain for the conveyance of the letter. A similar system, except that the numeral was not struck on the stamp, seems to have prevailed in Trinidad, as Mr. A. W. Chambers has shown me a letter-sheet forwarded from that colony to London in 1861, franked by a sixpenny stamp, the letter-sheet bearing a large red figure " 5 " by the side of the adhesive.

Mr. Luard tells me he has seen two specimens of the eight cents issued in 1860, cut in half diagonally, and used in November, 1861 : one being on an entire envelope postmarked November 21st of that year. It seems probable from this fact that the supply of the four cents value had become exhausted at this date.

The lithographic stones for the six, twenty-four, and forty-eight cents stamps issued in 1863, Mr. Rapkin tells me, were prepared in precisely the same way as those for the 1860 set previously described, but the die for these three stamps was engraved differently to that of the former, the inscriptions on the latter showing up in colour on white, in place of in white on colour. The sheets of these three values contained fifty stamps, arranged in five horizontal rows of ten.

The stamps in use from 1863 down to the year 1876 were, with the exception of the provisionals of 1862, printed by Messrs. Waterlow and Sons, and were all produced, as I have previously said, by lithography. Since 1876, Messrs. De la Rue and Co., of London, have held the contract for supplying the stamps and other postal stationery. With regard to the three provisionals issued in 1862, I have nothing new to add, except that I think it is possible the issue took place in September instead of October. I have seen a specimen of the four cents postmarked September, but the day of the month and year were undecipherable. I have also seen another copy of the same value obliterated October 1st, 1862. The excellent paper by Mr. Philbrick, which he read before the Society on July 2nd, 1881, which describes every variety found on the sheet of each value, leaves little or nothing wanting in our information about these interesting stamps.

The following list of Government appointments is taken from *The Colonial Office Lists* for the various years. Mr. E. H. G. Dalton succeeded Mr. E. T. E. Dalton as Colonial Postmaster in 1874. The former became Registrar and Clerk of the Supreme Courts—Demerara and Essequibo—in 1876, and Mr. N. Darnell Davis was appointed Colonial Postmaster in 1877. The latter became Comptroller of Customs and Rum Duties, and Registrar of Shipping in 1882; and Mr. F. M. Hodgson became Postmaster-General the same year. He was succeeded by Mr. F. W. Collier, the present Postmaster-General, who was appointed on October 19th, 1888.

As regards the volumes of *The Gazette* from 1871, the first important notice is that found in the number for April 17th, 1878:—

"GENERAL POST OFFICE, GEORGETOWN, 16th *April*, 1878.

"1-CENT AND 2-CENTS POSTAGE STAMPS.

"THE attention of the public is hereby called to the following temporary arrangement which has been made for a supply of 1-CENT and 2-CENT POSTAGE STAMPS.

"FOR 1-CENT STAMPS.—The Government will cause 6 cents Stamps to be defaced by two broad, black Lines being drawn across them, and then such defaced Stamps will be issued as 1-Cent Stamps.

"FOR 2-CENTS STAMPS.—The Government will cause 4 cents Stamps to be Cut right down the Centre, and then each Half can be used as a 2 cents Stamp.

"(Signed)   N. DARNELL DAVIS,
                              "*Colonial Postmaster.*"

The six cents, brown, stamp mentioned in the above decree, surcharged with two horizontal bars, must have been in use for a very short time, as obliterated copies are very scarce.

With regard to the provisional two cents, what I said in my previous paper turns out to be quite correct, as Mr. Luard informs me the intended issue never took place, a fresh supply of the ordinary two cents being received from England.

The next notice is taken from *The Gazette,* June 19th, 1878. It refers to certain reductions made in some of the rates for inland postage, and reads as follows:—

"GENERAL POST OFFICE,
" GEORGETOWN DISTRICT, 17*th June*, 1878.
" INLAND RATES OF POSTAGE.

"THE ATTENTION of the Public is called to the following Resolution of
the Combined Court, at its session on the 14th June, 1878 :—

"*Resolved.*—'That the postage on letters posted in Georgetown, for
delivery in Georgetown, and posted in New Amsterdam, for delivery in New
Amsterdam, shall be fixed at One Cent for each half ounce or portion of
half an ounce.

"'That the postage on Books, Pamphlets, Packets of printed matter, or
Packets of manuscript matter not in any respect partaking of the nature
of a letter, sent from one part of the Colony to another part of the Colony,
shall be fixed at One Cent for any weight under four ounces, and Two
Cents for every additional four ounces, or portion of four ounces.

"'That all Letters, Book packets, Pamphlets, or other Official Documents transmitted either to or from the Government Secretary shall be free
of Inland Postage ; and the Governor and Court of Policy may from time
to time authorise the transmission, free of Inland Postage, of the Correspondence on public business, of any Public Department or Public Officer.

"'All inland postage shall be prepaid. Letters posted without any prepayment will not be forwarded.'

"(Signed) N. DARNELL DAVIS,
" *Colonial Post Master.*"

The two next notices authorise the issue of fresh provisional stamps, which were
required towards the end of 1878. The first is taken from *The Gazette*, November
6th, 1878, and the second from the number for November 23rd of the same year.

"BRITISH GUIANA,
"GENERAL POST OFFICE, 6*th November*, 1878.

"UNTIL further intimation is given, the Government has authorised the
use of 6 cent Postage Stamps in lieu of 1 cent stamps. The Stamps so
converted will have a bar drawn across the value and another bar down the
centre.

"(Signed) E. D. WIGHT,
" *Acting C.P.M.*"

NOTICE.

"UNTIL further intimation is given, Government has authorised the
issue of 4 cent Stamps in lieu of 1 cent, and 8 cent Stamps in lieu of 2
cent. The Postage Stamps so converted will be defaced by a line drawn
across the value, and another down the centre.

"(Signed) E. D. WIGHT,
" *Acting Colonial Post Master.*

"GEORGETOWN, 23*rd November*, 1878."

Neither of these " Notices " specify which issue of stamps were to be surcharged ;
so we may conclude that any adhesives in stock of the specified values were to be
used in this way. With regard to the first notice, we know both the 6 cents, blue,
of Waterlow's design, and the 6 cents, brown, of De la Rue's were so defaced. The
latter stamp is also found with the word OFFICIAL obliterated with an extra black
bar. The stamps employed for defacement, in accordance with the second notice, are
the 8 cents of Waterlow's design, and the 4 cents and 8 cents of De la Rue's. All
three stamps bear the word OFFICIAL. In the two former it is obliterated with a

black bar, but the latter variety has the word unobliterated. There is nothing in the surcharge of the two 8 cents whereby their new value of 2 cents could be told, were it not for *The Gazette* notice.

Besides the above stamps, the 1 cent, black, of Waterlow's design, and the 1 cent and 2 cents of De la Rue's, surcharged OFFICIAL, were issued to the public at the same time, with this word obliterated with a black bar.

The admittance of British Guiana into the Postal Union took place on April 1st, 1879, after being notified in *The Official Gazette*, March 15th, 1879, as follows:—

" BRITISH GUIANA,

" GENERAL POST OFFICE, GEORGETOWN, *8th March*, 1879.

NOTICE.

" ON and after 1st April, 1879, the following changes will take place in the rates of postage and conditions of transmission of correspondence of various kinds forwarded from this Colony to Countries comprised in the General Postal Union :—

LETTERS.

" The rate on paid letters will be 8 cents per half-ounce, instead of 12 cents. Letters wholly unpaid will be charged 16 cents on delivery. Short paid letters will be charged double the amount of the deficiency of the prepaid rate.

POST CARDS.

" Rate—3 cents each.

" Only cards issued by the Government will be received. The front, or stamped side, is intended for the address only. There must be nothing else written, printed, or otherwise impressed on it, nor must there be any writing or printing across the stamp. On the reverse side any communication of the nature of a letter or otherwise may be written or printed. Nothing whatever may be attached; nor may the card be folded, cut, or otherwise altered. If any of these rules be infringed, the card will be treated as an insufficiently paid letter.

COMMERCIAL DOCUMENTS.

" Rate for a packet not over 4 ounces—5 cents.

" Every additional 2 ounces—2 cents.

" Prepayment is compulsory.

" The limit of size is 24 inches in length, and 12 inches in width or depth.

" The limit of weight is 4 lbs.

BOOK POST.

" Includes all printed papers (except newspapers), books, patterns, and samples of merchandise.

" Rate for every 2 ounces—2 cents.

" The limit of size and weight for books is the same as for commercial documents. The limit of weight for patterns and samples is 8 ounces, as before ; but the limit of size has been reduced to 8 inches in length, 4 inches in breadth, and two inches in depth. No article exceeding these limits can be forwarded.

NEWSPAPERS.

" No alteration. For each newspaper under 4 ounces—2 cents.

REGISTRATION FEE.

" The fee is 8 cents, as before.

PROHIBITED ARTICLES.

" Letters or packets containing gold or silver bullion, pieces of money, jewellery, precious articles, or any articles whatever liable to customs duty, cannot be forwarded.

" On the 1st April, 1879, the following will be the countries comprised in the General Postal Union, and to which the foregoing rates are applicable : —

" The whole of Europe.

" The whole of the French, Dutch, Spanish, Portuguese, and Danish Colonies, Possessions and Dependencies.

" The United States of North America.

" The whole of British North America.

" British India, and the Colonies of Bermuda (British Guiana), British Honduras, Jamaica, Trinidad, Mauritius, the Gold Coast, Sierra Leone Gambia, Lagos, Falkland Islands.

" The Argentine Republic.

" Brazil.

" Chili.

" Peru.

" Salvador.

" Mexico.

" Japan.

" Persia.

" (Signed)   " E. D. WIGHT,
" *Acting Colonial Postmaster.*"

Notwithstanding this notice, the 3-cent Post Card was not ready for issue until July 3rd. This is proved by the following notice, taken from *The Gazette*, July 2nd, 1879 :—

POST OFFICE NOTICE.

" GENERAL POST OFFICE,
" GEORGETOWN, *2nd July*, 1879.

" POST cards will be ready for issue at the General Post Office, George-town, to-morrow, the 3rd July, and at the several District Post Offices on Saturday, the 5th July. Post Cards will not be sold at the Post Offices in quantities of less than ten for thirty-six cents, or of one hundred for three dollars and fifty cents. Licensed vendors can obtain Post Cards from the Colonial Receiver General.

" (Signed)   E. D. WIGHT,
" *Acting Colonial Postmaster.*"

The next notice gives us the date of issue of the Registration Envelopes. It may be found in *The Gazette* for March 26th, 1881.

NOTICE.

" GENERAL POST OFFICE,
" GEORGETOWN, *24th March*, 1881.

" ENVELOPES for the purpose of Registration are now ready for issue at the General Post Office, Georgetown, at the Post Office, New Amsterdam, Berbice, and at all the District Post Offices.

" These Envelopes will be sold in Packets, each containing 10 Envelopes, and each Envelope having a Registration Fee Stamp of 4 Cents impressed thereon.

For a Packet of 10 Envelopes, Size G, 6 ×3½, 48 cents.
    „   „   „   Size H, 8 ×5, 56 „
    „   „   „   Size J, 10 ×7, 65 „
    „   „   „   Size K, 11½×6, 65 „
                     " (Signed)   E. D. WIGHT,
                                  " Acting Postmaster-General."

The next three notices of importance refer to the provisional stamps issued in December, 1881, and January, 1882. The first two appeared in *The Gazette* of December 24th and 28th respectively, and the third was published in *The Gazette* of January 7th, 1882.

NOTICE.

" BRITISH GUIANA, GENERAL POST OFFICE,
           " GEORGETOWN, *21st December*, 1881.

" A supply of POSTAGE STAMPS, ordered sometime ago, not having arrived, it has been deemed necessary to issue the following temporary STAMPS until the regular supply is received, namely :—

" 96 cent STAMPS, having the face value obliterated, and the figure 1 printed in the centre, will be issued as One Cent STAMPS.

" 96 cent STAMPS, having the face value obliterated, and the figure 2 printed in the centre, will be issued as Two Cent STAMPS.
          " (Signed)   E. D. WIGHT,
                      " Acting Postmaster-General."

NOTICE.

" BRITISH GUIANA, GENERAL POST OFFICE,
           " GEORGETOWN, *28th December*, 1881.

" THE following POSTAGE STAMPS will be issued as One and Two cents STAMPS, namely :—

12 cents STAMPS (Official).
48   „   „   „   and
48   „   „   will be used as One Cent STAMPS.
12   „   „   (Official).
24   „   „   „   will be used as Two Cents STAMPS.
          " (Signed)   E. D. WIGHT,
                      " Acting Postmaster-General."

NOTICE.

" BRITISH GUIANA, GENERAL POST OFFICE,
           " GEORGETOWN, *7th January*, 1882.

" AN issue of Provisional One and Two Cents Postage Stamps having been authorised, Notice is hereby given, that such Provisional Stamps are now ready for issue, but that they will be issued in such quantities only as the Acting Postmaster-General is satisfied are required for the actual purpose of prepaying postal matter.
          " (Signed)   E. D. WIGHT,
                      " Acting Postmaster-General."

There is no further notice to be found in *The Gazette* authorising the surcharge of the 12 cents and 24 cents, " official " Waterlow's type, with a figure 1 and 2 respectively, and with the original value obliterated. Mr. Luard says, in one of his letters to me, " The 1860 12 cents, lilac, surcharged 1, and the 1863 24 cents, green, surcharged 2, were not sold to the public, but all bought in by the present acting postmaster himself. The postmarks on a great number of these provisional stamps are not genuine, inasmuch as many speculators, when they bought the stamps, got the clerk to postmark them, and I have an acquaintance here who has the entire sheet of *unsevered* 96 cents stamps surcharged 2, each stamp in the sheet being carefully postmarked."

Mr. Luard further tells me that the one cent, black on rose, and the two cents, black on yellow, mentioned in the last notice, which were produced in the colony, were printed by Messrs. Baldwin and Co., a firm of booksellers, stationers, and printers, in Georgetown. He says, "After the stamps in question were printed they were taken to the Receiver General's Office, in the Guiana Public Buildings, and there the word '*Specimen*' was added. The very punching machine employed to punch the word 'specimen' is now used as a door weight in the office. A few sheets escaped the punch, and as many as were detected were returned from the Post Office to the Receiver General's Office to be punched."

These stamps were type-set, and the entire sheet of each value consists of twelve varieties, arranged sometimes in six horizontal rows of two, sometimes in four horizontal rows of three. I am unable to say which arrangement was first adopted, neither can I give the reason of the alteration. It may be that the printers found the sheets of paper would take more blocks one way than the other, and a saving of paper thus effected by the change. The same setting up did duty for both the one and two cents, the value only being altered; but in the alteration, some of the stamps have the remainder of the type shifted more or less. Taking the sheets of stamps two in a row, and comparing them with those having three in a row, the types on the former will be found placed as follows on the latter:—

No.	1	becomes No.	10
„	2	„	1
„	3	„	7
„	4	„	4
„	5	„	2
„	6	„	3
„	7	„	5
„	8	„	6
„	9	„	8
„	10	„	9
„	11	„	11
„	12	„	12

In addition to the changes noted above, there is a third setting up for the two cents value which was pointed out to me some two years ago by Mr. A de Reuterskiöld, an eminent Swiss Philatelist. This gentleman has succeeded in getting together eight out of the twelve types belonging to this arrangement, and has kindly allowed me to have an "autotype" taken of the varieties for publication in this work. The illustration is numbered 112. It will be seen on comparing this illustration with numbers 111 and 114, that the value "2 cents" is differently spaced as regards the border at the bottom of each of the stamps, and number six has a small figure 2 in place of a large one, while number nine has a large 2 in place of a small one. Whether there are any marked differences in numbers 1, 2, 4 and 5 is not known, as these varieties have still to be found. No third setting up of the one cent has yet been discovered.

The next notice, taken from *The Gazette*, April 15th, 1882, authorises Registration Envelopes and foreign Post Cards to be sold singly.

REGULATIONS.

"On and after Monday, the 1st May, Registration Envelopes and foreign Post Cards will be sold at every Post Office in the Colony, and by Stamp Vendors, at the following prices :—

REGISTRATION ENVELOPES.

		Small Size.				*Medium Size.*		*Large Size.* (*square & oblong*).
For	1	Envelope,	5 cents	...		6 cents	...	7 cents.
,,	2	,,	10 ,,	...		12 ,,	...	14 ,,
,,	3	,,	15 ,,	...		18 ,,	...	21 ,,
,,	4	,,	20 ,,	...		24 ,,	...	28 ,,
,,	5	,,	25 ,,	...		30 ,,	...	35 ,,
,,	6	,,	30 ,,	...		36 ,,	...	42 ,,
,,	7	,,	35 ,,	...		42 ,,	...	49 ,,
,,	8	,,	40 ,,	...		48 ,,	...	56 ,,
,,	9	,,	45 ,,	...		54 ,,	...	63 ,,
,,	10	,,	50 ,,	...		60 ,,	...	70 ,,

POST CARDS.

For	1	Card,	4 cents.
,,	2	,,	8 ,,
,,	3	,,	12 ,,
,,	4	,,	16 ,,
,,	5	,,	20 ,,
,,	6	,,	24 ,,
,,	7	,,	28 ,,
,,	8	,,	32 ,,
,,	9	,,	36 ,,
,,	10	,,	40 ,,

"The Post Cards are not available for circulation within the Colony, but are to be used only for communications to persons in England, and other countries in the Postal Union.

"(Signed)   F. M. HODGSON,
                         "*Postmaster General.*

"General Post Office,
       "Georgetown, *April*, 1882."

The next notice gives us the date of issue of the reply paid card 3+3 cents, and makes a reduction in the price of the 3 cents single cards. It is taken from *The Gazette*, August 25th, 1883.

POSTAL NOTICE.

Reduction in the Price Charged for Foreign Post Cards and Issue of Double Post Cards, that is, Cards Having a Prepaid Reply Attached.

"On and after the 1st September the foreign Post Cards hitherto sold at 4 cents each will be sold at 3 cents each. These cards are available for despatch to the United Kingdom, the Islands in the West Indies, and to all countries in the Postal Union. On and from the same date, Post Cards having a reply card attached will be sold at all Post Offices in the Colony for 6 cents each double card. The object of the double card is similar to that of prepaying the reply to a telegram ; namely, that the person to whom the card is sent may be placed in a position to send a reply without having to pay for it. Persons using the double card must be careful not to write on the reply card.

"The double card is available for use to the United Kingdom, the West India Islands, and to all countries in the Postal Union with the following exceptions: Brazil, Egypt, Guatemala, Japan, Mexico, Nicaragua, Peru, Russia, Venezuela, United States.

" (Signed)   F. M. HODGSON,

" GENERAL POST OFFICE,   " *Postmaster General.*

" GEORGETOWN, 24*th August*, 1883."

The 1 cent and 2 cents Newspaper Wrappers were issued on February 1st, 1884, in accordance with the terms of the following notice given in *The Gazette* of January 19th, 1884.

NOTICE.

SALE OF NEWSPAPER WRAPPERS.

"ON and after Friday, the 1st February, the sale of Newspaper Wrappers will be undertaken at the following Post Offices :—

Georgetown	...	...	...	(General Post Office.)
Belfield	...	...	...	
Buxton	...	...	...	
Mahaica	...	...	...	East Coast, Demerara.
Mahaicony	...	...	...	
Plaisance	...	...	...	
Fort Wellington	...	...		
New Amsterdam	...	...		Berbice.
Reliance	...	...	...	
Skeldon	...	...	...	
Leonora	...	...	...	
Tuschen	...	...	...	West Coast, Demerara.
Vreed-en-Hoop	...	...	...	
Leguan	...	...	...	
Good Success	...	...	...	(Wakenaam.)
Anna Regina	...	...	...	
Suddie	...	...	...	Arabian Coast, Essequibo.
Taymouth Manor	...	...		

" The Wrappers are in packets of 10, and will be sold as follows :—

1 cent stamp wrappers, per packet 12 cents.

2 ,,   ,,   ,,   24 ,,

" (Signed)   F. M. HODGSON,

" *Postmaster General.*

" GENERAL POST OFFICE,

" GEORGETOWN, 18*th January*, 1884."

On the 1st May, in the same year, the above wrappers were slightly reduced in price by the following :—

NOTICE.

ALTERATION IN THE PRICE OF NEWSPAPER WRAPPERS.

"ON and after the 1st May, Newspaper Wrappers will be sold at the following rates :—

1 cent wrappers in packets of 10 for 11 cents.

2 ,,   ,,   ,,   10 ,, 21 ,,

" (Signed)   E. D. WIGHT,

" *Acting Postmaster General.*

" GENERAL POST OFFICE, 30*th April*, 1884."

In *The Gazette* for August 19th, 1885, the following notice was inserted, withdrawing all provisional and other postage stamps from use, excepting those of the then current issue, the 96 cents of which had previously been withdrawn by the Post Office. Mr. Luard tells me this value was so withdrawn because a large number of the stamps were stolen from the Post Office.

H

POST OFFICE NOTICE.

WITHDRAWAL OF POSTAGE STAMPS FROM CIRCULATION.

"GENERAL POST OFFICE,
"GEORGETOWN, 20*th August*, 1885.

"ON and from the 1st October, 1885, "Provisional Issue Postage Stamps," and all Postage Stamps other than those of current issue, which are described below, will not be available for the prepayment of Postage.

"Postage Stamps, which by this notice will become obsolete, can be exchanged for current issue stamps of equal value on application at the Public Counter of the General Post Office up to the 30th September.

CURRENT ISSUE OF BRITISH GUIANA POSTAGE STAMPS.

"1 cent, gray
2 „ yellow
4 „ blue
6 „ light brown
8 „ red
12 „ mauve
24 „ green
48 „ chocolate

Ship in full sail turned to the right on shaded oval, with the motto *Damus Petimusque Vicissim* round it; value in cents on lower part; the words postage on top, and British Guiana at side.

"(Signed)   F. M. HODGSON,
"*Postmaster General.*"

The next notice I am able to give is that authorising the issue of inland post cards. It appeared in *The Gazette* of August 26th, 1885.

COURT OF POLICY NOTICE.

"HALL OF THE COURT OF POLICY,
"26*th August*, 1885.

"AT a Meeting of the Honourable the Court of Policy, held on the 19th instant, the following Rules and Regulations with respect to the use of Inland Post Cards were settled and approved, and are hereby published for general information :—

RULES AND REGULATIONS WITH RESPECT TO THE USE OF INLAND POST CARDS.

"1. Post Cards impressed with a 1 cent Stamp may be obtained at any Post Office in the Colony, and are available for transmission between places in the Colony.

"2. The front (or stamped) side is for the address only, in addition to the words printed thereon by the Government, and nothing else must be written, printed, or otherwise impressed on it, or on the stamp.

"3. On the reverse side any communication, whether of the nature of a letter or otherwise, may be written, printed, engraved or lithographed. Nothing whatever may be attached to the card, nor may a card be folded, cut, or otherwise altered.

"4. If the Rules in paragraphs 2 and 3 are infringed, the card will be treated as a letter, and charged 2 cents on delivery.

"5. Adhesive Stamps are not accepted in payment of postage on post cards.

"6. The Postmaster General may cause any Post Cards which contain communications obscenely or indecently worded, or which have upon them any marks or designs of an indecent, obscene, libellous, or offensive character to be stopped or destroyed.

" 7. Inland Post Cards shall be sold at the following rates:—

1 Card for three farthings.
2 Cards for 1½d.
3 Cards for two pence and one farthing.
4 Cards for three pence.
6 Cards for four pence.

" By Command,

" (Signed)   FRANCIS VILLIERS,

" *Acting Secretary.*"

The 1 cent cards not having arrived from England at the date of this notice, the 3 cents Postal Union card was issued provisionally, with the stamp surcharged across the centre ONE CENT, in two lines, in block letters, and the original value obliterated with a black bar.

On October 1st, 1888, a new " Stamp Duties " Ordinance came into force, Clause 7, of which reads as follows:—

" 7. The stamps to be used under any Ordinance imposing a stamp duty shall be impressed or adhesive as the Governor and Court of Policy may from time to time direct, and adhesive stamps made applicable on the face thereof for Postage and Revenue purposes may as soon as the same can be procured be issued and used to denote such duty."

The Gazette for October 3rd, 1888, contains the notice of issue of the first set of stamps for combined fiscal and postal use.

STAMP NOTICE.

" THE public are hereby notified that on and after Friday, the 5th instant, the Chief Commissary will be prepared to stamp Cheque Books, in part or in whole, in the possession of private individuals: and that stamps of the undermentioned values can be obtained, viz.:—

1 Cent.		40 Cent.
2 ,,		72 ,,
3 ,,		$1
4 ,,		$2
6 ,,		$3
8 ,,		$4
10 ,,		$5
20 ,,		

" Bills of Lading are now being stamped.

" (Signed)   W. S. TURNER,

" *Chief Commissary.*"

" CHIEF COMMISSARY'S OFFICE, GUIANA PUBLIC BUILDINGS,

" *3rd October*, 1888."

Mr. Luard informs me the values from seventy-two cents upwards were issued for postal purposes on October 1st, 1888, and that several of the other values were sold at the Post Offices, as the supply of the old stamps became exhausted; viz.: the two cents on the 25th May, 1889, the same stamp with an additional large *red* numeral " 2 " on the 5th June, and the one cent and eight cents in August the same year. He makes no mention of the issue of the three, four, six, ten, twenty, and forty cents by the Post Office, and it seems probable that these values were only sold for " revenue " purposes, although no doubt they would have franked letters if so applied. I have seen postmarked copies of these values, but whether these were obliterated " to order," or paid postage in the usual way, I am unable to say.

The following notice appeared in *The Gazette* of January 1st, 1890.

POST OFFICE NOTICE.

"GENERAL POST OFFICE,

"GEORGETOWN, *28th December*, 1889.

"NOTICE is hereby given for general information, that the following adhesive stamps issued by the Government for Revenue purposes, are not available for prepayment of Postage, and Postal matter franked with such stamps only will be regarded by the Post Office as unpaid, and treated accordingly.

REVENUE STAMPS.

$2·40	$9·60
$4·80	$12·00

"(Signed)　　　　F. W. COLLIER,

"*Postmaster General.*"

In July, 1890, the supply of one cent stamps again became exhausted, and recourse had once more to be made to a provisional issue. The stamp first selected to do duty for the required value, was the current one dollar, which was surcharged in red in two lines "One Cent," and the former value was obliterated by two straight bars. It was first issued on July 15th, 1890, according to *Stanley Gibbon's Monthly Journal*. As in the case of some of the previous provisional issues, these stamps were greedily bought up by speculators, who thought to make a good thing out of their purchase. The demand was in fact so excessive that the Stamp Commissioners published the following notice in *The Gazette* of July 30th, 1890.

STAMP NOTICE.

"THE Commissioners of Stamps hereby give notice that the issue of provisional stamps to licensed vendors will, for the present, be suspended, as the supplies already issued are amply sufficient for revenue and postal purposes; where stamps of the one cent value are required for such purposes, they may be obtained at the Post Offices.

"(Signed)　　　CHARLES PIERCY AUSTIN, ⎫
　　　　　　　　W. S. TURNER, 　　　　⎬ *Commissioners of Stamps.*
　　　　　　　　F. W. COLLIER, 　　　　⎭

"*28th July*, 1890."

The publication of this notice called forth loud remonstrances from the Press, and the absurdity of refusing to supply stamps to all comers was pointed out. Among other articles which appeared in the newspapers, was the following, which may be found in *The Argosy* of August 2nd, 1890.

"In our correspondence columns to-day is a letter from a Water Street merchant relating an incident which is likely to be memorable in the history of our postage stamps. Our system of Government is known to be paternal, most paternal. A man may buy at one time only a small measure of opium and only one quart of rum. And now— Heaven bless them for their kindness—our authorities have decided that the people shall not be allowed to buy more than a certain number of postage stamps !!! This is not a joke. It is a positive fact. The three Stamp Commissioners, Messrs. Austin, Turner and Collier (we mention their names with reluctance) have issued a notice that as a sufficient number of one cent stamps for the postal requirements of the colony has been issued, the further sale will be conducted only at the Post Office, under regulations. From the founding of that useful commodity the postage stamp, its sale in all countries in the world has been according to the wants of the buyers; the one desire of the issuers of it being to have as many as possible sold. All over the globe the stamp collector's album is to be found, in the smallest cottage and in the Royal palace; stamp collection (*sic*) has been elevated into a science, and at the present moment the treasures of a philatelic exhibition in London is delighting the most intellectual people of the empire. Because collectors and those who collect for collectors bought up large quantities of a provisional issue of one-cent stamps which our Government had to issue, a month ago, the Commissioners have lost their head entirely, and see in this important contribution to the revenue of the Post Office, an attempt to trifle with the Fiscal machinery. One of the Commissioners stated in Court that the printer could supply 60,000 of the new stamps per day (and considering that the printing is done at the rate of 60 in one impression, the Commissioner might have said 300,000 a day so far as the printer is concerned) and at this rate the local demands could soon have been met in full. But however long or deep the local demands were, the Government ought to have continued to supply them as long as there was any paper left in the colony. The Commissioners are deliberately interfering with a legitimate branch 'of postal revenue, and if strict justice were meted out to them, they would be called upon to make good the loss their misapprehension of the range and utility of the postage stamp, has caused and is causing the colonial revenue."

The Stamp Commissioners apparently soon realised their mistake, the same surcharge of "One Cent" being applied to the current two, three, and four dollar adhesives in turn, as the supply of each value became used up, and the following notice was published in *The Gazette* of August 23rd, 1890.

STAMP NOTICE.

"THE Commissioners of Stamps hereby give notice that the issue of the provisional One Cent Stamps to Licensed Vendors will be continued from and after this date.

"(Signed)   CHAS. PIERCY AUSTIN,   ⎫
                 W. S. TURNER,   ⎬ *Commissioners of Stamps.*
                 F. W. COLLIER,   ⎭

"21st August, 1890."

Stanley Gibbon's Monthly Journal for June, 1891, gives the number of the four varieties issued as follows :—

1 cent on 1 dollar, 121,800.	1 cent on 3 dollars, 111,000.
1 „ „ 2 „ 111,000.	1 „ „ 4 „ 54,000.

On October 1st, 1890, Postcards and Newspaper Wrappers were sold at their face value, in accordance with the following two notices, the former of which was published in *The Gazette* of September 27th, and the latter in the issue of that paper for October 1st, for the year mentioned.

GOVERNMENT NOTICE.

"26th September, 1890.

"NOTICE is hereby given for general information that the Court of Policy at its 'meeting on the 19th September, approved of Inland Post Cards and Newspaper Wrappers being sold 'at their face value, and of only the *small sized registration envelopes being issued in future,* the charge for which will be five cents each.

POST OFFICE NOTICE.

POST CARDS AND NEWSPAPER WRAPPERS.

"GENERAL POST OFFICE, 27th September, 1890.

"ON and after Wednesday, the 1st October, proximo, Post Cards and Newspaper Wrappers may be purchased at any Post Office in the Colony at the face value, as follows :—

POST CARDS.

Inland	...	...	...	... 1 cent each.
Foreign	...	...	...	... 3 cents each.
Do. Reply paid	...		...	... 6 cents each.

NEWSPAPER WRAPPERS.

" 2 cents and 1 cent each.

" These wrappers may be used for Newspapers, or for such Documents as are allowed to be sent at the book rate of postage.

     " (Signed)   F. W. COLLIER,

                       " *Postmaster General.*"

In conclusion, I give a list of the Colony's present *Inland* Postal Rates, taken from the current *Post Office Guide*, published on May 1st, 1884, making the necessary alterations advertised in *The Gazette* of April 21st, 1886.

LETTERS.

For a letter not exceeding 1 oz.   ...   .   2 cents.

   "   "   above 1 oz., but not exceeding 2 oz.   3   "

   "   "   2 "   "   "   4 oz.   4   "

And at the rate of 1 cent for every additional 2 oz. up to 2 lbs.

Letters not exceeding ¼ oz. in weight, posted in Georgetown for delivery in Georgetown, or in New Amsterdam for delivery in New Amsterdam, can be sent for a prepaid postage of ...   1 cent.

For letters exceeding ¼ oz. in weight, the rate is the same as for letters to other parts of the Colony.

NEWSPAPERS.

For each Newspaper posted in the Colony   ...   1 cent.

CIRCULARS AND PRICES CURRENT.

For each article   ...   .   1 cent.

BOOK PACKETS.

For a packet not exceeding 4 oz.   ...   1 cent.

   "   each additional 4 oz.   ...   ...   2 cents.

REGISTRATION.

The fee for each article is   ...   .   4 cents.

On comparing the above rates with those current at the time of the introduction of postage stamps, we shall see the great reductions made in the postal service since 1850.

REFERENCE LIST OF THE PHILATELIC SOCIETY, LONDON.

Issue I. July 1st, 1850.

Four values. Locally printed from a series of blocks. The numerals of value were moveable, and were fitted in as the stamps of each value were required. The stamps were printed in black, on coarse, coloured wove paper, varying considerably in substance, and the four cents is also found upon pelure paper. The stamps are unperforated. Design : An irregular single lined circle or oval contains the inscription BRITISH GUIANA in Roman capitals, following the curve of the circle on the inside. The value in numerals and the word *Cents* in small italic type are in a straight line across the centre. Each stamp was initialled before issue by the Postmaster or one of the clerks in the Post Office at Georgetown. Shape, circular or oval. (*Illustrations* 57-60.)

A. On medium wove paper.

     (1st March, 1851), 2 c., black on pale rose.

            4 c., black on orange (shades).

            4 c., black on lemon-yellow.

            8 c., black on green (shades).

            12 c., black on blue, indigo, pale blue (shades).

B. On pelure paper.

4 c., black on pale lemon-yellow.

Varieties. a. Without initials.

8 c., black on green.

b. With large figure 2 with straight foot. (*Illustration* 60.)

12 c., pale blue.

Remarks.—There are several varieties of type of these stamps, see *Illustrations* 60—67, information concerning which will be found given in Mr. E. D. Bacon's Paper.

Issue II.   January 1st, 1852.

Two values. Designed and lithographed by Messrs. Waterlow and Sons, of London. Black impression on medium surface-coloured wove paper, unwatermarked and unperforated, brown gum. Design: A plain shield containing a ship sailing to the right, a fort being depicted in the left background, and another ship in the distance in the right background. Above the shield is the value in numerals and block letters, and below is the motto of the Colony signifying, "WE GIVE AND ASK IN TURN," in smaller block letters. On the left and right is the name of the Colony, and the whole design is contained in a single lined rectangular frame. Shape, large upright rectangular. (*Illustrations* 68, 69.)

T. "1 CENT."   "4 CENTS."   B. "DAMUS PATIMUSQUE VICISSIM."   L. "BRITISH," reading upwards.   R. "GUIANA," reading downwards.

1 c., black on magenta (shades).

4 c., black on bright blue (shades).

Remarks.—There are two varieties of type of each value printed side by side, which in the case of the one cent may readily be distinguished from each other by the absence on one variety of the period after GUIANA. In both values other slight differences are readily discernible in the details of the forts and the shading of the waves. It will be noticed that in the legend PATIMUSQUE is printed in error for PETIMUSQUE. This mistake must be attributed to the workman who engraved the original dies.

Issue III.   1853.

Two values. Lithographed by Messrs. Waterlow and Sons, of London, and printed on white wove paper varying in substance, unwatermarked and unperforated. Yellowish gum. Design: A barque sailing to the left on a background of lines crossed obliquely within a linear oval band, containing the legend, "DAMUS PETIMUSQUE VICISSIM," in small coloured block letters. Straight coloured labels above and below, contain an inscription and the value in white Roman capitals, and similar labels at the sides contain the name of the Colony in the same lettering. In the four corners there are small square blocks, each containing one of the figures of the date 1853. The figures are in white and are printed upon an eight rayed star upon a diagonally lined ground, and the space between the corner blocks and the inscriptions at the sides is filled in with a white reticulated pattern. The spandrels are filled in with concentric circular ornamentation, and the design is completed by a single outer line of colour. Shape, upright rectangular. (*Illustration* 70.)

T. "POSTAGE."   B. "ONE CENT."   "FOUR CENTS."   L. "BRITISH," reading upwards.
R. "GUIANA," reading downwards.

1 c., vermilion, brownish-red (shades).

4 c., blue, pale to dark.

Varieties.   *a.* With white line above the value. (*Illustration* 71.)

     1 c., red, red-brown (shades).

     4 c., blue, pale to dark.

b. With letter o of ONE further away from the left corner block. (*Illustration* 72).

     1 c., red, red-brown (shades).

c. With small letter o to ONE. (*Illustration* 73.)

     1 c., red, red-brown (shades).

Remarks.—The four cents is also found with a period between the letters s and T of POSTAGE. This variety is due to a defect in transferring the impressions to the lithographic stone from the engraved die. Full particulars concerning the method employed for printing the stamps of this issue, with an explanation as to how the varieties *a*, *b*, and *c* may be accounted for, are given in Mr. E. D. Bacon's Paper.

Issue IV.   Early in 1856.

Two values. Designed and typographed locally. Black impression on medium coloured paper, unwatermarked and unperforated. Brownish gum. Design : A ship sailing to the right. Above are the words "Damus Petimus," and below "Que Vicissim" in two straight lines in lower case type, the initial letter of each word being a capital. The whole is in an oblong rectangular frame composed of four lines, which usually do not meet at the corners. Outside the frame, and surrounding it, is an inscription in Roman capitals. As in the case of the first issue, each stamp was initialled before use. Shape, large, oblong, rectangular. (*Illustration* 82.)

     T. "BRITISH."   B. "GUIANA."   L. "POSTAGE, reading upwards.   R. "ONE CENT."

     "FOUR CENTS," reading upwards.

     A. On paper coloured on the surface only.

     1 c., black on magenta.

     4 c.,   ,,   ,,   ,,   (shades).

     4 c.,   ,,   ,,   carmine-rose (,,   )

     4 c.,   ,,   ,,   pale blue   (,,   )

     B. On paper coloured right through.

     4 c., black on dark blue.

Remarks.—Several varieties of type of the four cents exist, chiefly distinguishable from each other by the relative positions and spacing of the inscriptions. At least eight are known to the Society, which are given as *Illustration* 82; but the number of varieties to the sheet, and their arrangement are still only matter of conjecture. Numbers one and five in the illustration, are a vertical unsevered pair in the collection of the late Mr. T. K. Tapling. Judging from postmarked specimens the issue took place in February, 1856. The stamps on the magenta surface paper seem to have been first used, then those on the blue paper "coloured right through," about August, 1856, and lastly those on the blue surface paper, which are usually found postmarked later on in that year.

Issue V.   1860 (?).

One value. Lithographed and printed by Messrs. Waterlow and Sons by transfer from a newly engraved die, on medium white wove unwatermarked paper. Unperforated. Yellowish gum. Design : Very similar to that of the four cents of Issue III., but the numerals in the corner blocks are upon a dotted ground, and the blocks are enframed by thin white lines. There is a white line above the value and numerous other minute differences in other details of the design. The vessel depicted is no longer a barque, but is square rigged. Shape, upright rectangular. (*Illustration* 74.)

     4 c., pale blue (slight shades).

Issue VI. May (?), 1860.

Six values. Designed and lithographed by Messrs. Waterlow and Sons, of London. Coloured impression on stout white wove unwatermarked paper, varying in substance. Machine perforated 12. Yellowish gum. Design : A ship sailing to the right on a background of horizontal lines enclosed by a garter of solid colour containing the inscription " DAMUS PETIMUSQUE VICISSIM " in white block letters. Above, below, and at the sides there are straight horizontal and vertical labels of solid colour containing an inscription and the value ; the latter, in the case of the three lower values being expressed in words, and in numerals on the higher values. The value is placed about 2 mm. distant from the word " CENTS," except in the four cents, where the distance is 1 mm. Inscriptions and values are printed in white Roman capitals or numerals. The spandrels are enclosed by a wavy line, and are filled in with reticulated ornamentation. The corners consist of square blocks of solid colour enframed by white lines, and each contains a white Arabic numeral of the date 1860. A single outer line of colour completes the design. Shape upright, rectangular. (*Illustrations* 75, 76.)

T. " GUIANA." B. " ONE CENT," ' TWO CENTS," ' FOUR CENTS," " VIII. CENTS," " XII. CENTS," " XXIV. CENTS." L. " BRITISH," reading upwards. R. " POSTAGE," reading downwards.

> 1 c., pale rose, violet-rose (shades).
> 2 c., orange.
> 4 c., light blue.
> 8 c., pale rose, brownish-rose (shades).
> 12 c., grey, lilac, brownish-lilac („)
> 24 c., yellow-green („)

Variety. The eight cents is known cut in half diagonally, and used (in November, 1861) for half the value.

> 4 c. (half 8 c.) rose.

Remarks. —The one, two, eight, and twelve cents exist on slightly toned paper. Full particulars concerning the twelve cents with " 5d." in red (*Illustration* 77) will be found in Mr. E. D. Bacon's paper.

Issue VII. 1861.

One value. Same in all respects as Issue VI., but changed in colour. Paper, perforation, etc., as before. (*Illustration* 75.)

> 1 c., red-brown (shades).

Remarks. —A pair of these stamps has been seen by the Society postmarked October 29th, 1861.

Issue VIII. 1862.

One value. Same design as Issue VII., but changed in colour, and the paper is very thin, almost pelure. Perforation, gum, etc., as before. (*Illustration* 75.)

> 1 c., dark chocolate-brown (slight shades).

Issue IX. October (?) 1862.

Three values. Provisional Issue. Designed and type printed in the Colony. Black impression on medium coloured wove paper, unwatermarked. Rouletted 6. Yellowish gum. Design : ONE CENT, TWO CENTS. A blank rectangular space bounded by plain lines constitutes the centre of the stamp. Surrounding this rectangular frame is an inscription and the value in Roman capitals and numerals. A bordering of various type pattern ornaments enframes the whole.

The varieties of bordering, which are known to printers under the name of " *Minion Flowers* "; may be described as follows :—

> (*a*) Border composed of small ovals, placed diagonally, and crossed with small lines.
> (*b*) Border composed of small shaded circles or pearls.
> (*c*) Border composed of grape pattern ornamentation.

I

FOUR CENTS. Very similar to the one and two cents, but the bordering pattern is different in design, and certain specimens on the sheet are without the lines forming the central rectangular frame.

The varieties of bordering, etc., may be classified as follows :—

(*d*) Border composed of a pattern called "hearts and pearls."

(*e*) Border composed of small crosses in rosaces.

(*f*) Border composed of a trefoil pattern.

Each stamp was initialled by Mr. Robert Mather, acting Receiver General of the Colony, before being issued to the public. Shape upright rectangular. (*Illustrations* 83, 84, 85.)

T. "GUIANA." B. "ONE CENT." "TWO CENTS." "FOUR CENTS." L. "BRITISH," reading upwards, R. "POSTAGE," reading downwards.

Borders (*a*) (*b*) (*c*) 1 c., black on dull rose.

   "   "   "   2 c.,   "   "   lemon yellow.

Borders (*d*) (*e*) (*f*) 4 c.,   "   "   dark blue.

PROMINENT VARIETIES.

1 c., variety 24, the word "POSTAGE" is misspelt "POSTAGE."

2 c.,   "   13, the word "TWO" is misspelt "TWC."

2 c.,   "   16, the "*s*" of "CENTS" is an italic letter.

2 c.,   "   18, the "*t*" of "TWO" is an italic letter.

2 c.,   "   24, the word "POSTAGE" is misspelt "POSTAGE."

4 c., varieties 8 & 14, the "*s*" of "CENTS" is an italic letter.

4 c., variety 15,   the "*s*" of "BRITISH" is an italic letter.

4 c., varieties 13 to 24, have no inner lines.

Remarks.—The information which follows has been taken from a paper read before the London Philatelic Society by the President on July 2nd, 1881. It was afterwards published in the *Philatelic Record, Vol. III., p. 108.* "The issue took place in October, 1862, in order to supply a temporary failure in the current issues of the one, two, and four cents values, the stock of which had become exhausted at the moment, no supply having arrived from England. The Post Office was then under the charge of Mr. E. T. E. Dalton as Postmaster, Mr. Robert Mather being Acting Receiver General of the Colony. Recourse was had to the printers of the *Royal Gazette* at Georgetown, and they were asked to supply the necessary substitutes, being instructed to print the stamps in the above values on red, yellow, and blue paper respectively. Accordingly Mr. George Melville caused the three denominations of value to be set up in type and printed off at the *Gazette* office. The resources of the establishment in the matter of ornamental type being limited, it was necessary to print off both the one and two cents value from the same designs, but for the four cents a change of type was available. The sheets were composed of 24 stamps, each separately set up, and of course showing as many varieties of type as there were stamps to the sheet. They were arranged in four horizontal rows comprising six stamps to the row. The supply of the one cent value having first been printed off, the two cents were printed after the lettering of the value had been altered from *one cent* to *two cents*. Thus it follows that all the varieties found on the sheet of the one cent, are repeated on that of the two cents, while all the twenty-four stamps of the four cents differ from those of the two lower values and from each other. The size of the sheets was $4\frac{1}{4} \times 5\frac{3}{4}$ inches, or 107×145 mm. The impression was printed by a small hand press, still in use in the *Gazette* office. When printed, the adhesive matter (a strong gum) was applied to the backs, and the perforation was effected by a roulette machine worked by hand, as is evident from the irregular angles formed by the lines of perforation: some are in lines running truly and forming right angles, in others the lines are more or less oblique, and cause the stamps to be out of the square. After reception at the Post Office, and before being issued for circulation, each stamp was separately initialled by Mr. Mather, " R.M., Ac., R.G.," in ink, black on the one cent, red on the two cents, and white (as it looks) on the four cents ; but the white appearance is due to the initials being written in an alkali, which discharged the colour of the paper. The stamps when the *paraphe* had been thus applied, were issued and sold for ordinary use at their facial value. In the great "find" of the older values of British Guiana stamps in 1877-8, which resulted in most of the great European collections supplying their *lacunae* in the stamps of this Colony, but very few of these provisionals were discovered. They have always been rare, and of late years their rarity has rather increased, although forgeries are exceedingly rife."

The author of the paper from which the above extracts have been quoted, next proceeds to give in detail the differences between each stamp on the sheets ; but the "autotype." illustrations of the entire sheets, obviates the necessity of their repetition here.

Issue X. 1862.

Six values. Same as to design, etc., as Issue VI., but the paper is thinner and more transparent. Machine perforated. (*Illustrations* 75, 76.)

A.—*Perf.* 12.

1 c., black, grey-black.
2 c., orange (shades).
4 c., dull blue, greenish-blue (shades).
8 c., rose (shades).
12 c., lilac, grey-lilac (shades).
24 c., yellow-green (shades).

B.—*Perf.* 12½.

Same values, colours and shades.

Varieties. The 1, 4, 8, and 24 cents exist imperforate.

Remarks.—All the values except the twenty-four cents are known to exist on toned paper, perforated (A) and perforated (B).

Issue XI. 1863.

Four values. Designed and lithographed by Messrs. Waterlow and Sons. Coloured impression on medium white wove paper, unwatermarked. Yellowish gum, machine perforated 12½. Design : Very similar to that of the preceding issue, but the value is placed closer to the word " CENTS," being about 1 mm. distant. In the preceding issue the distance was about 2 mm., though there were slight differences between the various values. In all other respects the types appear to be the same, making allowance for printing by lithography. (*Illustrations* 78, 79.)

1 c., black.
2 c., orange (shades).
8 c., rose, violet-rose (shades).
12 c., grey, lilac, brownish-lilac (shades).

Varieties. All four values exist imperforate.

Issue XII. August, 1863.

Three values. [Designed and lithographed by Messrs. Waterlow and Sons. Coloured impression on medium white, or toned wove paper, unwatermarked. Yellowish gum. Machine perforated. Design : Ship sailing to right, with a background of clouds, within a white circular band, containing the words " DAMUS PETIMUSQUE VICISSIM " in coloured block letters. The corners consist of square blocks of solid colour, enframed with white lines, and each containing an Arabic numeral of the date 1863. Straight white labels above and below contain the abbreviated name of the Colony, and the value, all in coloured Roman capitals or numerals. The spandrels are filled in with white arabesque ornamentation, and the design is completed by a double outer line of colour. Shape, large upright rectangular. (*Illustration* 80.)

T. "B. GUIANA." B. "VI. CENTS." "XXIV. CENTS." "XLVIII. CENTS."

A.—*Perf.* 12.

24 c. green, yellow-green (shades).

B.—*Perf.* 12¼.

6 c., blue, dark blue, ultramarine (shades).

24 c., green, yellow-green (shades).

48 c., rose-red (shades).

Varieties. The 6 and 24 cents exist unperforated, and all three values are found on toned paper perf. 12¼. The 48 cents exists with a full stop after the "r." of "PETIMUSQUE."

Issue XIII. 1868.

Eight values. The designs are those of Issues VI., XI., and XII., but the stamps are perforated 10. The paper, toned or white, varies in substance. (*Illustrations* 76, 78, 79, 80.)

A.—*Designs of Issue* VI.

4 c., pale blue, blue, greenish-blue (shades).

12 c., dull lilac (shades).

B.—*Designs of Issue* XI.

1 c., black, grey-black.

2 c., orange, orange-yellow (shades).

8 c., rose, rose-red, violet-rose (shades).

12 c., grey, lilac, (shades).

C.—*Designs of Issue* XII.

6 c., blue, dark blue, ultramarine (shades).

24 c., yellow-green (shades).

48 c., rose-red (shades).

Varieties. All these stamps exist on toned paper.

Issue XIV. 1875.

Seven values. Same in all respects as the preceding issue, but perforated 15. (*Illustrations* 78, 79, 80.)

A.—*Design of Issue* VI.

4 c., pale blue.

B.—*Designs of Issue* XI.

1 c., black.

2 c., orange (shades).

8 c., rose-red (shades).

12 c., dull lilac („).

C.—*Designs of Issue* XII.

6 c., ultramarine.

24 c., yellow-green.

Issue XV. July 1st, 1876.

Nine values. Engraved and surface printed by Messrs. De la Rue and Co., of London. Coloured impression on medium white wove paper, watermarked Crown C.C. White gum. Machine perforated 14. Design: Ship sailing to right on a background of horizontal lines within an upright rectangular double lined frame, curved at the top and bottom and straight at the sides. Around the frame and following its shape, there is a narrow coloured band containing an inscription in white block letters and white arabesque ornamentation. L. DAMUS (reading upwards). T. PETIMUSQUE. R. VICISSIM (reading downwards). B. White arabesque ornamentation. Straight white labels at the top, bottom, and sides contain an inscription and the value in coloured block letters and numerals. The spandrels consist of coloured triangular blocks containing white floriate ornaments, and the design is completed by a double outer line of colour. Shape upright rectangular. (*Illustration* 81.)

T. "POSTAGE." L. "BRITISH," reading upwards. R. "GUIANA," reading upwards. B. "1 CENT." "2 CENTS." "4 CENTS." "6 CENTS." "8 CENTS." "12 CENTS." "24 CENTS." "48 CENTS." "96 CENTS."

        1 c., grey, indigo-grey (shades).
        2 c., orange, yellow   („   )
        4 c., ultramarine   („   )
        6 c., chocolate-brown   („   )
        8 c., rose   („   )
       12 c., lilac, grey-lilac („   )
       24 c., green   („   )
       48 c., red-brown   („   )
       96 c., olive-yellow   („   )

Variety. M. Moens catalogues the 2 cents surcharged "1D" in red. No specimen is known to the Society. It is probably either a "bogus" surcharge altogether, or else a mark of insufficiently prepaid postage, applied at the Post Office after the letter was posted.

Issue XVI. 1878.

Two values. Provisional issue. The supply of one and two cent stamps having given out, the Government authorised the surcharging of several of the higher values of Issues XIII. and XV. as issued to the public, and of certain values of Issues I. and II. of the "OFFICIAL" stamps, described later under a separate heading. The surcharge consists of one or two broad bars of black ink, apparently applied with a brush, and obliterating either the value, the surcharged word "OFFICIAL," or both. Watermark, perforation, etc., as previously or subsequently described for the respective issues.

I.—Ordinary stamps not bearing the word "OFFICIAL."

A. With a horizontal bar over the value, and another across the upper portion of the stamp, both 3 mm. in width.

(April 16th, 1878) (1 c.) black surcharge, on 6 c., brown Issue XV. (*Illustration* 86.)

B. With a horizontal bar over the value, and a vertical bar down the centre both 3mm. in width.

(Nov. 6th, 1878) (1 c.) black surcharge, on 6 c., ultramarine. Issue XIII. (*Illustration* 87.)
(„ „ „) (1 c.) „ „ „ 6 c., brown „ XV. („ 88.)

II.—Surcharged upon stamps surcharged "OFFICIAL."

C. With a horizontal bar, 3mm. in width, obliterating the word "OFFICIAL."

(Nov., 1878) 1 c., black surcharge, on 1 c., black, surcharged "OFFICIAL" in red, Issue I. (a) (*Illustration* 89.)
(„ „) 1 c., „ „ „ 1 c., grey, „ „ „ black „ II. („ 90.)
(„ „) 2 c., „ „ „ 2 c., orange, „ „ „ „ II. („ 90.)

D. With a thick horizontal bar, 6mm. in width, over the value and "OFFICIAL"; and a thinner vertical bar, 3mm. in width, down the centre.

Nov., 1878) (1 c.) black surcharge, on 4 c. ultramarine, surcharged "OFFICIAL" in black. Issue II. (*Illus.* 91.)
„ „) (1 c.) „ „ „ 6 c. brown, „ „ „ „ II. („ 91.)
„ „) (2 c.) „ „ „ 8 c. rose, „ „ „ „ I. (c) („ 92.)

E. With a horizontal bar over the value. The word "OFFICIAL" not obliterated. Vertical bar down the centre. Both bars are 3mm. in width.

(Nov. 23rd, 1878). (1 c.) black surcharge, on 4 c. ultramarine, surcharged "OFFICIAL" in black. Issue II. (*Illus.* 93.)
(„ „ „). (2 c.) „ „ „ 6 c. rose, „ „ „ „ II. („ 93.)

Remarks.—The four cents with surcharge *variety E* is unknown to the Society. It is catalogued by M. Moens.

Issue XVII. December, 1881.

Two values. Provisional issue. Various stamps of Issues XIII. and XV., and of the series surcharged " OFFICIAL" Issues I. and II., with the value obliterated by a black or red bar and a numeral " 1 " or " 2 " surcharged in black in the centre of the stamps. The numerals are found in two sizes, and with the exception of the larger size of the one cent, two prominent varieties of type of each numeral in each size exist side by side on the same sheet. The obliterating bars also vary in thickness. Paper, perforation, etc., the same as previously or subsequently described for the respective issues.

I.—Ordinary stamps not bearing the word " OFFICIAL."

A. Numeral 4mm. in height.

(a.) Obliterating bar 1mm. thick.

1 (c.), black surcharge, on 48 c., rose-red Issue XIII. surcharge type I.   (*Illustration* 94.)
1 (c.),   „   „   „ 48 c.,   „   „ XIII.   „   „ II.   („   95)

Remarks.—The latter variety of type appears to be only found on the stamp with the dot after the F of FETIMUSQUE. The former exists on stamps with and without the dot.

(b.) Obliterating bar 2½mm. thick.

1 (c.), black surcharge, on 48 c., rose-red Issue XIII. surcharge type I.   (*Illustrat on* 94)
1 (c.),   „   „   „ 48 c.,   „   „ XIII.   „   „ II. (95.)

Remarks.—As in the former case, the latter type probably exists only on the variety with a dot after the F of FETIMUSQUE. The surcharge type I. exists on stamps with and without the dot.

(c.) Obliterating bar 4mm. thick.

1 (c.), black surcharge, on 48 c., rose-red Issue XIII. surcharge type I.   (*Illustration* 94.)
1 (c.),   „   „   „ 48 c.,   „   „ XIII.   „   „ II.   „   93.)

Remarks.—As in the former case, this latter type probably exists only on the variety with a dot after the F of FETIMUSQUE. The surcharge type I. exists on stamps with and without the dot.

B. The numerals are 7mm. in height.

(a.) Obliterating bar 1mm. thick.

1 (c.), black surcharge, on 96 c., olive-yellow Issue XV. one type only of surcharge. (*Illustration* 96.)
2 (c.),   „   „   „ 96 c.,   „   „ XV. surcharge type I.   („   97.)
2 (c.),   „   „   „ 96 c.,   „   „ XV.   „   „ II.   („   98.)

(b.) Obliterating bar 3mm. thick.

1 (c.), black surcharge, on 96 c., olive-yellow Issue XV. one type only of surcharge. (*Illustration* 96.)
2 (c.),   „   „   „ 96 c.,   „   „ XV. surcharge type I.   („   97.)
2 (c.),   „   „   „ 96 c.,   „   „ XV.   „   „ II.   („   98.)

Varieties. Both varieties of type of numeral of the 2 cents exist with a double obliterating bar over the value, in two colours, black and red. The black bar is 3mm. in width, and the red 1mm. (*Illustration* 99.)

II.—Surcharged upon stamps surcharged "OFFICIAL."

A. Numeral 4mm. in height.

(a.) Obliterating bar 1mm. thick.

1 (c.), black surcharge, on 12 c., lilac, surcharged " OFFICIAL " in black Issue I. (c.) (*Illustration* 100.)
1 (c.),   „   „   „ 48 c., red-brown „   „   „   „   „ II., (,   102.)
2 (c.),   „   „   „ 12 c., lilac   „   „   „   „   „ II. surcharge type I. (*Illus.* 103.)
2 (c.),   „   „   „ 12 c.,   „   „   „   „   „   „ II.   „   „ II. („ 104.)
2 (c.),   „   „   „ 24 c., green   „   „   „   „   „ II.   „   „ I. („ 103.)
2 (c.),   „   „   „ 24 c.,   „   „   „   „   „   „ II.   „   „ II. („ 104.)

(b.) Obliterating bar 2mm. thick.

1 (c.), black surcharge, on 12 c., lilac,   surcharged " OFFICIAL " in black Issue I., (c.) (*Illustration* 101.)
1 (c.),   „   „   „ 48 c., red-brown „   „   „   „   „ II.   „   102.)

(c.) Obliterating bar 3mm. thick.

2 (c.), black surcharge, on 12 c., lilac, surcharged "OFFICIAL " in black Issue II. surcharge type I. (*Illus.* 103.)
2 (c.), ,, ,, ,, 12 c., ,, ,, ,, ,, II. ,, ,, II. (,, 104.)
2 (c.), ,, ,, ,, 24 c., green ,, ,, ,, ,, II. ,, ,, I. (,, 103.)
2 (c.), ,, ,, ,, 24 c., ,, ,, ,, ,, II. ,, ,, II. (,, 104.)

Varieties. *(a)* Double surcharge, type I., on 12 c., lilac.

(b) ,, ,, types I. & II., on 12 c., lilac.

(c) No surcharged numeral of value (2), on 24 c., green.

B. Numeral 7mm. in height.

Obliterating bar 3mm. thick.

2 (c.), black surcharge, on 24 c., green, surcharged "OFFICIAL" in black Issue I., (c.) (*Illustration* 105.)

Remarks.—In the foregoing complicated list it is perhaps open to question whether the variations in the width of the obliterating bars are worthy of separate classification. The variations, however, are constant, and the sets perfectly distinct, and lead to the conclusion that the process of surcharging took place on several separate occasions.

Issue XVIII. January 7th, 1882.

Two values. Provisional issue. Type set and printed by Messrs. Baldwin and Co., Georgetown. Black impression on medium coloured wove paper, unwatermarked, machine perforated 12. Design : Ship or brig sailing to right on plain ground within a single-lined rectangular frame. Surrounding the frame there is an inscription and the value in block letters and numerals. Outside each corner of the frame there is an Arabic numeral of the date 1882. The whole is enframed by a fancy border of type pattern ornamentation. Each stamp was perforated across the face with the word "SPECIMEN." Shape, large square. (*Illustrations* 110, 111, 112, 113, 114.)

T. "POSTAGE." D. "1 CENT." "2 CENTS." L. "BRITISH," reading upwards.

R. "GUIANA," reading downwards.

(*a*) With "SPECIMEN" reading downwards from left to right.

1 c., black on rose.

2 c., ,, ,, yellow.

(*b*) With "SPECIMEN" reading downwards from right to left.

1 c., black on rose.

2 c., ,, ,, yellow.

(*c*) With "SPECIMEN" reading upwards from left to right.

1 c., black on rose.

2 c. ,, ,, yellow.

(*d*) With "SPECIMEN" reading upwards from right to left.

1 c., black on rose.

2 c., ,, ,, yellow.

Varieties. With "SPECIMEN" struck twice. 1 and 2 cents, variety (*d*).

With "SPECIMEN" struck three times. 1 cent, variety (*d*).

Without "SPECIMEN". 1 and 2 cents.

Remarks.—There were twelve stamps of each value to the sheet, and as each was separately set up, there are twelve varieties of type of each value. In addition, there were two separate settings up of the sheet of the one cent, and three of the two cents ; thus making twenty-four varieties in all of the one cent, and thirty-six of the two cents. Full particulars of this issue will be found given in Mr. E. D. Bacon's Paper.

Issue XIX.   June, 1882.

Eight values. Same as the stamps of Issue XV., but the watermark is changed to Crown C.A.   Printing, paper, perforation, etc., as before.   (*Illustration* 81.)

           1 c., grey   (shades).
           2 c., orange   („)
           4 c., ultramarine   („)
           6 c., brown   („)
           8 c., rose   („)
          24 c., green.

Remarks.—No specimens of the other values with this watermark are known to the Society.

Issue XX.   1888 - 1889.

Fifteen values. Designed and surfaced-printed by Messrs. De la Rue and Co., upon medium white wove paper, watermarked Crown C.A.   White gum.   Machine perforated, 14. Design : The design is the same as that of the last issue, but the bottom label is left blank, and the stamps are surcharged in the following way, in black block letters and numerals.   INLAND over POSTAGE in the top label, REVENUE in the vacant bottom label, and the value in a straight line above the last word, in numerals, and the word CENT, CENTS, DOLLAR, or DOLLARS.   (*Illustrations* 106, 107.)

          (Aug.,   1889)   1 c., black surcharge, on lilac.
          (25th May, 1889)   2 c.,   „   „   „   „
                             3 c.,   „   „   „   „
                             4 c.,   „   „   „   „
                             6 c.,   „   „   „   „
          (Aug.,   1889)   8 c.,   „   „   „   „
                            10 c.,   „   „   „   „
                            20 c.,   „   „   „   „
                            40 c.,   „   „   „   „
          (1st Oct., 1888) 72 c.,   „   „   „   „
          („   „) 1 S.,   „   „   „ green.
          („   „) 2 S.,   „   „   „   „
          („   „) 3 S.,   „   „   „   „
          („   „) 4 S.,   „   „   „   „
          („   „) 5 S.,   „   „   „   „

Remarks.—The above set of stamps was available for both postage and fiscal purposes.   The various values were issued by the Post Office as the supply of the old stamps became exhausted.   Some doubt seems to exist whether the three, four, six, ten, twenty, and forty cents were ever issued to the public for the prepayment of *postage*, although obliterated copies are known.

Issue XXI.   June 5th, 1889.

One value. The two cents of the preceding issue surcharged locally with an additional large figure 2 in red in the centre of the stamp. (*Illustration* 108.)

                2 c., black and red surcharge, on lilac.

Remarks.—After 34,500 of the two cents stamps of the preceding issue had been sold the further sale was stopped until an additional figure 2 had been surcharged by the Government printer in red on the remaining portion.   This precaution was taken, as it had been pointed out to the authorities that the stamp was easily convertible into one of seventy-two cents by the application of a numeral 7 before the 2.

Issue XXII. September, 1889-1890.

Ten values. Engraved and surface-printed by Messrs. De la Rue and Co., on medium white wove paper, watermarked Crown C.A. White gum. Machine perforated 14. Design: Ship sailing to right on background of horizontal lines within a double lined circular frame. Above and following the shape of the circle there is a narrow coloured band containing the words DAMUS PETIMUSQUE VICISSIM in white block letters. The lower portion of the stamp contains an oblong octagonal tablet with horizontal lined ground, enframed by a white octagonal line, which impinges upon the circle. The tablet contains the value in white block letters and numerals, shaded by lines of the same colour as that of the linear ground. Perpendicular white labels at the sides contain an inscription in coloured block letters. The lower portions of the bands are terminated by small coloured semi-circles and arabesque ornaments, and the upper portions by a coloured straight line which extends across the stamp, and which, together with portions of the outer frame lines of the design, enframes a straight white label containing an inscription in coloured block letters. The spandrels contain white floriate ornaments, and the design is completed by an outer line of colour. Shape upright rectangular. The stamps are bi-coloured, the main portion of the design being printed in lilac, and the top inscription, the tablet, and the value, being printed in various colours. (*Illustration* 109.)

T. " POSTAGE AND REVENUE." D. "1 CENT," "2 CENTS," "4 CENTS," "6 CENTS," "8 CENTS," "12 CENTS," "24 CENTS," "48 CENTS," "72 CENTS," "96 CENTS." L. " BRITISH," reading upwards. R. " GUIANA," reading upwards.

> 1 c., lilac and green.
> 2 c., „ „ orange.
> 4 c., „ „ ultramarine.
> 6 c., „ „ chocolate.
> 8 c., „ „ pale red.
> 12 c., „ „ mauve.
> 24 c., „ „ bright green.
> 48 c., „ „ red.
> 72 c., „ „ chestnut brown.
> 96 c., „ „ carmine.

Remarks.—The two, eight, seventy-two, and ninety-six cents were issued in September, 1889, the remaining values coming into use as the stock of the old issues became exhausted.

Issue XXIII. July 15th, 1890.

One value. The one, two, three, and four dollars adhesives of Issue XX., surcharged in the Colony as provisional one cent stamps. The surcharge is applied in the centre of the stamp, and consists of the word " One—Cent," in two lines in lower case type with capital initial letters, the word " One" measuring $8\frac{1}{2}$ mm. and the word " Cent" 10 mm. in length. The original value of the stamp is obliterated by two straight bars. (*Illustration* 115.)

> 1 c., red surcharge on 1 dollar, black surcharge on green.
> 1 c., „ „ „ 2 „ „ „ „ „
> 1 c., „ „ „ 3 „ „ „ „ „
> 1 c., „ „ „ 4 „ „ „ „ „

K

Issue XXIV. December, 1890.

Two values. Printed by Messrs. De la Rue and Co. upon medium white wove paper, watermarked Crown C.A. White gum, machine perforated 14. The design is the same as that of Issue XXII., the colour of the overprint of the eight cents alone being changed. The five cents is printed all in one colour. *(Illustration* 109.)

5 c., bright blue.

(13th December, 1890.)   8 c., lilac and bronze-green.

OFFICIAL STAMPS.

Issue I. June, 1875.

Five values. Same in all respects as the stamps of Issue XIV., but surcharged "OFFICIAL." in black or coloured block letters varying in height. Owing to slight differences in the spacing of the letters, the word "OFFICIAL." also varies in length. Paper, perforation, &c., as previously described.

I.—Surcharged in red. (Illustration 116.)

(a) Surcharge 3 mm. in height and 12 mm. in length.

1 c., red surcharge on black.

Variety.   Unperforated vertically.

1 c., red surcharge on black.

II.—Surcharged in black. (Illustration 117.)

(b) Surcharge 2 mm. in height and 13 mm. in length.

2 c.,	black surcharge on orange.		
8 c.,	„	„	„ rose.
12 c.,	„	„	„ lilac.
24 c.,	„	„	„ yellow-green.

(c) Surcharge 2 mm. in height and 14 mm. in length. *(Illustration* 118.)

2 c.,	black surcharge on orange.		
8 c.,	„	„	„ rose.
12 c.,	„	„	„ lilac.
24 c.,	„	„	„ yellow-green.

Issue II. 1877.

Eight (?) values. Same in all respects as the stamps of Issue XV., but surcharged "OFFICIAL" horizontally in black block letters 2 mm. in height, the word "OFFICIAL" being 16 mm. in length. Paper, perforation, &c., as previously described. *(Illustration* 119.)

1 c.,	black surcharge on grey.		
2 c.,	„	„	„ orange.
4 c.,	„	„	„ ultramarine.
6 c.,	„	„	„ brown.
8 c.,	„	„	„ rose.
12 c.,	„	„	„ lilac (?)
24 c.,	„	„	„ green (?)
48 c.,	„	„	„ red-brown (?)

Remarks.—The three highest values were certainly surcharged for "Official" use, as these stamps were afterwards issued with an additional surcharge for ordinary postal service, but it is doubtful whether they were ever employed as "Official" stamps, at any rate no copies are known to the Society.

Issue III. 1885.

Two values. Same in all respects as the stamps of Issue XX., but surcharged " official " obliquely in black block letters 3mm. in height, the word " official." being 20 mm. in length. Paper, perforation, &c., as previously described. (*Illustration* 120.)

1 c., black surcharge on grey.

4 c., „ „ „ ultramarine.

Remarks.—The authenticity of this surcharge is, at present, open to doubt.

ESSAY AND PROOFS.

Issue III., 1853. An essay exists of the four cents having the figures in the angles inscribed on a plain diamond shaped ground within the shaded square. It is evidently from the same manufactory, but differs slightly in details from the issued stamps. Thinnish white wove paper.

4 c., black.

Proofs exist of the stamps as issued to the public. (*Illustration* 70.)

1 c., red-brown.

1 c., black.

4 c., „

4 c., „ (Type of Issue V.) (*Illustration* 74.)

REPRINTS.

Issue II., 1852. The stamps of this issue were reprinted in 1865. The reprints are perforated 12½, and are printed on paper of rather a brighter colour and more highly surfaced. Both varieties of type were reprinted. (*Illustrations* 68, 69.)

1 c., black on magenta.

4 c., „ „ blue.

Issue III., 1853. These reprints are stated to have been also made in 1865. The paper is rather thinner than that of the originals, and somewhat brighter colours were used. (*Illustration* 70.)

A.—*Unperforated.*

1 c., vermilion.

4 c., blue.

B.—*Perf.* 12½.

1 c., vermilion.

4 c., blue.

Issue VI., 1860. One value of this issue was reprinted also in 1865, on *thin* paper perforated 12½. (*Illustration* 75.)

1 c., dull rose.

REGISTRATION ENVELOPES.

Issue I. March 24th, 1881.

One value. Bag-shaped envelopes of white wove, linen-lined paper; crossed lines on the back and an inscription along the upper margin of the address side, reading—BRITISH GUIANA REGISTERED LETTER, in large Roman capitals, with a line beneath, followed by This letter must be given to an officer of the Post Office—to be registered, and a receipt be obtained for it, in two lines of block letters. Beneath are two straight lines, one much thicker than the other, which extend across the envelope. In the right upper corner is the rectangle for the adhesive stamp, with the usual inscription, and in the left lower corner is a space inscribed NAME AND ADDRESS—OF SENDER, in two lines of block letters. The stamp is embossed on the flap, and is in the same colour as the inscriptions, &c. Design: Diademed profile of Queen Victoria to left, in plain relief on a solid ground of colour, surrounded by a circular band, bearing inscriptions in coloured block letters on a reticulated ground. *(Illustrations* 123, 124.)

T. " BRITISH GUIANA REGISTRATION FEE." B. " FOUR CENTS."

A.—With flap to left ; inscription under the flap :—

" McCorquodale & Co's.,   PATENT REGISTERED   in *red*
         LIMITED.   ENVELOPE."

4 c., vermilion ; size G.

B.—With flap to right ; same inscription.

4 c., vermilion ; size G.
4 c.   ,,   ,, H.
4 c.   ,,   ,, I.
4 c.   ,,   ,, K.

Issue II. 1888.

One value. The same as before ; the envelopes are differently constructed, the lower flap being placed outside the side flaps. The stamped flap is to the right, and under it is the inscription " THOS. DE LA RUE & Co., PATENT " in *red*. A new size is added, H², 9×4 inches (229×102 mm.), and the paper has a yellowish tinge. *(Illustrations* 123, 124).

4 c., vermilion : size G.
4 c.   ,,   ,, H².

WRAPPERS.

February 1st, 1884.

Two values. Designed and printed by Messrs. De la Rue and Co. upon light buff wove paper. Similar to the wrappers of Barbados, with the exception that the stamp is of the type of the adhesives of British Guiana of 1876. *(Illustration* 121.)

T. " POSTAGE." B. " 1 CENT," " 2 CENTS." L. " BRITISH." R. " GUIANA."

1 c., sage-green.
2 c., carmine.

POSTCARDS.

Issue I. July 3rd, 1879.

One value. Designed and printed by Messrs. De la Rue and Co. upon stout straw card. Size, 139×89 mm., or 5½×3½ inches. The inscription is in four straight lines commencing at the top of the card ; 1st, UNIVERSAL POSTAL UNION, in small block letters. 2nd, BRITISH GUIANA, GUYANE BRITANNIQUE in tall Roman capitals. The words GUIANA and GUYANE are separated by the arms of the Colony, (a plain circular band inscribed with the motto of the Colony, DAMUS PETIMUSQUE VICISSIM in small coloured block letters, with an ornament below, the centre of the circle containing a three masted ship in full sail to right.) 3rd, " POST CARD " in early English type, with capital initial letters. 4th, At the right hand side of the card in Italics, *Only the address to be written on this side.* Beneath this is a thick straight line extending quite across the card underneath which, in the centre, is the word ADDRESS in Roman capitals. The stamp, type of adhesives, issue 1876, is in the right upper corner. (*Illustration* 56.)

3 c., carmine (shades).

Issue II. August 26th, 1885.

One value. The card of the preceding issue surcharged in the Colony for provisional use, until the arrival of the new value from England. The surcharge consists of the words ONE CENT, in two lines, in block letters 3mm. in height, struck over the centre of the stamp, the original value of which is obliterated by a line. (*Illustration* 122.)

(*a*) The original value is struck out by a thick line drawn with pen and ink.

1 c., black surcharge on 3 c. carmine (shades).

(*b*) The original value is struck out by a narrow printed line applied at the same time as the surcharge.

1 c., black surcharge on 3 c. carmine (shades).

Issue III. May (?), 1886.

One value. Designed and printed by Messrs. De la Rue and Co. upon stout straw card. Size 139×89 mm., or 5½×3½ inches. The inscription is in three straight lines at the top of the card. 1st, INLAND POST CARD in Roman capitals. 2nd, BRITISH GUIANA, in thick block letters, the two words being separated by the arms of the Colony, (a three-masted ship in full sail to right within a plain narrow circular band, inscribed with the motto DAMUS PETIMUSQUE VICISSIM, in small coloured block letters, with an ornament at the bottom.) 3rd, THE ADDRESS ONLY TO BE WRITTEN ON THIS SIDE, in thin block letters. The stamp, type of adhesives, issue 1876, is in the right upper corner. (*Illustration* 136.)

1 c., grey (slight shades).

Issue IV. April (?), 1887.

One value. Designed and printed by Messrs. De la Rue and Co. upon stout straw card. Size, 139×88 mm., or 5½×3½ inches. The inscription is in four straight lines at the top of the card. 1st, UNION POSTALE UNIVERSELLE in small block letters. 2nd, BRITISH GUIANA—GUYANE BRITANNIQUE in tall Roman capitals. 3rd, POST CARD in large fancy capitals. 4th, THE ADDRESS ONLY TO BE WRITTEN ON THIS SIDE, in small block letters. Stamp, type of adhesives, issue 1876, in the right upper corner. (*Illustration* 137.)

3 c., rose-carmine (shades).

REPLY PAID CARD.

Issue I. September 1st, 1883.

One value. Designed and printed by Messrs. De la Rue and Co. upon stout straw card. Size, 130×88 mm., or 5½×3½ inches. The design is the same as that of the single card of Issue IV., but each half has the usual additional inscription like the reply cards of Antigua. The cards are joined along the top, perforated 4, and the design is impressed upon the first and third pages. (*Illustration* 137.)

3 c.+3 c., rose-carmine (shades).

BRITISH HONDURAS.

PRELIMINARY NOTES.

By E. D. BACON.

THE earliest number of the *Honduras Gazette* I have found in London is that for January 6th, 1866, since which date the series is complete to the present time. The first stamps are described in the *Timbre-Poste* for January, 1866, so no doubt the issue took place towards the end of 1865.

The Colony joined the Postal Union on April 1st, 1879, when the four penny adhesive and three halfpenny card should have been issued, but as neither are described in the journals until some months later, it is possible they had not arrived from England when the new rates came into force. I have found no actual notice of their issue in the *Gazette*, neither have I come across any mention of the three penny adhesive, which first made its appearance in 1872. A change in the currency, from the English to the American system, took place in the Colony on January 1st, 1888. The values of the stamps consequently required alteration, and as the ones ordered from England had not arrived at the above date, the stamps and card then in use were surcharged in the Colony with fresh values. A list of the new Postal rates is given in the *Supplement to the Honduras Gazette* of December 10th, 1887.

"COLONIAL SECRETARY'S OFFICE,
"BELIZE, *8th December*, 1887.

"THE following Rates of Postage to be collected on Letters, Post Cards, Newspapers, Books, Patterns and Parcels posted in British Honduras on and after the 1st January, 1888, are published for general information.

"By command,

"(Signed)   HUBERT E. H. JERNINGHAM,
"*Colonial Secretary.*"

RATES OF POSTAGE.

To be collected on Letters, Post Cards, Newspapers, Books, Patterns and Parcels posted in British Honduras on and after the 1st January, 1888.

To ALL PLACES ABROAD, except the undermentioned :—

Letters per ½ oz.	10 cents.
Post Cards, each	5 cents.
Newspapers, each	2 cents.
Books and Patterns, per 2 ozs.	3 cents.
Commercial Documents, not exceeding 2 ozs. ...	6 cents.
Every additional 2 ozs...	3 cents.
Registration Fee	10 cents.
Late Letter Fee	10 cents.

	Letters per ½ oz.	Newspapers each.	Books and Patterns, per 4 ozs	Registration Fee.
Ascension ... ... Australia ... ... Cape of Good Hope ... China ... ... Fiji ... ... Natal ... ... New Zealand... ... ... St. Helena	23 cents.	5 cents.	8 cents.	12 cents.

PARCELS TO THE UNITED KINGDOM.

For every pound... ... ... 20 cents

INLAND POSTAGE.

Letters, per ½ oz ... ... 3 cents.
Books and Patterns, per 2 ozs. ... 2 cents.
Newspapers, each ... ... 1 cent.

GENERAL POST OFFICE,
BELIZE, *1st December*, 1887.

As no stamp of one cent was provided, the two cents value was cut in half for the Inland Newspaper rate. The number of these half stamps has no doubt been multiplied for the benefit of collectors, still the fact remains that one cent stamps were really required for the postal service. All varieties of the two cents are found divided, and even to the present time of writing (October, 1890), no one cent stamp has been issued.

The standard of value of the present currency is the Guatemalan dollar, which is the same in value as the Chilian, Columbian, or Uruguayan peso, and the Peruvian sol ; the English equivalent of each being 3s. 11½d. : 10 cents therefore equals 4¾d.

REFERENCE LIST OF THE PHILATELIC SOCIETY, LONDON.

Issue I. End of 1865.

Three values. Engraved and surface-printed by Messrs. De la Rue and Co., of London, on medium white wove surfaced paper, unwatermarked. White gum, machine perforated 14. Design : Profile of Queen Victoria, with Gothic crown, to left, on ground of horizontal lines, enclosed within a white oval garter, shaded round the buckle, the garter is inscribed, in coloured block letters, with the name of the colony in the upper and the value in words in the lower curve. A small ornament, which differs in each value, separates the two inscriptions at either side. The spandrels contain arabesques, and the design is completed by two plain outer coloured lines. Shape, upright rectangular. (*Illustrations* 125, 126, 127.)

T. "BRITISH HONDURAS." B. "ONE PENNY," "SIX PENCE," "ONE SHILLING."

1d., blue (shades).
6d., rose (,,)
1s., green (,,)

Issue II. 1872-1873.

Four values. Of the same design as the preceding issue, but printed upon medium white wove paper, watermarked Crown C.C. (*Illustrations* 125, 126, 127, 128.)

A.—*Perforated* 12½.

(End 1873,) 1d., blue   (shades).
(March, 1872,) 3d., red-brown („)
(End 1873,) 6d., rose   („)
(„   „   ) 1s., green   („)

B.—*Perforated* 14.

1d., blue   (shades).
3d., red-brown („)
6d., rose   („)
1s., green   („)

Variety. The one penny, perforated 14, is to be found with the vertical perforation between some of the stamps missing.

Issue III. July, 1879.

One value. Precisely the same in design as the three pence of Issue II., but for the change of value. Watermark Crown C.C., machine perforated 14. (*Illustration* 128.)

4d., mauve (shades).

Remarks.—This stamp is found upon paper with lines in it, resembling the lines in laid paper. This peculiarity appears to be due to some unintentional variation in the manufacture.

Issue IV. 1882-84.

Two values. Identical in design with the preceding issues, but printed upon medium white wove surfaced paper, watermarked Crown C.A., machine perforated 14. (*Illustrations* 125, 128.)

(April,   1884,) 1d., blue   (shades).
(October, 1882,) 4d., mauve („)

Issue V. 1884-1887.

Three values. The same in design as the former issues, the colours being changed. Watermark Crown C.A., machine perforated 14. (*Illustrations* 125, 126, 127.)

(October (?), 1884,) 1d., carmine   (shades).
(May (?),   1885,) 6d., yellow   („)
(January,   1887,) 1s., slate-grey („)

Issue VI. January 1st, 1888.

Five values. Being stamps of Issues II., IV. and V., surcharged in the Colony, with a new value in "cents," for provisional use. The surcharge consists of an Arabic numeral of value 3 mm. high, with the word CENTS in Roman capitals beneath, the letters being 2½ mm. in height, and the whole word measuring 14¾ mm. in length. (*Illustration* 129.)

I.—Surcharged on the stamps of Issue II., watermarked Crown C.C.

(*a*) *Perforated* 12½.

2 c., black surcharge, on 6d. rose.
3 c., „   „   „ 3d. red-brown.

(b) Perforated 14.

2 c., black surcharge, on 6d. rose.

3 c.   ,,   ,,   ,, 3d. red-brown.

Variety. Half stamp 2 c., on 6d. rose, used as 1 c.

II.—Surcharged on the stamps of Issues IV. and V., watermarked Crown C.A.

Perforated 14.

2 c., black surcharge, on 1d. carmine.

10 c.,   ,,   ,,   ,, 4d. mauve,

20 c.,   ,,   ,,   ,, 6d. yellow.

50 c.,   ,,   ,,   ,, 1s. slate-grey.

Error for 50 c.   5 c., ,,   ,,   ,, 1s. slate-grey.

Varieties.   *a.* Double surcharge.

2 c., black surcharge, on 1d. carmine.

b. Half stamp 2 c. on 1d. carmine, used as 1 c.

c. Inverted surcharge.

2 c , black surcharge, on 1d. carmine.

10 c.,   ,,   ,,   ,, 4d. mauve.

Issue VII. May, 1888.

One value. The fifty cents of Issue VI., with an additional surcharge of the word "TWO" in black or red Roman capitals struck over the numerals "50." The word measures $8\frac{1}{2}$ mm. in length, and the letters are 3 mm. in height. Watermark Crown C.A., perforated 14. (*Illustration* 130.)

2 c., black surcharge, on 50 c. black surcharge, on 1s. slate-grey.

2 c., red surcharge, on 50 c. black surcharge, on 1s. slate-grey.

Variety. Half stamp 2 c. on 50 c., on 1s. slate-grey, used as 1 c.

Issue VIII. May, 1888.

Five values. Surcharged by Messrs. De la Rue and Co., of London, upon stamps of the old design. The surcharge is in two lines as in Issue VI., but the numerals of value are $4\frac{3}{4}$ mm. in height, and the word CENTS is in Roman capitals measuring $12\frac{1}{2}$ mm. in length, and the letters 3 mm. in height. The stamps are all watermarked Crown C.A. and machine perforated 14. (*Illustration* 131.)

2 c., black surcharge, on 1d. carmine.

3 c.,   ,,   ,,   ,, 3d. red-brown.

10 c.,   ,,   ,,   ,, 4d. mauve

(1889) 20 c , ,,   ,,   ,, 6d. yellow.

50 c ,   ,,   ,,   ,, 1s. slate-grey.

Variety. Half stamp 2 c. on 1d. carmine, used as 1 c.

POSTCARDS.

Issue I. End of 1879

One value. Designed and printed by Messrs. De la Rue and Co. upon medium light buff and also on straw card. Size 122×87 mm., or $4\frac{4}{5} \times 3\frac{2}{5}$ inches. The inscription is in four lines at the top of the card—1st, UNION POSTALE UNIVERSELLE in in small thick block letters. 2nd, BRITISH HONDURAS (HONDURAS BRITANNIQUE) in Roman capitals. 3rd, POST CARD in large fancy capitals. 4th, THE ADDRESS ONLY TO BE

WRITTEN ON THIS SIDE, in small block letters with a straight line underneath. The stamp, type of adhesives, Issue I., is in the right upper corner. (*Illustration* 138.)

> A.— On medium light buff card.
> 1½d., light brown (shades).
>
> B.—On straw card.
> 1½d., light brown (shades).

Issue II. 1st January, 1888.

One value. Variety B, of the card of Issue I., with the stamp surcharged across the centre $_{\text{CENTS}}^{5}$. The numeral is 3 mm. high, and the word CENTS, which is in Roman capitals, measures 2½ mm. in height and 15 mm. in length. The numeral is usually found directly in a line above the letter N, and a sub-variety has it over the left part of that letter. (*Illustration* 139.)

> 5 c., black surcharge, on 1½d. light brown (shades).

Variety. Surcharged twice, once on the stamp and once in the left lower corner of the card, the last surcharge being inverted.

> 5 c., black surcharge, on 1½d. light brown.

Remarks.—The above card was surcharged in the Colony for provisional use until the arrival of the new card ordered from England.

Issue III. November (?), 1888.

One value. Designed and printed by Messrs. De la Rue and Co., upon stout straw card. Size 139×88 mm., or 5½×3½ inches. The inscription is the same as that on the card of Issue I., and the stamp is the same type as that found on the second issue cards of Antigua, except that the upper label is inscribed BRITISH HONDURAS, and the lower FIVE CENTS. (*Illustration* 146.)

> 5 c., dark brown (slight shades).

DOMINICA.

PRELIMINARY NOTES.

By E. D. BACON.

POSTAGE STAMPS were first introduced in this island in May, 1874. The notice of issue is found in *The Official Gazette*, Dominica, of May 5th of that year.

"DOMINICA POST OFFICE,

"*May 4th*, 1874.

.   .   .   .

"STAMPS may now be had at this office, at 1d., 6d., and 1s. each. Letters, &c., dropped into the letter-box insufficiently paid will be DETAINED.

"ALL LETTERS, &c., MUST NOW BE FULLY PREPAID BY STAMPS."

The Official Gazette, unfortunately for our purpose, was discontinued at the end of 1876, and as the second issue of stamps did not take place until the latter part of 1879, the above is the only notice respecting stamps to be found in that paper. Dominica, and the other Leeward Islands joined the Postal Union on the 1st July, 1879, when the rates for foreign correspondence were considerably reduced, and a three halfpenny post card first came into use. The halfpenny, two pence halfpenny, and four penny adhesives and the three halfpenny card, if not ready for issue at this date, were probably received from England shortly afterwards. About May or June, 1882, the rate for half-ounce letters for Islands distant not more than 300 nautical miles, was reduced to two pence halfpenny, and post cards to one penny. As the new card had not arrived from England at the required date, a provisional card was printed at Roseau, the chief town in the island, by the Government printer, and issued with the then current one penny adhesive attached to it. Mr. R. F. Garraway, the present Postmaster, tells me there were only 100 of these provisional cards printed. He also informs me that all the provisional stamps were surcharged by the same printer, and that there were 18,000 of the sixpence green surcharged " Halfpenny," while the number of the one shilling crimson surcharged " One Penny " was 15,000.

REFERENCE LIST OF THE PHILATELIC SOCIETY, LONDON.

Issue I. May 4th, 1874.

Three values. Engraved and surface-printed by Messrs. De la Rue and Co. of London, on medium white wove surfaced paper, watermarked Crown C.C. White gum, machine perforated. Design: Diademed profile of Queen Victoria to left, on ground of horizontal lines, enclosed within a circular band of solid colour, which touches the top, right, and left sides of the stamp. The band is inscribed with the name of the Colony above, and with POSTAGE below in white block letters, the two inscriptions being separated at either side by a small white ornament. Beneath the circle there is a white label the width of the stamp, containing the value in words in coloured block letters. The spandrels contain conventional ornaments on ground of solid colour, and a plain outer line of colour completes the design. Shape upright rectangular. (*Illustration* 132.)

T. "DOMINICA." B. "POSTAGE." "ONE PENNY." "SIX PENCE." "ONE SHILLING."

A.—*Perforated* 12½.

1d., lilac   (shades).
6d., green   („)
1s., violet-rose   („)

B.—*Perforated* 14.

1d., lilac   (shades).
6d., green   („)
1s., violet-rose   („)

Remarks.—All three values surcharged with the word "REVENUE" in block letters, are known postally used. The one penny is known with a "bogus" surcharge in black of "2d."

Issue II.   End of 1879.

Three values. The same design as the preceding issue, printed upon medium white wove surfaced paper, watermarked Crown C.C., machine perforated 14. (*Illustrations* 132, 133.)

T. "DOMINICA." B. "POSTAGE." "HALFPENNY." "2½ PENNY." "FOUR PENCE."

½d., olive-yellow (shades).
2½d., red-brown („)
4d., blue   („)

Issue III.   November 25th, 1882.

One value. The one penny of Issue I., perforated 14, surcharged in the Colony for provisional use as a halfpenny value. The stamp is divided vertically down the centre, and each half is surcharged "½" in small type, 4 mm. in height. (*Illustration* 134.)

½ (d) black surcharge, on right half of 1d., lilac.
½ (d)   „   „   „ left   „ „ 1d., „
Varieties.   a. The above surcharge is found inverted.

b. Halves of the one penny stamp are found used without any surcharge.

Issue IV.   End of 1882.

One value. Issued provisionally as a halfpenny stamp. The one penny of Issue I., perforated 14, is divided, as in the preceding issue, and each half is surcharged "½" in large type, 13½ mm. in height. (*Illustration* 135.)

½ (d) red surcharge, on right half of 1d., lilac.
½ (d)   „   „   „ left   „ „ 1d., „
Variety.   The above surcharge is found inverted.

Issue V.   March, 1883.

One value. A further provisional halfpenny stamp, made by dividing the one penny of Issue I., perforated 14, as in the two preceding issues, and surcharging each half HALFPENNY in small Roman capitals, with a larger capital initial letter H. The surcharge measures 14 mm. in length, and is found reading both upwards and downwards. (*Illustration* 140.)

A.—The surcharge reads upwards.

½d., black surcharge, on right half of 1d., lilac.
½d. ,, ,, ,, left ,, ,, 1d., ,,

B.—The surcharge reads downwards.

½d., black surcharge, on right half of 1d., lilac.
½d. ,, ,, ,, left ,, ,, 1d., ,,

Issue VI. 1883-1884.

Two values. The halfpenny and two pence halfpenny of Issue II., printed upon medium white wove surfaced paper, watermarked Crown C.A., machine perforated 14. (*Illustrations* 132, 133.)

(April, 1883,) ½d., olive-yellow, bistre-yellow (shades).
(Dec., 1884,) 2½d., red-brown (shades).

Issue VII. March, 1886.

Two values. The sixpence and one shilling of Issue I. perforated 14, surcharged in the Colony for provisional use as "Halfpenny" and "One Penny" stamps. The surcharge is in two lines of ordinary lower case type with an initial Roman capital to each word, and the original value is obliterated by a thin black bar. The word "Half" measures 10½ mm., "One" 8½ mm., and "Penny" 13½ mm. in length. (*Illustration* 141.)

½d., black surcharge, on 6d., green.
1d., ,, ,, ,, 6d., ,,
1d., ,, ,, ,, 1s., violet rose.

Variety. The one penny on one shilling exists with a space of 4 mm. between the letters "n" and "e" of "One;" the letter "O" being directly above "P" instead of "e" of "Penny."

Issue VIII. May and July, 1886.

Three values. The one penny of Issue I., and the halfpenny and fourpence of Issue II., printed upon medium white wove surfaced paper, watermarked Crown C.A., machine perforated 14. (*Illustration* 132.)

(July, 1886,) ½d., dull green (slight shades).
(,, ,,) 1d., lilac (,, ,,)
(May, 1886,) 4d., grey (,, ,,)

Issue IX. 1887-1888.

Four values. Same design as the preceding Issue, printed upon medium white wove surfaced paper, watermarked Crown C.A. Yellowish and white gum, machine perforated 14. (*Illustrations* 132, 133.)

(May, 1887,) 1d., carmine-rose (slight shades).
(Sept., 1888,) 2½d., ultramarine (,, ,,)
(Oct. ,,) 6d., orange (,, ,,)
(1888) 1s., violet-rose (,, ,,)

Remarks.—In June, 1889, the one penny carmine was surcharged in the Colony with the word "Revenue" in lower case type, some of these stamps being used for postal purposes.

POSTCARDS.

Issue I. July 1st (?), 1879.

One value. Designed and printed by Messrs. De la Rue and Co. upon medium light buff card. Size, 121×87 mm., or 4⅔×3⅔ inches. The design is the same as that of the first issue card of Antigua, but the second line of the inscription is altered to DOMINICA (DOMINIQUE), and the name of the Colony at the top of the stamp is changed. *(Illustration 147.)*

1½d., light brown (shades).

Issue II. June (?), 1882.

One value. Printed in the Island, as a provisional issue, upon stout white card. Size, 122×88 mm., or 4⅔×3⁹⁄₂₀ inches. The inscription is the same as that on the card of Issue I., but the type employed is different. The first and second lines are in Roman capitals, the former being much smaller than the latter. The third is in large double lined shaded capitals, and the Royal Arms are differently emblazoned. The fourth is in Roman capitals, and there is no period at the end. Beneath the fourth, in a straight line, is the following additional inscription in small Roman capitals :— FOR COUNTRIES WITHIN 300 MILES SERVED BY BRITISH PACKETS. The card is franked by an adhesive stamp, fixed in the right upper corner. *(Illustration 148.)*

Without expressed value (1d.) carmine impression (shades) franked by a 1d. lilac adhesive (Issue I.)

Issue III. April (?), 1883.

One value. In every way the same as the card of Issue I., but for the change of value in the bottom label of the stamp. *(Illustration 147.)*

1d., lilac-mauve (shades.)

Issue IV. May (?), 1886.

Two values. Designed and printed by Messrs. De la Rue and Co., upon stout straw card. Size 139×88 mm., or 5½×3½ inches. The inscription is the same as that on the cards of Issues I. and III., and the stamp is similar in design to that on the second issue cards of Antigua, but for the change of name in the top label. *(Illustration 149.)*

1d., carmine (slight shades).
1½d., dark brown (slight shades).

REPLY PAID CARDS.

Issue I. May (?), 1886.

Two values. Precisely similar to the single cards of Issue IV., but with the additional inscription on each half, the same as on the reply cards of Antigua. The cards are joined along the top, perforated 4½, and the design is impressed upon the first and third pages. *(Illustration 149.)*

1d.+1d., carmine (slight shades).
1½d.+1½d., dark brown (slight shades).

Remarks.—The postal emissions of this Colony became obsolete at the end of October, 1890, when a uniform set for all the various Islands composing the Leeward Group, took their place.

FALKLAND ISLANDS.

REFERENCE LIST OF THE PHILATELIC SOCIETY, LONDON.

Issue I. June 19th, 1878.

Four values. Designed and printed by Messrs. Bradbury, Wilkinson and Co., of London, upon greyish white wove unwatermarked paper. Yellowish gum, machine perforated 14½. Design : Diademed profile of Queen Victoria to right, on ground of horizontal lines, within a narrow white upright oval band. A curved coloured label above following the shape of the oval, and a straight coloured label below, contain the name of the Colony and the value in words, respectively, in white block letters. The two lower corners of the stamp contain circular discs of solid colour, which are surrounded by a white and a coloured line. The discs contain a white Arabic numeral of value. The spandrels are filled in with conventional ornaments, and there is a beaded frame to right and left of the oval, and at the top, right, and left sides of the stamp. Shape, upright rectangular. (*Illustration* 142.)

T. " FALKLAND ISLANDS." B. " ONE PENNY." " FOUR PENCE." " SIX PENCE." " ONE SHILLING."

	1d , claret-red	(shades).		
(Sept., 1879,)	4d., brown-grey	(	,,	)
	6d., green	(	,,	)
	1s., yellow-brown	(	,,	)

Remarks.—The dates of the emission of the above stamps, as well as those of the postcards, have been obtained by Mr. E. D. Bacon from Mr. F. S. Sanguinetti, the Acting Colonial Secretary and Postmaster of the Falkland Islands. Mr. Sanguinetti states that the sheets of all four values contain 60 stamps each, in rows of six by ten. He adds, " On the 25th June, 1858, the rate of sixpence was fixed for postage of all letters, books, and papers not exceeding half an ounce, to be prepaid by affixing the following stamp." (*Illustration* 143.) This mark, as well as others of a similar nature, was struck on letters, etc., at the Post Office, after the charges had been prepaid in *money.* It is nothing more than a hand-stamp employed for the convenience of the Post Office like other postmarks.

Issue II. Early in 1884.

Two values. Printed by Messrs. De la Rue and Co., from the plates of the previous issue, upon medium white wove paper, watermarked Crown C.A. Machine perforated 14½. (*Illustration* 142.)

1d., claret-red   (shades).
4d., brown-grey (,,   )

Issue III.   1886-1888.

Three values.   The same as those of Issue I., but printed upon medium white wove paper, watermarked Crown C.A.   Machine perforated: 14½ for the one penny; 14, for the four pence and six pence.   The watermark on the stamps of this issue, is found placed sideways.   (*Illustration* 142.)

(1886) 1d., claret-red   (shades).
(1888) 4d., brown-grey („)
(1887) 6d., black   (..)

POSTCARD.

Issue I.   January, 1884.

One value.   Designed and printed by Messrs. De la Rue and Co., upon stout straw card.   Size 139×88 mm., or 5½×3½ inches.   The design is the same as that for the second issue cards of Antigua, except that the second line of the inscription reads FALKLAND ISLANDS (ILES FALKLAND), and the name of the Colony at the top of the stamp is changed.   (*Illustration* 150.)

1½d., dark brown (slight shades).

REPLY PAID CARD.

Issue I.   October, 1885.

One value.   Same as the single card just described, but each half has an additional inscription like the reply cards of Antigua.   The cards are joined along the top, perforated 4½, and the design is impressed upon the first and third pages. (*Illustration* 150.)

1½d.+1½d., dark brown (slight shades).

GRENADA.

PRELIMINARY NOTES.

By E. D. BACON.

THE *Grenada Gazette* only commenced publication on January 10th, 1883, so no information concerning the stamps issued prior to that date, can be looked for from that source.

Previous to 1883, all the stamps used in the Colony were printed by Messrs. Perkins Bacon and Co., from steel plates of their own construction. Those of the one penny and six pence each contained 120 stamps in ten horizontal rows of twelve, while the plate used for the halfpenny, two pence halfpenny, four pence and one shilling, contained the same number similarly arranged. This latter plate was finished in February, 1875. All three plates were handed over to the Crown Agents on April 13th, 1889. Proof impressions in black struck from the dies upon white card are known of the one penny, six pence, and that without value, while proof impressions also in black, taken from the plate of the latter, upon plain white paper exist. A proof in purple (the colour of the issued stamp) without the surcharged value has also been met with. The *one penny* and six pence may both be found imperforate, and printed upon plain white paper, in dull red, the same shade as that used for some of the earlier six penny stamps, but whether these varieties must be looked upon as proofs, or stamps issued for use, it is difficult to determine. No collector has, I believe, come across a used specimen of either variety, but it is not impossible some may yet turn up. The first supply of stamps, which consisted of one penny green and six pence red, were sent out to the Island on April 27th, 1861 ; so the date 1860 usually given in the Catalogues as that of the first issue is incorrect. Looking at the date the stamps were despatched, it seems probable they first came into use on or about June 1st, 1861. The first supply of the halfpenny, two pence halfpenny, and four pence, were printed off in February, 1881, according to the date given in one of Messrs. Perkins Bacon and Co.'s books, to which specimens are attached. The postcards first issued in the Colony were not, as was stated in *The Philatelic Record* of May, 1881, the work of Messrs. De la Rue and Co., but were produced by Messrs. Perkins Bacon and Co. Subsequent issues, as well as other postal stationery, and adhesives from 1883, have been obtained from the former firm.

The following, taken from the *Grenada Gazette* of March 12th, 1884, shows the inland postal rates in force at that time.

RULES AND REGULATIONS.

.   .   .   .

"On every letter arriving in this Colony from any place out of this Colony, and delivered at any branch office, and on letters posted at any

M

branch office for transmission out of this Colony, and on all letters transmitted from any one place to any other place within this Colony, there shall be charged as follows:—

On every letter not exceeding ½ ounce, the sum of .... 1d.

   „   „   „   ½ ounce, but not exceeding 1 ounce 2d.

   „   „   „   1 ounce, but not exceeding 2 ounces 4d.

The sum of 2d. being charged for every additional ounce or fractional part thereof.

"On all newspapers, whether printed in the Colony or otherwise, one halfpenny each. It shall not be compulsory to send all newspapers by post.

      "(Signed)   C. FALCONER ANTON,

                           " *Clerk of Councils.*"

Mr. James Anton was Postmaster in 1883, and Mr. John Griffith the present Colonial Postmaster was appointed on August 31st, 1885. No notice appeared in the *Gazette* (the title of which by-the-bye was changed to *Grenada Government Gazette* on May 6th, 1885,) of the issue of any of the various provisional stamps which have been employed at different periods. The first notice of postal issues I have found, is one published in *The Gazette* of June 9th, 1886, which gives the date Reply Cards, Registration Envelopes, and Newspaper Wrappers came into use, the third set of single postcards being issued at the same time.

NOTICE.

"REPLY Post Cards for Europe and the Colonies, also for Inland use, Registered Envelopes, and Newspaper Wrappers may now be obtained at the General Post Office.

      "(Signed)   J. GRIFFITH,

                       " *Colonial Postmaster.*

" GENERAL POST OFFICE,

    " ST. GEORGE, 8*th June,* 1886."

The next notice relating to postage stamps I have come across is the following, taken from *The Gazette* of June 23rd, 1886.

NOTICE.

"REVENUE and Postage Stamps will now be sold separately, at this Department with an allowance of discount as follows, viz.:—

      Five per centum on £5 to £9 19s. 11½d.

      Ten   „   „   „ £10, and upwards.

      "(Signed)   J. GRIFFITH,

                       " *Colonial Postmaster.*

" GENERAL POST OFFICE,

    " ST. GEORGE, 22*nd June,* 1886."

This reduction in price, on taking the quantities named, remained in force until August, 1890, when a notice was published in *The Gazette* of the 20th of that month, stating the allowance would be discontinued.

POST OFFICE NOTICE.

"NOTICE is hereby given that the arrangement notified in *Gazette* Notice, dated the 22nd June, 1886, under which discount of 5 per cent. and 10 per cent. respectively was allowed on purchases of Revenue and Postage Stamps exceeding £5 and £10 respectively has been cancelled.

      " (Signed)   W. P. ANTON,

                       " *Acting Postmaster.*

" GENERAL POST OFFICE,

    " ST. GEORGE'S, 13*th August,* 1890."

REFERENCE LIST OF THE PHILATELIC SOCIETY, LONDON.

Issue I. June 1st (?), 1861.

Two values. Engraved and printed in *taille-douce* by Messrs. Perkins Bacon and Co., of London, on white wove unwatermarked paper, varying considerably in substance. Yellowish gum, machine perforated 15. Design: An almost full faced bust portrait of Queen Victoria, looking to left, adorned with diadem, necklace, and earrings, on ground of crossed lines, enclosed within a narrow upright white oval band. Straight labels of solid colour at top and bottom contain respectively the name of the Colony, and the value in words, in white block letters. A white Maltese cross at either end of the inscriptions, forms the corners of the design, the remainder of which is filled in with reticulations, bordered by an outer single line of colour. Shape upright rectangular. (*Illustration* 144.)

T. " GRENADA." B. " ONE PENNY." " SIX PENCE."

1d., green   (shades).
6d., rose-red („)

Variety. Imperforate.

6d., rose-red.

Remarks.—The one penny is found printed in rose-red, imperforate. It is not known whether this stamp is an error of colour, or a printer's proof. The sixpence *imperforate* has been seen in pairs.

Issue II. 1864.

Two values. Identical with the preceding issue, but printed upon white wove paper watermarked with a six-rayed star, the perforation being 14,—15 compound. (*Illustration* 144.)

1d., green (shades).
6d., rose, rose-red, orange-vermilion (shades).

Remarks.—The shape and size of the star watermark in the paper varies considerably, and it is not improbable that these variations occur on the same sheet. The one penny is known divided in two, and each half used as a halfpenny value.

Issue III. September, 1875.

One value. Engraved and printed in *taille-douce* by Messrs. Perkins Bacon and Co., of London, on white wove paper, watermarked with a six-rayed star. Yellowish gum, machine perforated 14. Design: The same portrait of Queen Victoria as in Issue I., but cut off at the neck and enframed by a narrow white circular band. A straight label of solid colour below the portrait, bears the name of the Colony in white block letters. A small square white block in each of the four corners contains an eight-rayed star. The remainder of the design is filled in with a reticulated pattern bordered by an outer line of colour. Shape, upright rectangular. The words POSTAGE and ONE SHILLING are overprinted in straight lines, respectively above and below the Queen's head, in blue block letters] $1\frac{1}{2}$ mm. in height. The word POSTAGE measures $11\frac{1}{2}$ mm., and the value $13\frac{1}{2}$ mm. in length, (*Illustration* 145.)

1s. blue surcharge, on purple.

Varieties. a. The word " SHILLING " is mis-spelt " SHILLIING."

b. The letter " o " of the word " ONE " is omitted.

Issue IV. March (?), 1881.

Three values. Identical in design with the last issue, and having the same watermark and perforation. In the two pence halfpenny, the overprinted value follows the lower curve of the central circle, in the other two stamps it is in a straight line. All the values are overprinted in black block letters, 1¼ mm. in height. (*Illustrations* 145, 151.)

> ½d.,   black surcharge, on purple (shades).
> 2½d.,   „   „   „   dull-red („   )
> 4d.,   „   „   „. blue   („   )

Varieties.   *a.* Imperforate.

> ½d.,   black surcharge, on purple.
> 2½d.,   „   „   „   dull-red.

> *b.* Imperforate vertically.

> 2½d., black surcharge, on dull-red.

> *c.* The halfpenny value with the letter P of POSTAGE omitted.

> *d.* The same value with the letter H of HALF omitted.

> *e.* The same value with the letters NY of HALFPENNY omitted.

> *f.* The same value with double surcharge.

Remarks.—Imperforate *pairs* of the halfpenny and two pence halfpenny exist in the collection of the late Mr. T. K. Tapling.

Issue V. January, 1883.

Two values. Owing to the stock of one penny and halfpenny labels being exhausted, the one penny fiscal stamp identical in design with the preceding Issues III. and IV., and having the same watermark and perforation, but overprinted in green with a " crown " above the central circle, and the words " ONE PENNY " beneath it, was utilised for postal purposes, with the additional surcharge of the word POSTAGE in Roman capitals 3¾ mm. in height, and 16½ mm. in length. The letter S is sometimes, and the letters POS are at other times, higher than the remaining portion of the word. The words ONE PENNY vary in length, but two distinct sets may be formed, one with the words measuring 9½ mm. in length, the other measuring 10¼ mm. In the latter the letters O and P are taller than the rest of the words. To form the halfpenny, the word POSTAGE was printed twice obliquely across the stamp, which was then divided diagonally, and each half served as a halfpenny value. The surcharge being found inconveniently large, when twice applied for the half-penny, the word POSTAGE for this value was afterwards struck in smaller Roman capitals measuring 2¾ mm. in height, and 16 mm. in length, the surcharge on the lower half being inverted as regards that on the upper part.

I.   With surcharge type 1. (*Illustrations* 152, 153.)

A.—The words ONE PENNY measure 9½ mm.

> ½ (d.), black surcharge, on upper half of 1d. green surcharge, on orange.
> ½ (d.), „   „   „ lower „   1d.   „   „   „   „   „
> 1d.,   „   „   „   1d. green surcharge, on orange.

Varieties.   *a.* With the surcharge POSTAGE inverted.

> 1d., black surcharge, on 1d. green surcharge, on orange.

> *b.* With the word POSTAGE written across the stamp with pen and black or red ink. (*Illustrations* 154, 155.)

> 1d., black surcharge, on 1d. green surcharge, on orange.
> 1d., red   „   „ 1d. „   „   „

c. Without the surcharge POSTAGE, postally used.

1d., green surcharge, on orange.

d. Same as *variety c*, divided in two and each half used as a half-penny.

½ (d.) (half 1d.) green surcharge, on orange.

B.—The words ONE PENNY measure 10½ mm. and the letters O and P are taller.

½ (d.) black surcharge, on upper half of 1d. green surcharge, on orange.
½ (d.) „ „ lower „ 1d. „ „ „
1d. „ „ 1d. green surcharge, on orange.

II. With surcharge type II. (*Illustration* 156.)

A.—The words ONE PENNY measure 9½ mm.

½ (d.) black surcharge, on upper half of 1d. green surcharge, on orange.
½ (d.) „ „ lower „ 1d. „ „ „

B.—The words ONE PENNY measure 10½ mm. and the letters O and P are taller.

½ (d.) black surcharge, on upper half of 1d. green surcharge, on orange.
½ (d.) „ „ lower „ 1d. „ „ „

Issue VI. 1883.

Seven values. Engraved and surface-printed by Messrs. De la Rue and Co., of London, on medium white wove surfaced paper, watermarked Crown C.A. White gum, machine perforated 14. Design: Diademed profile of Queen Victoria to left, on ground of horizontal lines, enclosed within an octagonal white line. Narrow upright straight labels of solid colour at the sides, contain vertical rows of white diamonds, and the spandrels are filled in with triangular white ornaments. Above the octagon are the words GRENADA POSTAGE in a straight line, in small block letters, and below the octagon is the value in words in larger block type. Both inscriptions are printed in colour, without either groundwork or border, which gives the stamp a very unfinished appearance. Shape, upright rectangular. These stamps are printed in sheets, having each alternate row of labels inverted, thus forming what is known as *tête-bêche*. (*Illustrations* 157, 158.)

T. "GRENADA POSTAGE." B. "HALFPENNY." "ONE PENNY." "2½ PENCE." "FOUR PENCE." "SIX PENCE." "EIGHT PENCE." "ONE SHILLING."

(February) ½d., green (shades).
(„) 1d., rose („)
(August) 2½d., ultramarine („)
(June) 4d., slate-grey („)
(August) 6d., mauve („)
(February) 8d., grey-brown („)
(April) 1s., lilac („)

Varieties. Têtes-bêches.

Same values and shades.

Remarks.—The one penny is known with a "bogus" surcharge in black of HALF—PENNY in two lines of Roman capitals, and the original value obliterated.

Issue VII. October, 1886.

One value. The supply of one penny postage labels becoming again exhausted, recourse was once more had to the series of fiscal stamps of the design described in Issue V., watermarked as before, with a six-rayed star, and machine perforated 14. The additional surcharge consists of the word POSTAGE, in Roman capitals, 2 mm. in height, and 16 mm. in length, struck over the original value of the stamp, and on the Queen's head is overprinted ½ the numeral and letter measuring together 8 mm. in height. (*Illustration* 159.)

1d., black surcharge, on 1½d. green surcharge, on orange.
1d.,   „   „   „   4d.   „   „   „
1d.,   „   „   „   1s.   „   „   „

Varieties.   *a.* With the word POSTAGE inverted.

1d., black surcharge, on 1½d. green surcharge, on orange.

    b. With the word REVENUE surcharged in place of POSTAGE, and postally used.

1d., black surcharge, on 2s. green surcharge, on orange.

Issue VIII.   January, 1887.

One value. The one penny of Issue VI. with the inscription at the top of the stamp altered to GRENADA—POSTAGE AND REVENUE in two lines of small block letters. Watermark Crown C.A., machine perforated 14. (*Illustration* 160.)

1d., rose (shades).

Variety.—Tête-bêche.

1d., rose.

Issue IX.   End of March, 1888.

One value. The two shilling fiscal stamp of the design described in Issue V. surcharged provisionally as a four penny value. The additional surcharge consists of the word POSTAGE in Roman capitals 2 mm. in height and 15½ mm. in length struck across the centre of the stamp, and "4d." overprinted above, the letter and numeral measuring 4 mm. in height. The sheet consists of sixty stamps in six rows of ten, and the sixth stamp of the lowest row from the left has a Roman letter "d." *Illustrations* 161, 162.)

4d., black surcharge, on 2s. green surcharge, on orange.

Variety. With Roman letter "d."

4d., black surcharge, on 2s. green surcharge, on orange.

*Remarks.—*This stamp has been chronicled with double and also with inverted surcharge, but the authenticity of these two varieties requires confirmation.

Issue X.   December, 1889.

One value. The two shilling fiscal stamp employed in the preceding issue, surcharged provisionally as a halfpenny value. The additional surcharge consists of HALF — PENNY — POSTAGE in three straight lines of Roman capitals 2 mm. in height, the first word measuring 9¼ mm., the second 12 mm., and the third 15½ mm. in length. (*Illustration* 163.)

½d., black surcharge, on 2s. green surcharge, on orange.

Issue XI.   December, 1890.

One value. The same two shilling fiscal stamp used in the last two issues, surcharged provisionally as a one penny value. The additional surcharge consists of POSTAGE — AND — REVENUE in three straight lines of Roman capitals, the first and last word 2 mm., and the word AND 1¼ mm. in height. The first word measures 15½ mm., the second 5 mm., and the third 17 mm. in length. Besides the above inscription, a new value of $\frac{d}{1}$ is surcharged, the numeral and letter each measuring 4 mm. in height. (*Illustration* 164.)

1d., black surcharge, on 2s. green surcharge, on orange.

Variety. With the numeral and letter "d" side by side, measuring 5¼ mm. in breadth.

1d., black surcharge, on 2s. green surcharge, on orange.

REGISTRATION ENVELOPES.

Issue I. June 8th, 1886-88.

One value. Bag-shaped envelopes of white wove, linen-lined paper, with the flap to the right. The inscriptions upon them are the same as those upon the envelopes of Barbados, Issue II., with the large "R" in an upright oval frame. The inscriptions, lines, &c., are in *red*. The stamp was designed and embossed in colour, on the flap, by Messrs. De la Rue and Co. Design: Diademed profile of Queen Victoria to left in plain relief on a solid ground of colour, enclosed by a single-lined octagon; surrounding this is a circular reticulated band, bearing the inscriptions in coloured block letters; outside this again is a single-lined octagon, with a projection in the centre of each side; and the whole is upon a disc of solid colour. (*Illustrations* 28, 165.)

T. " GRENADA REGISTRATION FEE." B. " TWO PENCE."

A.—The inscription under the flap is "McCorquodale & Co., Contractors." in *red*.

LIMITED.

(1886) 2d., grey-blue ; size F.
2d.,   ,,   ,, G.
2d.,   ,,   ,, H.
2d.,   ,,   ,, H².
2d.,   ,,   ,, I.
2d.,   ,,   ,, K.

B. The inscription under the flap is " Thos. De La Rue & Co. Patent," in *red*.

(1888) 2d., grey-blue ; size F.
2d.,   ,,   ,, G.

WRAPPERS.

Issue I. June 8th, 1886.

Four values. Designed and printed by Messrs. De la Rue and Co. Similar to the wrappers of Barbados, but with stamp of a different type. Design: Diademed profile of Queen Victoria to left in a circle, enclosed in a rectangular frame, with inscriptions in uncoloured block letters on straight labels at top and bottom, foliate ornaments in the spandrels, all on a solid ground of colour. Shape upright rectangular. (*Illustration* 169.)

T. " GRENADA." B. " HALFPENNY." " ONE PENNY." " PENNY HALFPENNY."
"TWO PENCE."

½d., green
1d., carmine.
1½d., red-brown.
2d., deep blue.

POSTCARDS.

Issue I. April, 1881.

Two values. Designed and printed by Messrs. Perkins Bacon and Co. upon thin straw card. Size 123×87 mm., or 4$\frac{17}{20}$×3$\frac{2}{5}$ inches. The inscription is in three lines at the top of the card, 1st, UNION POSTALE UNIVERSELLE. 2nd, GRENADA. (DE GRENADA.)

3rd, THE ADDRESS ONLY TO BE WRITTEN ON THIS SIDE. The first and third lines are in block letters, the type of the latter being the smaller of the two, and the second is in Roman capitals. The stamp is in the right upper corner. Design : Diademed head of Queen Victoria to left, upon ground of horizontal lines, enclosed within an upright oval. Surrounding the oval is a border of an eccentric pattern, containing at the top and bottom scrolls of solid colour shaded at the ends, the upper inscribed POSTAGE, and the lower with the value in words, both in plain block letters. At either side of the border is a small block of solid colour containing a star, above and below which are conventional ornaments. A plain outer line of colour rounded at the four corners completes the design. (*Illustration* 170.)

> 1d., light blue (shades).
> 1½d., pale brown („   )

Issue II. December, 1881.

Two values. Designed and printed by Messrs. De la Rue and Co., upon medium light buff card. Size, 122×87 mm., or 4⅗×3½ inches. The design is the same as that of the first issue card of Antigua, except that the second line of the inscription is altered to GRENADA (LA GRENADE), and the name of the Colony at the top of the stamp is changed. The one penny, but for the alteration of the value at the bottom of the stamp, is precisely similar to the three halfpenny. (*Illustration* 188.)

> 1d., blue   (shades).
> 1½d., pale-brown („   )

Issue III. June 8th, 1886.

Three values. Designed and printed by Messrs. De la Rue and Co., upon stout straw card, the halfpenny being somewhat thinner. Size of the halfpenny 122×74 mm., or 4⅗×2⅞ inches, that of the one penny and three halfpenny 139×88 mm., or 5½×3½ inches. The design of the two latter is the same as that of the second issue cards of Antigua, except for the modification of the name of the Colony, as mentioned in the preceding issue. The inscription on the halfpenny is in three lines—1st. POST CARD in large Roman capitals, separated by the arms and supporters of Great Britain. 2nd. GRENADA in smaller Roman capitals. 3rd. THE ADDRESS ONLY TO BE WRITTEN ON THIS SIDE, in thin block letters. The stamp is similar in design to that on the other two values. (*Illustrations* 189, 190.)

> ½d., green   (slight shades).
> 1d., carmine   („   „   )
> 1½d., dark brown („   „   )

REPLY PAID CARDS.

Issue I. June 8th, 1886.

Three values. Similar in every way to the single cards of Issue III., but the one penny and three halfpenny have the usual additional inscription on each half like the reply paid cards of Antigua. The first half of the halfpenny has only, THE ANNEXED CARD—IS INTENDED FOR—THE ANSWER, in three lines in small block type in the left lower corner, without the French translation. The cards are joined along the top, perforated 4½, and the design is impressed on the first and third pages. (*Illustrations* 189, 190.)

> ½d.+½d. green   (slight shades).
> 1d.+1d. carmine   („   „   )
> 1½d.+1½d. dark brown („   „   )

JAMAICA.

PRELIMINARY NOTES.

By E. D. BACON.

THE file of *The Jamaica Gazette* I have had access to, commences with "Volume I. new series," which is dated June 3rd, 1869. I am consequently unable to furnish any particulars concerning the issue, &c., of the earlier postage stamps from that source. Thanks, however, to Mr. George H. Pearce, the chief clerk in the General Post Office at Kingston, Jamaica, I am enabled to give the following information.

The first issue of postage stamps in Jamaica took place on May 8th, 1858, when the notice, of which I append a copy, was published :—

NOTICE TO THE PUBLIC.

"GENERAL POST OFFICE, *8th May*, 1858.

"THE Postmaster General having been pleased to sanction the introduction of Postage Stamps for the prepayment of Packet Postage, notice is hereby given that from this date the Public will be supplied with stamps of the respective value of 1d., 4d., and 6d., on application at the General Post Office, Kingston, between the hours of 8.30 a.m. and 2.30 p.m.

"For the present the use of stamps is restricted to packet correspondence.

"Arrangements will be made for supplying the several Postmasters throughout the Island with Postage Stamps as soon as possible.

"(Signed)   MAURICE O'CONNOR MORRIS,

"*Deputy Postmaster General.*"

The Jamaica Post Office was at this date under the control of the English Government, and the labels referred to in the notice were the then current Great Britain stamps of the values mentioned.

On the 1st August, 1860, the Post Office was transferred to the Colonial Government, and Mr. Pearce tells me the first set of Jamaica postage stamps was issued on the 23rd November of that year, the values being one penny, two pence, four pence, six pence, and one shilling, the three penny stamp not coming into use until the 10th September, 1863.

The notice of the issue of the halfpenny adhesive is found in the number of *The Gazette* for November 7th, 1872.

HALF PENNY POSTAGE LABEL.

"GENERAL POST OFFICE, *29th October*, 1872,

"POSTAGE LABELS, of the value of One Half Penny each, having been provided, the Special Rule, under which one Half of a Penny Stamp has been permitted to be used in payment of the Half Penny Rate of Postage is no longer necessary.

" The Public are, therefore, hereby notified : That on and after the 1st day of December next, the half part of a Penny Postage Label will cease to be recognized in the payment of Postage, and any Paper, &c., posted with the part only of the Penny Stamp affixed thereon, will be treated as unpaid.

" The Half Penny Postage Label has been issued for use as of this date, the 29th day of October, 1872, and can be obtained at the several Post Offices on application.

" (Signed)   FRED. SULLIVAN,

" *Postmaster for Jamaica.*"

It is evident from the above notice, that previous to the arrival of the halfpenny stamp from England, the then current one penny adhesive was allowed to be divided, and each portion used for half the value. It also appears that the halfpenny stamp was used to prepay newspapers, and, probably, other printed matter of small weight. I am unable to say for what period the provisional stamp was in use, as although I have searched *The-Gazette* for some months previous to October 29th, 1872, I have found no further reference to this variety.

The number of *The Gazette* for September 2nd, 1875, contains the notice of issue of the two and five shilling adhesives.

NOTICE TO THE PUBLIC.

ISSUE OF NEW DENOMINATIONS OF POSTAGE STAMPS.

" GENERAL POST OFFICE, 27*th August*, 1875.

" HIS EXCELLENCY THE GOVERNOR, for the greater convenience of the Public, having been pleased to authorize the introduction of new Denominations of Postage Stamps of the Value of 5s. and 2s. respectively, the Public are hereby informed that such Stamps have this day been issued, and can be obtained at this Office.

" (Signed)   GEO. H. PEARCE,

" *pro Postmaster for Jamaica.*"

The authorisation for the issue of postcards is found in *The Gazette* of March 29th, 1877.

ORDER IN PRIVY COUNCIL AS TO POSTCARDS WITHIN THE COLONY.

" PRIVY COUNCIL CHAMBER, 28*th March*, 1877,

" WHEREAS by the Twelfth Section of Law 18 of 1868, the Governor is empowered, with the advice and consent of the Privy Council, from time to time to vary or alter the Rates of Postage set forth in the Schedule to that Law annexed : *Provided*, That the Rates in the said Schedule shall not be at any time exceeded. The Lieutenant-Governor is this day pleased, by and with the advice and consent of his Privy Council, to direct that, on and after 'the first day of April, 1877, POST CARDS may be sent by post *between places within Jamaica* upon the following conditions : —

" 1. POST CARDS, with an Impressed Stamp denoting their face value, shall be issued by the Postmaster for Jamaica ; and the Cards so issued, and no others, shall be deemed to be POST CARDS, within the meaning of this order.

" 2. The address, and nothing else, shall be written, printed, or otherwise impressed on the side of the Post Card which bears the Post Office Stamp and Instructions, and no part of the address shall be written, printed, or otherwise impressed across such Stamp.

" 3. Anything (including a Letter, or Communication in the nature of a Letter), may be written, printed, or otherwise impressed on the Reverse Side of the Post Card.

" 4. Nothing whatever shall be in any manner attached to a Post Card, nor shall a Post card be cut, or folded, or otherwise altered.

" 5. In case any one of the required conditions has not been fulfilled the Card will be charged at Letter Rates of Postage.

" And the LIEUTENANT-GOVERNOR is further pleased, with the advice aforesaid, to order that the Rate of Postage upon such *Inland Post Cards* shall be as under :—

" For a Post Card Posted for Town or Office Delivery. } One Half Penny.

" For a Post Card to be conveyed any distance within the Colony. } One Penny.

And that such Rate shall not be payable either in whole or in part by adhesive Stamps, but only as aforesaid.

" (Signed)   R. B. LLEWELYN,
" *Acting Clerk of Privy Council.*"

At the same date as the Inland postcards were issued—1st April, 1877—Jamaica was admitted into " The General Postal Union," and a card of the value of three pence was required for use between Countries in the Union. As it was impossible to get the cards from England by the required date, all three values had to be obtained in the Island ; and as Messrs. De la Rue and Co.'s cards did not arrive until November of that year, several printings of these provisional cards took place.   Mr. G. H. Pearce informs me that those with frame of " lozenges " were supplied from the Government Printing Office, in the General Penitentiary, and that those with the floriate pattern border were procured from Mr. George Henderson, the then Government printer.   He further tells me the number of temporary cards issued was as under :—

3d.   4,701
1d.   16,228
½d.   5,727
        ———
        26,656

A new Postal Convention, constituting the " Universal Postal Union," was signed at Paris, on the 1st June, 1878, for the revision of the Treaty of Berne, which had previously established the " General Postal Union." The new Convention, which came into force on the 1st April, 1879, made many alterations ; amongst others, the issue of postcards for Countries in the Union, instead of being optional, was made compulsory, and the rate was reduced from three pence to three halfpence. No card of the latter value being available, the three penny card of Messrs. De la Rue and Co.'s make, was surcharged, in the Island, with the necessary alterations. This surcharged card continued in use for over four years, as it was not until June 16th, 1883, that the new one, ordered from England, was issued. Registration Envelopes were first issued on January 1st, 1881, at the General Post Office. Contrary to the usual custom, these envelopes bear no stamp upon the flap, and there is nothing in the inscription on the face to denote that they emanate from this Colony. Precisely similar envelopes were issued for use in Turks Islands the same year, so it is necessary to have postmarked copies to prove which Island they were used in. The notice of issue as regards Jamaica, is found in *The Gazette* of February 17th, 1881.

REGISTERED LETTERS.

" GENERAL POST OFFICE, *1st January*, 1881.

" BY Law the Post Office is not liable, for the loss of any Registered Letter or of its contents, but in order to meet the requirements of the Postal Union Treaty the Postmaster for Jamaica will be prepared to make good the contents of a Registered Letter lost while passing through the Post *to the extent of Two Pounds*, in certain cases :—

Provided.—1. That the sender duly observed all the conditions of Registration required.

2. That the Letter was securely enclosed in a reasonably strong Envelope ; and, if it contained *money*, that it was enclosed in one of the special Registered Letter Envelopes, approved by the Post Office for the purpose.

3. That application was made to the Postmaster for Jamaica immediately the loss was discovered. (When the complaint is that the contents of a letter have been abstracted the envelope must accompany the application, otherwise the question cannot be entertained.)

4. That the Postmaster for Jamaica (whose decision shall be final) is satisfied that the loss occurred while the letter was in the custody of the Jamaica Post Office, and was not caused by any fault on the part of the sender.

The approved Registered Letter Envelopes are of two sizes.

Size G—6 inches by 3¾ inches. Price ½d. each or 5d. per dozen.

Size H—8 inches by 5 inches. Price ¾d. each or 7d. per dozen.

These envelopes can be obtained at the General Post Office and will be delivered Post Free at the prices stated.

"(Signed)   FRED. SULLIVAN,
" Postmaster for Jamaica."

The following notices are taken from *The Gazette* of June 21st, 1883, and amongst other particulars give the date of issue of reply paid postcards.

<h3 align="center">INLAND POST CARDS.</h3>

" GENERAL POST OFFICE, 16th June, 1883.

"THE following Regulation, in respect of the transmission of Post Cards in Jamaica, has been approved by Government :—

"In future the Halfpenny Post Card, intended for Town or Office delivery, may be used for general circulation within the Colony if the deficient Postage thereon, say one halfpenny, be added thereto by an adhesive Postage Stamp.

"(Signed)   FRED. SULLIVAN,
" Postmaster for Jamaica."

<h3 align="center">REPLY PAID POST CARDS.</h3>

" GENERAL POST OFFICE, 16th June, 1883.

"THE issue of Reply Paid Post Cards, for use between places in Jamaica, as well as between certain places in the Universal Postal Union, having been authorised by Government, such Cards can be obtained at each Post Office in the Island at the following rates :—

<h3 align="center">INLAND CARDS.</h3>

For Town or Office delivery ...   . at 1d.
For use between Post Offices in the Island ...   ... at 2d.

<h3 align="center">UNIVERSAL POSTAL UNION CARDS.</h3>

For transmission to any place in the Postal Union which
  is included in the list below   ...   . at 3d.

"The Reply Paid Post Card consists of a double card folded in the centre, one portion being intended for use by the poster, and the other portion to be torn off and used in reply by the addressee. Each portion of the card is impressed with a Stamp, representing the amount of the postage chargeable thereon. The conditions of transmission by post of Reply Paid Post Cards are the same as those which are in force with respect to the transmission of Single Post Cards.

"It must be distinctly understood, however, that Inland Post Cards, whether Single or Reply Paid, are not available for transmission to Postal Union Countries, even though the additional Postage be prepaid by means of adhesive Postage Stamps.

"List of places to which Reply Paid Post Cards may be forwarded:—

Argentine Republic.
Austria-Hungary.
Belgium.
Canada.
Chili.
Colombia, United States of,
Cyprus.
Dominican Republic.
France, but not including Colonies of Martinique, &c.
Germany.
Gibraltar.
Great Britain and Colonies.
Honduras, Republic of,
India, British.
Italy.
Liberia.

Luxemburg.
Malta.
Netherlands and Colonies.
Norway.
Paraguay.
Persia.
Portugal and Colonies.
Roumania.
Salvador.
Servia.
Spain and Colonies of Cuba and Porto Rico.
Switzerland.
Turkey.
Uruguay.
Venezuela.

"An additional rate of 1½d. on both the Card and its reply must be affixed, by means of adhesive Postage Stamps, on Reply Post Cards sent to the following places:—

Ceylon.
Hong-Kong.
India.

Java, and other Netherlands Colonies in Indian Ocean.
Straits Settlements.

"(Signed)   FRED. SULLIVAN,
"*Postmaster for Jamaica.*"

In October, 1887, Postage and Revenue Stamps were authorised to be used for either branch of the service, according to the following Law, a copy of which was published in *The Gazette* of October 13th, 1887.

"JAMAICA. LAW 18 of 1887.

The Postage and Revenue Stamp Law, 1887.

[*6th October,* 1887.]

"WHEREAS it is desirable to make postage stamps available for denoting payment of Revenue Stamp Duties, payment of which may be denoted by Adhesive Stamps, and also to make Revenue Stamps available for Postage purposes, and also to provide that, as from time to time stamp plates get worn out, new stamps shall be provided that shall be available for either Postage or Revenue purposes, and also to make further provision respecting the custody, issue and use, of Adhesive Stamps:—

"Be it enacted by the Governor and Legislative Council of Jamaica, as follows:—

"From and after the passing of this Law, any stamps of the pattern heretofore in use for expressing and denoting payment of rates or duties of Postage, and issued by the Treasurer and Commissioner of Stamps under and pursuant to the provisions of Law 18 of 1868, may be also lawfully used for expressing and denoting payment, to the amount expressed by the same, of any Stamp Duties, payment of which may be lawfully expressed and denoted by Adhesive Stamps; and any stamps of the pattern heretofore in use, and issued under the Provisions of Law 33 of 1868 for expressing and denoting payment of the Stamp Duties imposed by the said Law, may be also lawfully used for expressing and denoting payment to the amount expressed by the same, of rates and duties of Postage."

There are six other clauses, making seven in all, to the above Law, but the remainder are not of sufficient interest to collectors to reproduce here. The first two stamps to be issued with the inscription changed to " Postage and Revenue," were the one penny and two pence, which are altogether of a new design. These stamps first came into use on March 8th, 1889, according to a notice published in *The Gazette* of March 14th of that year.

GOVERNMENT NOTICE.

No. 112.   "*8th March*, 1889.

"THE OFFICER ADMINISTERING THE GOVERNMENT directs it to be notified, for general information, that the issue of the following Unified Postage and Revenue Stamps has been authorized, viz. :—

"1d. Colour, light purple, Queen's head within a circle containing the words 'Jamaica Postage and Revenue,' with the denomination '1d.' at the base.

"2d. Colour, light green, similar in other particulars to the 1d. stamp as above described, with the denomination '2d.' at the base."

On the 1st January, 1890, the postal rates for Inland letters and postcards was reduced, according to the following notice, extracted from *The Gazette* of September 26th, 1889.

REDUCTION OF POSTAGE ON LETTERS AND POST CARDS FOR INLAND CIRCULATION.

" HIS EXCELLENCY THE GOVERNOR, by and with the advice and consent of the Privy Council, has been pleased to direct that the Rate of Charge on Letters and Post Cards carried by Post for delivery within Jamaica shall be, as under :—

LETTERS.

For each half-ounce in weight ...   . One penny.

POST CARDS.

| Single | ... | ... | ... | ... | ... | ... | Half-penny. |
| Reply paid | ... | ... | ... | ... | ... | ... | One penny. |

" Such Regulation to come into force on the 1st day of January, 1890.

"(Signed)   FRED. SULLIVAN,
                              " *Postmaster for Jamaica.*

" GENERAL POST OFFICE, 24th September, 1889."

An alteration was made in the system of franking correspondence in the various Government Departments on the 1st April, 1890, when stamps surcharged with the word " *Official* " were issued in accordance with the following notice, published in *The Gazette* of April 3rd that year.

GOVERNMENT NOTICE.

No. 144.   *2nd April*, 1890.

"THE GOVERNOR directs it to be notified, for general information, that from and after the 1st instant, the privilege of sending or receiving Official Correspondence free of Postage in this Island is withdrawn.

"2. The following are the Rules which have been approved by His Excellency with respect to the payment of Official Postages.

"By command,

"(Signed)   NEALE PORTER,

"*Colonial Secretary.*"

Rules with respect to the Payment of Official Postages.

"From and after Tuesday the 1st day of April, 1890, the permission either to send or to receive Official Correspondence *Free of Postage* will be cancelled, with the following exceptions:—

"His Excellency the Governor, his Private Secretary, and his A.D.C.; and also (for the convenience of the general community and the general management of the Postal Department) the Postmaster for Jamaica.

"2. The Honourable the Colonial Secretary will also retain the right to frank, by his own signature, correspondence posted by himself in his official capacity.

"3. Correspondence to or from Heads of Departments or other Public Functionaries who have not been specially exempted, will be liable to the following Rates of Postage:—

Letters	...	...	...	...	1d. per half-ounce.
Book Packets not exceeding 5 lbs.			...	½d. per 4 ounces.
Parcels not exceeding 8 ounces ...			...	1d. per 2 ounces.

"4. Prepayment of postage on correspondence to or from a Head of a Department or other Public Functionary is *optional*, except in the case of registration; but, when prepayment is effected it must be by means of '*Official Postage Stamps*' which can be purchased from any Post Office. If the ordinary Postage Stamps be made use of the article so prepaid will not be recognised as '*Official*,' but will be surcharged as an *ordinary letter.*

"5. Official Postage Stamps are *only* available for the prepayment of postage by Heads of Departments or other Public Functionaries. Prepayment of correspondence *from* the Public *to* such Officials must be effected by means of the ordinary Postage Stamps.

"6. Correspondence which may be wholly unpaid or partially prepaid will be surcharged at the above stated prepaid rates of postage. The postage on such unpaid correspondence must be paid for, *in cash*, before delivery.

"(Signed)   FRED. SULLIVAN,

"*Postmaster for Jamaica.*"

"GENERAL POST OFFICE, 11*th March*, 1890.

TELEGRAPH STAMPS.

Telegraph Stamps and stamped forms were first issued on October 20th, 1879, according to the following announcement published in *The Gazette* of October 30th of that year.

"PRIVY COUNCIL CHAMBER, 20*th October*, 1879.

"UNDER the provisions of Law I. of 1879—

"(1.) The following Rules have been approved by the Lieutenant-Governor, in Privy Council.

"(2.) It is ordered that the following Rules shall come into operation on the 20th day of October, 1879.
"(Signed)   J. ALLWOOD, JNR.,
                          "Acting Clerk Privy Council."

TARIFF FOR INLAND TELEGRAMS.

" 1. The charge for Telegrams throughout Jamaica is 1s. for the first twenty words, and 3d. for every additional five words, *i.e.,* for every additional group of not more than five words, the names and addresses of the sender and receiver not being counted.

TELEGRAPH STAMPS.

" 2. Distinctive Telegraph Stamps of the values of One Shilling and Three Pence are issued for the payment of the charges on Telegrams. Postage Stamps are not accepted in payment of Telegrams, nor are Telegraph Stamps accepted in payment of Postage. Telegraph Stamps are not purchased from the public at Post Offices, nor can they be exchanged for Postage Stamps. Telegrams must be stamped before they can be accepted for transmission, and Telegrams will not be received unless so stamped.

RECEIPTS.

" 3. Receipts for the charges on Telegrams can be obtained at a cost of 3d. each.

TELEGRAM FORMS.

" 4. Inland Telegram Forms are of two kinds, namely, the 'A. 1.' Form embossed with a stamp of the value of 1s., and the 'A' Form given gratis with no stamp embossed thereon. The 'A. 1.' Forms, bound up into books of 20 forms interleaved and with a sheet of carbonic paper, price £1 0s. 3d each book, can be obtained on application to the Head Office."

There are altogether 35 clauses of the above Rules, but there is no reason for reproducing the remainder here.

REFERENCE LIST OF THE PHILATELIC SOCIETY, LONDON.

Issue I.   November 23rd, 1860.

Five values. Engraved and surface-printed by Messrs. De la Rue and Co., of London, on white wove surfaced paper, watermarked with a pine-apple, white gum ; machine perforated 14. Designs: A laureated profile of Queen Victoria to left, on a ground of horizontal lines, enclosed in a frame of a different design for each value ; all inscribed JAMAICA POSTAGE above, and with the value in words below, in small block letters. ONE PENNY.—The profile is enclosed in a single-lined circle ; beyond this is a circular band of colour broken by the sides of the rectangular frame ; there is a pearled outer edge to the space thus formed, and it contains the inscriptions in white letters ; the corners are reticulated and a single-lined rectangle forms the border and completes the design. TWO PENCE.—The profile is in a single-lined circle as on the One Penny; the inscriptions are in colour, on curved white labels above and below, not concentric with the circle, the spandrels being filled in with solid colour ; the whole is enclosed in a single-lined frame, with straight sides and curved at the top and bottom. FOUR PENCE.—The centre of the stamp is identical with that of the two last values; the inscriptions are in white block letters on straight coloured labels at the top and bottom of the stamp. Each spandrel is formed of a triangle shaded with slanting lines, bordered by a white line and framed with pearls. A square with a white outline encloses the central disc and the spandrels; there is no outer frame to the stamp. SIX PENCE.—The profile is enclosed in a hexagonal pearled frame, following the shape of which are white labels above and below, with the inscriptions in coloured letters. The corners are filled in with arabesques, and a single line of colour forms the outer border. ONE SHILLING.—The profile is surrounded by an oval frame of solid colour, with the inscriptions in white letters, a white dot separating them on each side. The spandrels are filled in with arabesques, and a single line of colour forms the outer border. Shape, upright rectangular. (*Illustrations,* 166, 167, 168, 171, 172.)

> T. " JAMAICA POSTAGE." B. "ONE PENNY." "TWO PENCE." "FOUR PENCE."
> " SIX PENCE." " ONE SHILLING."
> 1d., blue (shades).
> 2d., rose (,,)
> 4d., dull orange (pale to deep).
> 6d., lilac, dull lilac (shades).
> 1s., brown to violet-brown (,,)

Issue II. September 10th, 1863.

One value. Engraved and surface-printed by Messrs. De la Rue and Co., on white wove surfaced paper, watermarked with a pine-apple. White gum, machine perforated 14. Design: Laureated profile of Queen Victoria to left, on a background of horizontal lines, enframed by an oval band of colour, with inscriptions in white block letters, a small star-shaped ornament and two dots dividing the two inscriptions on either side. The spandrels are filled in with foliate ornaments, and an outer border of two coloured lines completes the design. Shape, upright rectangular. (*Illustration* 173.)

> T. " JAMAICA POSTAGE." B. " THREE PENCE."
> 3d., green (shades).

Issue III. 1871-1872.

Seven values. The six stamps of the two previous issues, with the addition of a HALFPENNY value engraved and printed in the same manner; all on paper watermarked Crown C.C.; machine perforated 14. Design: For the additional value, laureated profile of Queen Victoria to left, on a ground of horizontal lines, within a frame of three concentric scallopped circles. At the top and bottom are straight white framed labels, with inscriptions in coloured Roman capitals and an eight-rayed star on each side of the value below. The spandrels are filled in with arabesques, and a plain coloured line completes the design. Shape, upright rectangular. (*Illustrations* 166, 167, 168, 171, 172, 173, 174.)

> T. "JAMAICA POSTAGE." B. " HALFPENNY."
> (29th October, 1872) ½d., brown-lake (shades).
> 1d., blue (,,)
> 2d., rose (,,)
> 3d., green (,,)
> 4d., dull orange (,,)
> 6d., lilac (,,)
> 1s., brown (,,)

Remarks.—The one penny is known divided vertically, as well as diagonally, and the halves used as halfpenny stamps.

Issue IV. August 27th, 1875.

Two values. Engraved and surface-printed by Messrs. De la Rue and Co., of London, on white wove surfaced paper, watermarked Crown C.C. White gum, machine perforated 14. Designs: TWO SHILLINGS.—Laureated profile of Queen Victoria to left, as before, on a ground of horizontal lines, enclosed within a single-lined circle with pearled border. The inscriptions are in coloured block letters on curved white labels above and below, concentric with the circle. The spandrels are filled with conventional white ornaments on solid ground, and the stamp is surrounded by a single-lined outer border. FIVE SHILLINGS.—Profile, as above, within a single-lined octagonal frame with a pearled border. The inscriptions are in white block letters, on straight coloured framed labels at top and bottom; the spandrels are filled by similar conventional ornaments to those on the two shillings, and the whole is enclosed by a single-lined outer border. Shape, upright rectangular. (*Illustrations* 175, 176.)

T. "JAMAICA POSTAGE." B. "TWO SHILLINGS." "FIVE SHILLINGS."
2s., red-brown (shades).
5s., deep lilac („)

Issue V. 1883-1884.

Three values. The same designs, printing, paper, and perforation as before, but with watermark Crown C.A. (*Illustrations* 166, 167, 168.)

1d., blue (shades).
2d., crimson („)
4d., deep orange-red („)

Issue VI. 1885-1886.

Four values. Designs, &c., as before, but with the colours changed. Watermark Crown C.A., perforation as before. (*Illustrations* 166, 167, 173, 174.)

½d., pale-green (shades).
1d., crimson („)
2d., grey („)
(1886) 3d., olive-green („)

Issue VII. March 8th, 1889.

Two values. Engraved and surface-printed by Messrs. De la Rue and Co., of London, on white wove surfaced paper, watermarked Crown C.A. White gum, machine perforated 14. Design: Diademed profile of Queen Victoria to left on a ground of horizontal lines, enclosed in a circular band inscribed "JAMAICA" above, "POSTAGE on the lower left, and "& REVENUE" on the lower right, in white block letters on a solid ground of colour; at each side of the name is a star or flower formed of dots, and the band is interrupted below by the upper part of an octagonal label, which contains the value in figures on a lined ground. The design is surrounded by a double-lined, pearled frame, encroached upon at the top and side by the circular band and at the bottom by the octagonal label. The spaces between these and the frame are filled with arabesques. The value is printed separately from the rest of the design, and in a different shade. (*Illustration* 177.)

T. "JAMAICA." B. "POSTAGE—1d. (2d.)—& REVENUE."
1d., mauve, value in lilac.
2d., green, „ green.

Remarks.—Since October, 1887, the *Revenue* stamps of Jamaica have been allowed to pay postage; they consisted of three halfpence and three pence, of ordinary size, with the Arms of the Colony, one penny of very similar design to the one shilling *postage*, and one, five, and ten shillings of large rectangular design. Of these only the one penny and three pence have been commonly thus used, the stocks of the other values having been practically exhausted before their use was authorised. Specimens of all, except perhaps the ten shillings, are known postally used either before or since permission was given.

Issue VIII. 1890.

Two values. The TWO PENCE HALFPENNY is formed by overprinting the four pence of Issue IV. with the words " TWO PENCE—HALFPENNY " in thin block letters, in two lines, in black. The SIX PENCE is of the same design as before, but in a new colour, and with the watermark Crown C.A. Perforation unchanged. (*Illustrations* 171, 178.)

> 2½d., black surcharge on 4d., deep orange-red.
> 6d., orange-yellow.

Variety. The 2¾d. is known with double, treble, and also with inverted surcharge.

OFFICIAL STAMPS.

Issue I. April 1st, 1890.

Three values. The HALFPENNY of Issue VI. surcharged in the Colony with the word " OFFICIAL " in thin block letters, the word measuring 17 mm. in length; and the ONE PENNY and TWO PENCE of Issue VII., printed in different colours, and surcharged by Messrs. De la Rue and Co., with the same word in thick block letters, the word measuring 16 mm. Both the surcharges are in black, and the stamps are watermarked Crown C.A., and perforated 14. (*Illustrations* 179, 180.)

> ½d., green, black surcharge.
> 1d., carmine „   „
> 2d., grey „   „

Remarks.—Varieties of the locally printed surcharge are known, due to irregular or defective printing, such as " FFICIAL " or " OFF C AL " for " OFFICIAL," and with the whole word inverted, and part of a second impression in the correct position on the same stamp.

REGISTRATION ENVELOPES.

Issue I. January 1st, 1881.

Two sizes. Bag-shaped envelopes of white wove linen-lined paper, with the flap on the left; crossed lines on the back and front, and along the upper margin of the address side is the instruction in two lines, as described for the envelopes of Barbados. Below this on the left is the word " REGISTERED " in large Roman capitals, in a narrow oblong rectangle; in the right upper corner is the inscribed space for the adhesive stamp. These inscriptions, &c., are all in *blue*. Under the flap is—

> " McCORQUODALE AND Co.,   PATENT REGISTERED
>   LIMITED.   ENVELOPE."

in black. There is no stamp, and both postage and registration fee are paid by means of adhesives. (*Illustration* 192.)

> Without expressed value (½d.) blue ; size G.
> „   „   „ (¾d.) „   „ H.

Variety. Size G is known with the face of the envelope entirely plain.

Issue II. 1885 (?).

Two sizes. Similar to the envelopes of Barbados, Issue II., with a large letter " R " in an upright oval frame, on the face in the left upper corner, and the flap on the right. Under the flap is—

" McCorquodale and Co.,   Contractors,"
Limited.

in blue. (*Illustration* 28.)

Without expressed value (½d.) blue ; size G.
     „   „   „   (¾d.)   „   „   H.

Remarks.—These envelopes are also used in the Turks Islands, which are a dependency of Jamaica, and could of course be used anywhere else with equal propriety. Copies are known to have been employed in the Bermudas.

WRAPPER.

Issue I. September 1st, 1888.

One value. Designed and printed by Messrs De la Rue and Co., upon light buff wove paper. Similar to the wrappers of Barbados, but with a stamp of the following design: Diademed head of Queen Victoria to left upon ground of solid colour enclosed within a circle. Straight labels of solid colour above and below the circle, the upper inscribed with the name of the Colony and the lower with the value in words, all in uncoloured block letters : conventional ornaments in the spandrels, and a single outer coloured line completes the design. (*Illustration* 191.)

T. " JAMAICA."   B. " HALFPENNY."
½d., green.

POST CARDS.

Issue I. April 1st, 1877.

Pending the arrival of post cards from England, provisional cards of native manufacture were issued. The cards were of three values —one halfpenny being for urban, one penny for inland, and three pence for postage to countries in the Postal Union, into which Jamaica was admitted on the above date. When the permanent issue of cards arrived from England, at the end of 1877, the requirements of collectors and stamp dealers were so excessive that the supply was soon exhausted, and for a time Type II. of the provisional cards was reverted to, these being for the most part printed during their re-issue on stout white paper instead of card.

TYPE I.

The inscription consists of three lines: (1st) POST CARD in large Roman capitals, the two words being separated by the Arms and Supporters of Great Britain ; (2nd) beneath the Arms, JAMAICA ; and (3rd) lower down, THE ADDRESS ONLY TO BE WRITTEN ON THIS SIDE, the two latter lines being in small Roman capitals. The franking stamp is in the right upper corner, and consists of a circular hand stamp inscribed in block capitals JAMAICA above, 1887 and PAID in two lines in the centre, and HALFPENNY, or ONE PENNY, or THREEPENCE below, and in the case of the last value there is a large period after JAMAICA. The whole is enclosed within a frame formed of lozenges between two straight lines, the outer of which is considerably thicker than the inner. The design is typographed in colour, on thick white card, and the hand-stamp is struck in red. The frame measures 113×68 mm., or $4\frac{9}{10} \times 2\frac{7}{10}$ inches, and the reverse side of the card is plain. (*Illustration* 193.)

½d., red and blue ; shades from light to dark slaty-blue.
1d.,   „   „   „   „
3d.,   „   „ .   „   „

Remarks.—The stamp being hand-struck is found in various positions, inverted and otherwise, and also varies greatly in shade. In some of the cards of this issue slight flaws may here and there be found in the borders, but there is but one type.

TYPE II.

Three values similar to the last, but differing in parts of the design. The Arms and Supporters of Great Britain are differently emblazoned, and JAMAICA and THE ADDRESS ONLY, &c., are printed in larger Roman capitals. The hand-stamp is the same, but the former frame of the card is replaced by an ornamental one of fancy floriate pattern. The design is typographed in colour on thick card or on stout white paper, and there are six varieties.

Variety I. The frame measures 111×72 mm., or $4\frac{3}{5} \times 2\frac{17}{20}$ inches. The second ornament from the top on the right-hand side is misplaced, and points to the bottom of the card instead of to the right. (*Illustration* 194.)

Printed on thick white card.

$\frac{1}{2}$d., red and blue ; shades from light to dark.
1d.,   ,,   ,,   ,,
3d.,   ,,   ,,   ,,

Sub-variety. The second ornament from the right in the top border is wholly missing.

3d., red and blue.

Variety II. The frame measures $106\frac{1}{2} \times 72$ mm., or $4\frac{1}{5} \times 2\frac{17}{20}$ inches. None of the ornaments are missing, but the second one from the bottom on the right side is incomplete, the two little *fleur-de-lys* like ornaments being almost entirely absent. (*Illustration* 195.)

(*a*) Printed on thick white card.

$\frac{1}{2}$d., red and blue ; shades light to very dark.
1d.,   ,,   ,,   ,,
3d.,   ,,   ,,   ,,

(*b*) Printed on thick bluish card.

$\frac{1}{2}$d., red and pale blue (shades).
1d.,   ,,   (,,)

Variety III. The frame measures $107 \times 72\frac{1}{2}$ mm., or about $4\frac{1}{5} \times 2\frac{17}{20}$ inches. All the broken ornaments and mistakes are now corrected, and the right-hand corner ornament at the top is placed pointing above, and forms part of the upper border instead of, as in Variety II., forming part of the right border, and pointing to the right. (*Illustration* 196.)

(*a*) Printed on thick white card.

$\frac{1}{2}$d., red and very pale to dark blue.
1d.,   ,,   ,,   ,,

(*b*) Printed on thick bluish card.

$\frac{1}{2}$d., red and very pale to dark blue.
1d.,   ·,   ,,   ,,

Variety IV. The frame measures 107×72 mm., or about $4\frac{1}{5} \times 2\frac{17}{20}$ inches. It is similar to Variety II., but has many additional ornaments of the left side border broken, and JAMAICA is followed by a colon, as is also CARD ; but the top period of the latter is much smaller than the lower one, and is consequently very indistinct on some of the cards. (*Illustration* 197.)

(*a*) Printed on thick white card.

$\frac{1}{2}$d., red and very pale to dark blue.
1d.,   ,,   ,,   ,,

(*b*) Printed on thick bluish card.

$\frac{1}{2}$d., red and very pale to dark blue.
1d.,   ,,   ,,   ,,

(*c*) Printed on thick yellowish-white glazed card.

$\frac{1}{2}$d., red and blue.

Variety V. The frame is similar to that of Variety II., and measures the same, but, in addition, the seventh ornament from the bottom in the left side border is broken. Colon after JAMAICA, and the top of the 1 in this word is wanting. Period after CARD. (*Illustration* 198.)

Printed on stout white *paper.*

½d., red and blue (shades).
1d.,   ,,   (,,)
3d.,   ,,   (,,)

Variety VI. The frame measures 107×73 mm., or about $4\frac{1}{4}×2\frac{9}{16}$ inches, and is similar to Variety II.; but the broken ornament in the right-hand border is corrected, and the ninth ornament from the top of the left border is misplaced, and points to the bottom of the card instead of to the left, and the bottom left-corner ornament is also misplaced, and forms part of the left border instead of the bottom. (*Illustration* 199.)

Printed on stout white *paper.*

½d., red and very pale to dark blue.
1d.,   ,,   ,,   ,,   (?)
3d.,   ,,   ,,   ,,

Remarks.—The cards printed on *paper* may be found watermarked with Gothic letters or with a shield, as well as unwatermarked; but, like the watermarks in the unstamped cards of Chili, are worthy only of passing notice, as they are simply portions of the trade mark of the paper-maker, and only a few of the cards printed on the same sheet of paper would consequently catch parts of the watermark.

Issue II. November 14th, 1877.

This issue also consists of three values, the inscriptions, &c., being disposed in the same way as those on the provisionals, although the type employed is different. POST CARD is in fancy capitals, and JAMAICA and THE ADDRESS ONLY, &c., in block letters. The Arms and Supporters of Great Britain are similar to those on Type II. of the provisional cards, but smaller. The stamp is in the right upper corner, and is the same type as the adhesive of corresponding value, Issues I., II., and III. The whole is enclosed within a fancy frame of ornamental chain pattern. The design is typographed in colour on thin buff card, and the reverse side is plain. Makers, Messrs. De la Rue and Co. Size of the frame, 113×66 mm., or $4\frac{9}{16}×2\frac{3}{5}$ inches. (*Illustration* 200.)

½d., red-brown (shades).
1d., blue   (,,)
3d., green   (,,)

Issue III. April 4th, 1879.

The postage to countries in the Postal Union having been reduced by half, the three penny card was surcharged UNIVERSAL POSTAL UNION in Roman capitals in a straight line at the top of the card above the Arms, and the stamp surcharged at the bottom in two lines in block capitals: (1st) ONE PENNY, (2nd) HALFPENNY. The surcharge is in black.

Variety I. The letters of UNIVERSAL POSTAL UNION are $3\frac{1}{2}$ mm. in height, and 78 mm. in length. (*Illustration* 201.)

1½d., black surcharge, on 3d. green.

Error. With double surcharge, one being inverted at the bottom of the card.

1½d., black surcharge, on 3d. green.

Variety II. The letters of UNIVERSAL POSTAL UNION are $4\frac{1}{4}$ mm. in height, and 74 mm. in length. (*Illustration* 202.)

1½d., black surcharge, on 3d. green.

Issue IV. June 16th, 1883.

One value. Designed and printed by Messrs. De la Rue and Co., upon stout straw card. Size 139×88 mm., or 5½×3½ inches. The inscription is the same as that on the first issue card of Antigua, except that the second line reads JAMAICA (JAMAÏQUE), The stamp is in the right upper corner, and is similar in type to the two shilling adhesive issued in August, 1875, but for the alteration of the value. The card is without frame. (*Illustration* 203.)

1½d., slate-grey (slight shades).

REPLY PAID CARDS.

Issue I. June 16th, 1883.

Three values. Designed and printed by Messrs. De la Rue and Co., the half-penny and one penny upon medium light buff, and the three halfpenny upon stout straw card. Size of the halfpenny and one penny 121×75 mm., or 4⅘×2¹⁰⁄₁₆ inches, that of the three halfpenny 139×88 mm., or 5½×3½ inches. The design of the halfpenny and one penny is similar to that of the single cards of the same values of Issue II., but the first half has in the left lower corner, in three lines, THE ANNEXED CARD—IS INTENDED FOR—THE ANSWER, in small block letters, and the second half has the word REPLY in Roman capitals under THE ADDRESS ONLY, &c. The three halfpenny is similar to the card of Issue IV., with the usual additional inscription on each half, as upon the reply cards of Antigua. The cards are joined along the top, perforated 4, and the design is impressed upon the first and third pages. (*Illustrations* 200, 203.)

½d.+½d., red-brown (shades).
1d.+1d., blue („)
1½d.+1½d., slate-grey („)

TELEGRAPH STAMPS.

Issue I. October 20th, 1879.

Two values. Designed and surface-printed by Messrs. De la Rue and Co. upon white wove surfaced paper, watermarked Crown C.C., which is placed sideways on the three penny value. White gum, machine perforated 14. Designs: THREE PENCE. --Laureated head of Queen Victoria to left upon ground of horizontal lines, enclosed within a white circular band, inscribed in small coloured block letters; a period at either side separating the upper inscription from the lower. Triangular coloured blocks in the spandrels contain white conventional ornaments. The blocks are surrounded by a white border of fancy design, which is continued down the right and left sides of the stamp. The design is completed by a single outer line of colour. Shape, small oblong rectangular. ONE SHILLING.—Laureated head of Queen Victoria to left upon ground of horizontal lines, enclosed within a plain circular coloured line. White arabesques in the lower spandrels. Surrounding the circle and resting upon it at the top is a broad arched band of solid colour, which touches the top, right and left sides of the stamp. The band contains an inscription in the upper curve in white block letters, and starlike ornaments at the bottom at either side. Straight label of solid colour below the circle contains the value in words in white block letters. The upper corners of the stamp contain coloured arabesque ornamentation: and the lower ones a small square of solid colour with four white dots surrounding a smaller one. The design is completed by an outer coloured line voided at either side of the two top corners. Shape, large oblong rectangular. (*Illustrations* 181, 182.)

T. "JAMAICA TELEGRAPHS." B. "THREE PENCE." "ONE SHILLING."

A.—On paper blued by the chemical action of the ink.

1s., brown.

B.—On white paper.

3d., lilac.
1s., brown.

Issue II. 1889.

One value. The three pence of the preceding issue printed upon white wove surfaced paper, watermarked Crown C.A. placed sideways. White gum, machine perforated 14. (*Illustration* 181.)

3d., lilac.

STAMPED TELEGRAPH FORMS.

Issue I. October 20th, 1879.

One value. A large sheet of white wove unwatermarked paper, measuring about 230×150 mm. or 9×6 inches, with instructions on the face and back, and spaces for the addresses of the sender and consignee and message on the face, all printed in black. The stamp is embossed in the right upper corner. Design : Diademed profile of Queen Victoria to left in plain relief on ground of solid colour, enclosed within an octagonal frame formed of a single plain line. Surrounding the octagon is a broad circular band, with inscriptions in white block letters on a reticulated ground, a period at either side separating the upper inscription from the lower. The space between the octagon and circular band is filled in with eight small white circles containing cross-like ornaments, with fancy ornamentation between the circles. A plain outer circular line of colour completes the design. Shape circular. (*Illustration* 183.)

T. "JAMAICA TELEGRAPHS." B. "ONE SHILLING."

1s., pink.

Remarks.—These forms were sold bound up in books of twenty, interleaved, and with a sheet of carbonic paper for taking copies of the messages, price £1 0s. 3d. each book. The forms vary somewhat in size.

STAMPED TELEGRAPH FORMS FOR OFFICIAL USE.

Issue I. October 20th, 1879.

One value. Similar to the forms supplied to the public ; but printed upon green wove unwatermarked paper. The instructions, &c., are the same and are also printed in black, but there are two additional lines for the message. The form measures about 230×170 mm., or 9×6 7/16 inches. The stamp is embossed in the right upper corner, and is of the same design as that on the forms for the public, but is surcharged across the centre OFFICIAL in thick black block letters, measuring 4 mm. in height by 20½ mm. in length. (*Illustration* 187.)

1s., pink, black surcharge.

Remarks.—These forms were also supplied bound up into books, and like the forms sold to the public vary somewhat in size.

LEEWARD ISLANDS.

COPIES OF OFFICIAL NOTICES.

Furnished by E. D. BACON.

The following appeared in *The Leeward Islands Gazette* of October 30th, 1890 :—

A PROCLAMATION.

" Whereas an Act was passed in the 53rd year of Her Majesty's Reign by the General Legislative Council of the Leeward Islands on the 3rd day of February, numbered 3, and entitled : 'An Act to make uniform the stamps used throughout the Colony for Postal Rates and Stamp Duties, and to amend the Stamp Act, 1887.'

" And whereas by the said Act it was provided that such Act as aforesaid should come into operation on a day to be mentioned by the Governor by Proclamation, but that such Proclamation should not be issued until due provision had been made for the issuing of stamps in accordance with the provisions of the Act as aforesaid.

" Now, therefore, I do by this, my proclamation, declare that the said Act shall come into operation on the 31st day of October, 1890 :—

" Given under my hand and the Public Seal of the Leeward Islands, at Antigua, this thirtieth day of October, 1890, in the fifty-fourth year of Her Majesty's Reign.

" By His Excellency's Command,

" (Signed)   Fred. Evans,

" *Colonial Secretary.*"

The *Leeward Islands Gazette* for December 4th, 1890, contains the following notice :—

REDUCED RATES OF POSTAGE.

" It is hereby notified for general information that on and after the 1st January next the postage to the United Kingdom will be two pence halfpenny per half-ounce instead of four pence, and that the postage in the Colony of the Leeward Islands from any one place within the Colony to to any other will be one penny per half-ounce.

" (Signed)   Fred. Evans,

" *Colonial Secretary.*"

REFERENCE LIST OF THE PHILATELIC SOCIETY, LONDON.

Issue I. October 31st, 1890.

Eight values. Designed and surface printed by Messrs. De la Rue and Co., upon surfaced white wove paper, watermarked Crown C.A. White gum, machine perforated 14. The entire sheet contains 120 stamps in two panes of 60, each consisting of ten horizontal rows of six. Design : Diademed profile of Queen Victoria to left upon ground of horizontal lines, enclosed within an octagonal frame, which is contained in a small oblong rectangle with a star and two dots at each of the four corners, and three dots at the centre of the right and left sides. Above the rectangle there is a straight white label, the width of the stamp, inscribed with the name of the Colony, in coloured block letters, and beneath there is an hexagonal tablet of horizontal lines with the value in white shaded Arabic numerals, and small white shaded letter "D," with short line below. In the one and five shilling values the tablet is white, and the value is in words in two lines of small coloured block letters. At the left side of the rectangle is the word "POSTAGE" reading upwards, and at the right side "& REVENUE" reading downwards all in small white block letters on ground of solid colour. At either side of the tablet is white ornamentation of a circular pattern upon ground of solid colour, and the design is completed by a single outer line of colour. The label containing the name of the Colony and the tablet with value are printed in a different colour to the rest of the stamp. Shape, upright rectangular. (*Illustrations* 184, 185.)

T. " LEEWARD ISLANDS."   D. " ½d., 1d., 2½d., 4d., 6d., 7d."   " ONE SHILLING."
              " FIVE SHILLINGS."

   ½d., blue, value and name in green.
   1d., ,,   ,,   ,,   carmine.
   2½d., ,,   ,,   ,,   blue.
   4d., ...   ,,   orange.
   6d., ,.   ,.   ,.   brown.
   7d., ..   ,,   ,,   bronze-green.
   1s., green   ..   ,   carmine.
   5s., ,,   ,,   ,,   blue.

WRAPPERS.

Issue I. October 31st, 1890.

Two values. Designed and printed by Messrs. De la Rue and Co. upon light buff wove paper. Similar to the wrappers of Barbados, but with stamp of the following design : Diademed head of Queen Victoria to left upon ground of solid colour, enclosed within a circle. Straight labels of solid colour above and below the circle, the upper inscribed with the name of the Colony and the lower with the value in words, all in uncoloured block letters. Conventional ornaments in the spandrels, and a single outer coloured line completes the design. (*Illustration* 204.)

T. " LEEWARD ISLANDS."   D. " HALFPENNY."   " ONE PENNY."

     ½d., dark green.
     1d., carmine.

POSTCARDS.

Issue I. October 31st, 1890.

Two values. Designed and printed by Messrs. De la Rue and Co. upon stout straw card. Size 139×88 mm., or 5½×3½ inches. The design is the same as that of the second issue cards of Antigua, except that the second line of the inscription is altered to LEEWARD ISLANDS (ILES SOUS LE VENT) and the name of the Colony at the top of the stamp is changed. (*Illustration* 205.)

> 1d., carmine.
> 1½d., dark brown.

REPLY PAID CARDS.

Issue I. October 31st, 1890.

Two values. Similar in every way to the single cards, but with the usual additional inscription on each half like the reply paid cards of Antigua. The cards are joined along the top, perforated 4½, and the design is impressed on the first and third pages. (*Illustration* 205.)

> 1d.+1d., carmine.
> 1½d.+1½d., dark brown.

Remarks.—The adhesives, wrappers, and postcards above described have replaced the distinctive issues of Antigua, Dominica, Montserrat, Nevis, St. Christopher, and the Virgin Islands.

MONTSERRAT.

Issue I. September, 1876.

Two values. Being the ONE PENNY and SIX PENCE of the first issue of Antigua. The name of that Colony is cancelled with a black bar, and MONTSERRAT surcharged in a straight line below, in black block letters, $2\frac{1}{4}$ mm. in height and $16\frac{1}{2}$ mm. in length. Watermarked Crown C.C., machine perforated 14. (*Illustration* 186.)

1d., lake-red (shades); *black* surcharge.
6d., yellow-green to green (shades); *black* surcharge.

Remarks.—Halves of the one penny stamp described above divided vertically were permitted by the Post Office, during the year 1881, to serve as Halfpenny stamps.

Issue II. January, 1880.

Two values. Engraved and surface-printed by Messrs. De la Rue and Co., of London, on medium white surfaced paper, watermarked Crown C.C.; machine perforated 14. Design : This consists of a diademed profile of Queen Victoria to left on a ground of horizontal lines, within a single-lined octagon. Straight white labels above and below contain the inscriptions. The side borders are coloured, with a row of white diamonds down the centre of each. The spandrels are formed of coloured triangles, with a white foliate ornament in the centre of each, and white borders. A single line of colour encloses the whole. Shape, upright rectangular. (*Illustrations* 207, 208.)

T. " MONTSERRAT." B. " $2\frac{1}{2}$ PENNY." " FOUR PENCE."

$2\frac{1}{2}$d., red-brown (shades).
4d., blue („)

Remarks.—In the month of March, 1883, the then current one penny stamps, divided vertically, and each half surcharged " $\frac{1}{2}$d." in small block type, were seen upon envelopes, which apparently had passed through the post between Montserrat and Dominica, but the authenticity of such a provisional issue was doubted at the time, and it has since been repudiated by the Postal Authorities.

Issue III. February, 1884.

Five values. The current stamps, with the addition of a HALFPENNY value, of design similar to the FOUR PENCE before described, began during this month to be issued with the watermark changed to Crown C.A. The various values made their appearance at intervals, between February and August. (*Illustrations* 186, 207, 208.)

A.—*Perf.* 14.

(February) $\frac{1}{2}$d., sea-green.
(„) 1d., lake-red: *black* surcharge.
(August) $2\frac{1}{2}$d., red-brown.
(February) 4d, blue (shades).

B.—*Perf.* 12.

(July) 1d., lake-red : *black* surcharge.

POSTCARDS.

Issue I. December, 1879.

One value. Designed and printed by Messrs. De la Rue and Co., upon medium light buff card. Size 121×87 mm., or 4⅘×3⅗ inches. The card is similar in every respect to the first issue of Antigua, but the second line of the inscription is replaced by MONTSERRAT (MONSERRAT) and the name of the Colony at the top of the stamp is changed. (*Illustration* 206.)

1½d., light own (shades).

Issue II. 1885-1887.

Two values. Designed and printed by Messrs. De la Rue and Co., upon stout straw card. Size 139×88 mm., or 5½×3½ inches. The cards are similar in design to the second issue of Antigua, except for the modification of the name of the Colony, mentioned above. (*Illustration* 233.)

(Jan., 1885) 1d., carmine (slight shades).
(„ 1887) 1½d., dark brown („ „)

REPLY PAID CARDS.

Issue I. 1884-1886.

Two values. Designed and printed by Messrs. De la Rue and Co., upon stout straw card. Size, 139×88 mm., or 5½×3½ inches. The cards are similar in design to the single ones of Issue II., except that they have additional inscriptions like the reply cards of Antigua. The cards are joined along the top, and the design is impressed upon the first and third pages. The perforation of the one penny is 4½, while that for the three halfpenny is only 4. (*Illustration* 233.)

(June, 1886) 1d.+1d., carmine (slight shades).
(1884) 1½d.+1½d., dark brown („ „)

Remarks.—The postal emissions of this Colony became obsolete at the end of October, 1890, when a uniform set for all the various Islands composing the Leeward Group, took their place.

NEVIS.

PRELIMINARY NOTES.

By E. D. BACON.

This Island, which was named after the mountain Nieves in Spain, to which it bears some resemblance, has never possessed an *Official Gazette*, and I am indebted to Mr. T. Maycock, a member of the Society, for the few remarks I am enabled to make concerning its stamps.

Messrs. Nissen and Parker, of London, supplied the stamps from their first issue in 1861 down to the end of 1878, since which date Messrs. De la Rue and Co. have provided for all the further requirements of the Island. The stamps first issued were printed from steel plates, each containing twelve stamps arranged in four horizontal rows of three. Each stamp was separately engraved on the plates, and thus there are twelve varieties of type for each value. Mr. Maycock is unable to give me any particulars concerning the stamps printed previous to 1866, but from that year down to the De la Rue series the following list is complete showing every consignment, with the date it was sent out from England.

December 18th, 1866.	10,000 (834 sheets) 1s.		
	20,000 (1,667 ,,) 4d.		
	20,000 (1,667 ,,) 1d.		
June 29th, 1871.	12,000 (1,000 ,,) 1d.		
April 29th, 1872.	12,000 (1,000 ,,) 1d.		
March 14th, 1873.	18,000 (1,500 ,,) 1d.		
August 10th 1874.	2,040 (170 ,,) 4d.		
May 18th, 1875.	6,180 (515 ,,) 1d.		
	2,544 (212 ,,) 4d.		
May 1st, 1876.	2,040 (170 ,,) 4d.		
June 16th, 1876.	1,008 (84 ,,) 1s.		
	6,000 (500 ,,) 1d.		
December 13th, 1876.	24,000 (2,000 ,,) 1d.		
	3,000 (250 ,,) 4d.		
	1,000 ($83\frac{4}{12}$,,) 1s.		
February 15th, 1878.	12,000 (1,000 ,,) 4d.		
	1,200 (100 ,,) 6d.		
	12,000 (1,000 ,,) 1d.		
	1,200 (100 ,,) 1s.		
November 21st, 1878.	2,004 (167 ,,) 1s.		
	1,200 (100 ,,) 1d.		

From information received by Mr. Maycock, it appears that the stamps, down to the consignment sent out in February, 1878, were all printed direct from the plates, with the exception of some of the later supplies of the one penny, which were printed from lithographic transfers taken from the plate. The stamps forwarded in February and November, 1878, were, on the other hand, all printed by the lithographic process I have just mentioned. It has generally been thought that these stamps in use since 1878 were lithographs, but it has not been known for certain whether or not this was really the case. The information Mr. Maycock has been able to obtain, however, upon this point is most conclusive, and there can now be no further doubt upon the question. The lithographed six pence will probably become a scarce stamp, as only 1,200 of this variety were ever printed.

REFERENCE LIST OF THE PHILATELIC SOCIETY, LONDON.

Issue I. 1861.

Four values. Engraved and printed in *taille-douce* by Messrs. Nissen and Parker, London, on stout greyish-white wove unwatermarked paper ; white and brown gum, machine perforated 13. Designs : ONE PENNY.—Central vignette, representing a stream of water issuing from a rock. In the foreground are three female figures, one is reclining on the ground, supported by a second, who is kneeling, whilst the third is pouring water from a pitcher into a cup ; the whole having reference to a medicinal spring in the Island. The border of the stamp is a rough imitation of that of the first issue of Great Britain : straight coloured labels at top and bottom inscribed with white Roman capitals, blocks in the four corners with star-shaped ornaments, and side borders of wavy reticulated lines. FOUR PENCE.—Similar vignette within a double-lined circle, which extends over the side borders of the stamp. Above and below the circle are curved coloured labels, with straight ends, inscribed in white Roman capitals. The spandrels are filled in with network, the borders are formed of alternate thin white and thicker coloured lines, and there is a small square chequered ornament in each corner. A single outer line of colour completes the design. SIX PENCE.—Vignette in a circle, as on the FOUR PENCE. Straight white labels, with rounded ends, above and below, inscribed in coloured block letters. The inner rectangle has the corners rounded, and the spandrels are filled in with reticulations ; the side frames are shaded with vertical wavy lines and rounded at top and bottom ; there is a foliate ornament in each corner, and the design is completed by a frame of two coloured lines. ONE SHILLING.—The vignette is enclosed in an oval frame, which touches the outer line of the stamp at top, bottom, and sides. The upper and lower curves of the frame form coloured labels with rounded ends, inscribed in white block letters. The sides of the oval are filled with a band of reticulations between two white lines. The spandrels are netted also, and the outer border is formed by two coloured lines. Shape, upright rectangular. With the exception of the centre the designs of the three higher values are evidently copied from the surface-printed stamps of Great Britain, of 1855-56. (*Illustrations* 219, 220, 221, 222.)

T. "NEVIS." B. "ONE PENNY." "FOUR PENCE." "SIX PENCE." "ONE SHILLING."
A.—On blued paper.
        1d., dull lake.
        4d., dull rose.
        6d., grey.
        1s., green.
B.—On white or greyish paper.
        1d., dull and brownish-lake (shades).
        4d., dull rose   (,,)
        6d., grey and brownish-grey (,,)
        1s., green   (,,)

Remarks.—The blue tinge in the paper is owing to the chemical action of some of the inks employed. All the values were printed in sheets of 12, four horizontal rows of three stamps. Each stamp was separately engraved, and there are consequently as many varieties of type as there are stamps on the sheet. The illustrations are from entire sheets, the varieties therefore appear in their correct order. Proofs of all the values exist on thick white card, in *black, purple, ultramarine, blue-green, carmine, orange,* and *dark blue.*

Issue II. 1867.

Three values. Being three of those of the previous issue, printed on stout white wove unwatermarked paper ; white gum, machine perforated 15, (*Illustrations* 219, 220, 222.)

> 1d., brick-red   (shades).
> 4d., orange-yellow   („)
> 1s., green, yellow-green („)

Variety. On thick white, vertically *laid* paper.

> 1s., bright yellow-green.

Remarks.—The only specimen of the one shilling on *laid* paper known to the Society, is that in the late Mr. Tapling's collection.

Issue III. 1879.

Four values. The designs are those of the preceding issues. Printed on stout white wove unwatermarked paper ; white and yellowish gum, machine perforated. These stamps may be distinguished from those already described by their coarser appearance, which is accounted for by their being printed from lithographic transfers taken from the original plates. (*Illustrations* 223, 224, 225, 226.)

> A.—*Perf.* 15.
> 1d., dull rose-red, vermilion (shades).
> 4d., orange-yellow (shades).
> 6d., brownish grey („)
> 1s., pale green, yellow-green (shades).
> B.—*Perf.* 11½.
> 1d., vermilion (shades).

Varieties. 1d., vermilion, imperforate.

> 4d., orange-yellow „
> 1s., yellow-green, imperf. vertically, perf. 15 horizontally.

Remarks.—The four pence, imperforate, is catalogued by M. Moens, it has not been seen by the Society.

Issue IV. 1879-1880.

Two values. Engraved and surface-printed by Messrs. De la Rue and Co., of London, on white wove surfaced paper, watermarked Crown C.C., white gum, machine perforated 14. Design : Diademed profile of Queen Victoria to left, on ground of horizontal lines, within a single-lined octagon. Straight white labels at top and bottom, inscribed in coloured block letters. Coloured side frames, with a row of white diamonds down the centre of each. Triangular ornaments fill the spandrels, and the whole is enclosed by a single outer line of colour. Shape, upright rectangular. (*Illustrations* 209, 210.)

> T. "NEVIS."   B. "ONE PENNY."   "2½ PENNY."
> (1880) 1d., bright lilac (shades).
> (1879) 2½d., red-brown („)

Remarks.—In the year 1882, several values of the fiscal stamps were used to defray postage. According to precedent, no list of these varieties is given by the Society. The ONE PENNY of both types is known divided in half, and the halves used as halfpenny stamps.

Issue V. 1882.

Three values. Engraved and surface-printed by Messrs. De la Rue and Co., on white wove surfaced paper, watermarked Crown C.A., white gum, machine perforated 14. The design is that of the last issue, the additional value being inscribed FOUR PENCE below in coloured block letters. (*Illustrations* 209, 210.)

1d., bright lilac (slight variations in shade).
2½d., red-brown (,, ,,)
4d., blue (,, ,,)

Issue VI. September, 1883.

One value. In the month of September, 1883, a provisional HALFPENNY stamp was formed by dividing the current one penny, lilac, vertically, and surcharging each half with the word " NEVIS " in Roman capitals and " ½d.", in black or purple aniline ink; the surcharge measures 12½ mm. in length, and is found reading upwards or downwards. (*Illustration* 211.)

½d., black surcharge, on right half of 1d., lilac.
½d., ,, ,, ,, left ,, ,, 1d., ,,
½d., purple ,, ,, right ,, ,, 1d., ,,
½d., ,, ,, ,, left ,, ,, 1d., ,,

Remarks.—Varieties are found with the surcharge printed twice on the same half stamp; and the surcharge is also known on halves of the one penny, lilac, overprinted REVENUE, postally used.

Issue VII. 1883-1884.

Five values. Design, &c., of Issue V., but with the colours changed, and two new values added, inscribed below HALFPENNY and SIX PENCE, in coloured block letters, respectively. White and yellowish gum. (*Illustrations* 209, 210.)

(1883) ½d., dull green (slight variations in shade).
6d., green (,, ,,)
(1884) 1d., rose (,, ,,)
2½d., ultramarine (,, ,,)
4d., grey (,, ,,)

Issue VIII. 1886.

One value. Design, &c., of the preceding issue, the colour only being changed. (*Illustration* 209.)

6d., red-brown.

Issue IX. 1890.

One value. Design, &c., as in the last issue; additional value, inscribed ONE SHILLING below in coloured block letters. (*Illustration* 209.)

1s., purple.

POSTCARDS.

Issue I. End of 1879.

One value. Designed and printed by Messrs. De la Rue and Co., upon medium light buff card. Size 121×87 mm., or 4⅓×3¾ inches. The card is similar in every way to that of the first issue of Antigua, but the second line of the inscription reads NEVIS, and the name of the Colony at the top of the stamp is changed. (*Illustration* 234.)

1½d., light brown (shades).

Issue II. 1886.

One value. Precisely similar to the previous issue, but the design is printed upon stout straw card, and the size is increased to 139×88 mm., or 5¼×3½ inches. (*Illustration* 234.)

1½d., light brown (slight shades).

Issue III. 1886-1887.

Two values. Designed and printed by Messrs. De la Rue and Co., upon medium stout straw card. Size 139×88 mm., 5½×3½ inches. The design is the same as that of the second issue cards of Antigua, except for the modification of the name of the Colony in the second line of the inscription, and at the top of the stamp. (*Illustration* 235.)

1d., carmine   (slight shades).
(1887) 1½d., dark brown („   „).

REPLY PAID CARDS.

Issue I. May (?), 1886.

Two values. Designed and printed by Messrs. De la Rue and Co., upon stout straw card. Size 139×88 mm., 5½×3½ inches. The cards are similar to the single ones of Issue III., but each half has the usual additional inscription like the reply cards of Antigua. The cards are joined along the top, perforated 4½, and the design is impressed upon the first and third pages. (*Illustration* 235.)

1d.+1d., carmine   (slight shades).
1½d.+1½d., dark brown („   „).

Remarks.—The postal emissions of this Colony became obsolete at the end of October, 1890, when a uniform set for all the various Islands composing the Leeward Group, took their place.

ROYAL MAIL STEAM PACKET COMPANY.

By E. D. BACON.

———+———

It seems only right, that in a work dealing with the history of the stamps of the British West Indies, notice should be taken of a private postage label employed in that part of the world, by an English Company, viz:—The Royal Mail Steam Packet Company. The Secretary of the Company informs me that the stamp was prepared in March, 1875, and issued to certain places in the West Indies, say Curaçao, Surinam, St. Domingo, Porto Plata, and Puerto Cabello, but the use of the stamp gradually ceased, till about the end of 1880, when it was done away with altogether. It originated in the Company's vessels calling at certain places for which the Company was not subsidised by the British or any other Government, and it was thought that the public at those places would be glad to send letters by such non-contract vessels, purchasing the stamps from the Company's Agents to whom they were issued from the London Office. The system, however, met with opposition from local Governments, and the British Post Office, and last of all, if there was then any life left in it, was knocked on the head by the Postal Union arrangements. The stamp prepaid a letter of half an ounce in weight. It was designed and surface-printed by Messrs. De la Rue and Co., upon medium white wove unwatermarked paper, machine perforated 12½, and the entire sheet contains thirty specimens arranged in five horizontal rows of six. The design consists of the Flag of the Company turned to the right, upon a background of horizontal lines, enclosed within a circular band of solid colour, inscribed with the name of the Company in small white block letters with a white ornament at the lower part. Broad, straight white label at the bottom of the stamp inscribed with the value in words in coloured block letters. Conventional ornaments in the spandrels, and a thick outer line of colour completes the design. Shape, upright rectangular. (*Illustration* 212.)

10 cents, rose.

Remarks.—M. Moens chronicles the stamp with a query as printed also in blue. I am assured by the Secretary of the Company, it was never issued in any other colour but rose, neither was a stamp of any other design ever used by the Company.

ST. CHRISTOPHER.

PRELIMINARY NOTES.

By E. D. BACON.

The Official Gazette of Saint Christopher was first published in January, 1879, and was discontinued in August, 1882. It contains but few notices of a postal nature, and I have found no mention of the issue of new stamps, or postcards.

A notice appeared at the end of June, 1879, stating that St. Christopher, like the other Leeward Islands, would be admitted into the Postal Union on the 1st July following. A list of the reduced rates that would then come into operation was given, and the rate for postcards was fixed at three halfpence. The two pence halfpenny, and four penny adhesives, and the three halfpenny card would, therefore, be issued on or soon after the 1st July, 1879, as the two new value stamps, and the card would be required to prepay the fresh rates. As we see from the following notice in *The Gazette* of March 11th, 1882, the rates to certain Islands were still further reduced at this date.

POST OFFICE NOTICE.

" AFTER this date the Postage to the under-mentioned places will be reduced to—

Letters per ½ oz., 2½d.—Post Cards, each 1d.

Newspapers, Printed Papers, Books, &c., per 2 oz. ½d.

" Commercial papers same as printed papers, except that the lowest charge for each packet is 2½d.

" Patterns same as printed papers, except that the lowest charge for each packet is 1d.

NAMES OF THE PLACES.

" Antigua, Dominica, Saint Lucia, Montserrat, Nevis, Tortola, Martinique, Guadeloupe, Saint Martin's, Saint Thomas, St. Croix, Crab Island, Porto Rico.

" *March 11th*, 1882."

We may conclude from the above notice, that the one penny card was issued on or about March 11th, 1882.

Mr. W. P. Pearce, the clerk in charge of the Post Office at Basseterre, St. Kitts, writes to me under date December 9th, 1890, saying that the provisional stamps were generally surcharged at the printing office of *The Advertiser*, but the surcharge " Halfpenny" on half of the one penny carmine, was applied at the Post Office. He further states that Revenue stamps have never been authorised to prepay postage, and that they have never been used for that purpose. He adds, " Postage and Revenue stamps combined were issued for sale in the Leeward Islands on the 1st of last month (November), and all the former issues of postage and revenue stamps called in on that date."

REFERENCE LIST OF THE PHILATELIC SOCIETY, LONDON.

Issue I. April 1st, 1870.

Two values. Engraved and surface-printed by Messrs. De la Rue and Co., on white wove surfaced paper, watermarked Crown C.C., white gum; machine perforated. Design: Diademed profile of Queen Victoria to left on a ground of horizontal lines, enclosed in a coloured circular band, touching the top and sides of the stamp, inscribed in small white block letters; a small ornament on each side separates the two portions of the inscription. The value is in coloured block letters on a straight white label below the circular band. The spandrels are filled in with arabesques, and the whole is surrounded by a single coloured line. Shape, upright rectangular. (*Illustration* 213.)

T. "SAINT CHRISTOPHER." B. "POSTAGE." "ONE PENNY." "SIX PENCE."

A.—*Perf.* 12½.
1d., rose, violet-rose (shades).
6d., green to yellow-green („)
B.—*Perf.* 14.
1d., violet-rose (shades).
6d., green to yellow-green („)

Variety. Imperforate vertically.
6d., green.

Issue II. November, 1879.

Two values. Design, &c., as in Issue I., inscribed 2½ PENNY and FOUR PENCE respectively, in coloured block letters, perf. 14. (*Illustrations* 213, 214.)
2½d., red-brown (shades).
4d., blue („)

Issue III. 1882.

Four values. The design, perforation, &c., are the same as those of the preceding issue, but the watermark is changed to Crown C.A. White and yellowish gum. A new value is added, inscribed HALFPENNY below in coloured block letters. (*Illustrations* 213, 214.)

½d., dull green (slight variations in shade).
1d., rose, violet-rose („ „ „)
2½d., red-brown („ „ „)
4d., blue („ „ „)

Remarks.—Some of the stamps of this issue are found on paper with lines in it resembling the lines in laid paper. This peculiarity appears to be due to some unintentional variation in the manufacture.

In 1883, the ONE PENNY stamps were cut in half, and the halves used as half-penny stamps; and about the same time several varieties of the fiscal stamps appear to have been used to defray postage.

Issue IV. 1884.

Two values. Design, watermark and perforation as in the preceding issue, the colours only being changed. White and yellowish gum. (*Illustrations* 213, 214.)
2½d., ultramarine (slight variations in shade).
4d., grey („ „)

Issue V.　March, 1885.

Two values. In March, 1885, two provisional stamps were issued, namely, the one penny of Issue III., divided in half diagonally, and each half surcharged in lower case Roman type with the word " Halfpenny," varying in length from 14 to 15 mm., and the sixpence of Issue I., perf. 14, surcharged FOUR—PENCE in two lines of Roman capitals 2 mm. in height. The surcharge on the former is printed irregularly, being found sometimes reading downwards and sometimes reading upwards. (*Illustrations* 215, 216.)

½d., black surcharge, on upper half of 1d., rose ; watermarked Crown C.A.
½d., 　,, 　　,, 　　,, lower ., 　1d., 　,, 　　　　,, 　　　,, 　　,,
4d., 　,, 　　,, 　　,, 6d., green ; watermarked Crown C.C.

Issue VI.　June, 1886.

Two values. In June, 1886, two new provisional stamps of one penny and four pence were issued, produced by surcharging the six pence green. The former surcharge consists of the words ONE PENNY in two lines of Roman capitals, 2 mm. in height, and the latter consists of a numeral " 4," 6 mm., and a letter " d " 4 mm. in height, with the original value cancelled by a bar. Watermark Crown C.C., perf. 14. (*Illustrations* 217, 218.)

1d., black surcharge, on 6d., green.
4d., 　,, 　　　,, 　　　,, 6d., 　,,

Varieties. The four pence is found without the period after the letter " d," and also with the period at some distance from the letter.

Issue VII.　February, 1887.

One value. Design as before ; watermark Crown C.A., machine perforated 14 (*Illustration* 213.)

1s. lilac.

Issue VIII.　May, 1887.

One value. In May, 1887, the halfpenny stamp of Issue III. was converted into a one penny by a surcharge consisting of the words ONE PENNY in black, in two lines of Roman capitals 2 mm. in height, with a bar across the original value. Watermark Crown C.A., perforated 14. (*Illustration* 227.)

1d., black surcharge, on ½d., green.

Issue IX.　May, 1888.

One value. In May, 1888, the two pence halfpenny of Issue IV. was surcharged in black with the words ONE PENNY in two lines of Roman capitals as before. There are two varieties of the surcharge, the first in letters 3 mm. in height, and with a bar across the original value, the second in letters 2 mm. in height, without the bar. (*Illustration* 228.)

1d., black surcharge, 3 mm. high, on 2½d., ultramarine.
1d., 　,, 　　,, 　2 　,, 　　,, 2½d., 　　,,

Variety. Surcharge inverted.

1d., black surcharge, 3 mm. high, on 2½d., ultramarine.

Issue X.　February, 1890.

One value. The one penny of Antigua, Issue VI., used provisionally in St. Christopher. Watermark Crown C.A., perforated 14. (*Illustration* 1.)

1d., rose-red.

Remarks.—A number of the one penny stamps was borrowed from Antigua, pending the arrival of a fresh supply from England. This provisional can be recognised by its bearing the postmark "A 12," the number peculiar to St. Christopher.

Issue XI. May (?), 1890.

One value. Design of the previous issues; watermark Crown C.A., perforated 14. *(Illustration 213.)*

6d., greenish-grey.

POSTCARDS.

Issue I. November 18th, 1879.

One value. Designed and printed by Messrs. De la Rue and Co., upon medium light buff card. Size, 121×87 mm., or $4\frac{4}{5}\times3\frac{2}{5}$ inches. The design is the same as that of the first issue card of Antigua, except that the second line of the inscription is replaced by ST. CHRISTOPHER (ST. CHRISTOPHE), and the name of the Colony at the top of the stamp is changed. *(Illustration 236.)*

$1\frac{1}{2}$d., light brown (shades).

Issue II. July, 1882.

One value. Designed and printed by Messrs. De la Rue and Co., upon medium light buff card. Size 121×87 mm., or $4\frac{4}{5}\times3\frac{2}{5}$ inches. The design is precisely the same as that of the last issue, except that the value at the bottom of the stamp is altered to ONE PENNY. *(Illustration 236.)*

1d., rose (shades).

Remarks.—In February, 1883, the supply of the three halfpenny card was exhausted, and the one penny was issued temporarily with half a one penny violet-rose, or a halfpenny green adhesive attached to it, until a fresh consignment of three halfpenny cards was received from England.

Issue III. 1887.

Two values. Designed and printed by Messrs. De la Rue and Co., upon stout straw card. Size 139×88 mm., or $5\frac{1}{2}\times3\frac{1}{2}$ inches. The design is the same as that of the second issue cards of Antigua, except for the modification of the name of the Colony mentioned above for Issue I. *(Illustration 237.)*

1d., carmine (slight shades).
$1\frac{1}{2}$d., dark brown („ „)

REPLY PAID CARDS.

Issue I. 1887.

Two values. Designed and printed by Messrs. De la Rue and Co., upon stout straw card. Size 139×88 mm., or $5\frac{1}{2}\times3\frac{1}{2}$ inches. The design is similar to the single cards of Issue III., with the usual additional inscriptions, similar to those found on the reply paid cards of Antigua. The cards are joined along the top, perforated $4\frac{1}{2}$, and the design is impressed upon the first and third pages. *(Illustration 237.)*

1d.+1d., carmine (slight shades).
$1\frac{1}{2}$d.+$1\frac{1}{2}$d., dark brown („ „)

Remarks.—The postal emissions of this Colony became obsolete at the end of October, 1890, when a uniform set for all the various Islands composing the Leeward Group, took their place.

ST. LUCIA.

PRELIMINARY NOTES.

By E. D. BACON.

BEFORE the introduction of distinctive stamps in St. Lucia, British Postage Stamps were employed for the prepayment of correspondence. The notice, from which I have gathered this information, was published in the *St. Lucia Gazette* of the 19th May, 1858. It reads as follows :—

" POST OFFICE,
" ST. LUCIA, 14th May, 1858.

"THE following Circular, from Her Majesty's Postmaster General, is published for general information.

" (Signed)   O. LAFFITTE,
" *Deputy Postmaster General.*"

(Circular.)

"GENERAL POST OFFICE, 16th April, 1858.

" SIR,—I am directed by the Postmaster General to acquaint you that the Lords of Her Majesty's Treasury have authorised British Postage Stamps to be used in payment of the Packet Postage of Letters and Newspapers posted in St. Lucia; and I am to request that you will cause this regulation to be made known throughout the Colony, by advertising it in the local journals and by affixing a notice in your Office Window.

" 2. It is to be hoped that this arrangement will greatly facilitate the carrying out of the recent regulation for the compulsory prepayment of Letters posted in the Colony addressed to the United Kingdom.

" 3. The following descriptions of British Postage Stamps must henceforth be kept at your Office for sale to the Public, viz :—

Sixpenny,
Fourpenny,
and
Penny Stamps.

" 4. The Postmaster General has directed that a supply of the above Stamps to the amount of £50, may be forwarded to you by the present mail. This stock of Stamps is calculated to be sufficient for two months' consumption, and it is intended to send you a supply of equal value by the mail of the 17th of May.

.   .   .   .

" 10. All Postage Stamps affixed to letters posted at your Office, must be carefully cancelled by means of the obliterating stamp sent to you herewith. Some black composition will also be forwarded to you for this purpose, the use of which must be limited to the obliteration of Postage Stamps, and your stock of this composition must never be allowed to become low. The surveyor will furnish a fresh supply when necessary.

"11. It is important that the distinguishing number and letter introduced into the obliterating Stamp to be used at your Office should be legibly impressed.
"12.   .   .   .   .   .
"13.   .   .   .   .   .
                    "(Signed)   ROWLAND HILL,
                                        "*Secretary.*"

I find from a Post Office notice in *The Gazette* of February 17th, 1858, that letters for the United Kingdom had to be prepaid from and after April 1st of that year. We see, on reference to my paper on British Guiana (*page* 40), that a similar course was adopted at the same date, and British Postage Stamps were issued in the latter Colony on May 11th, 1858. Jamaica issued British Postage Stamps for Packet Service on May 8th, 1858, as may be seen from my paper on that Colony (*page* 89); and I have no doubt, that the same arrangements were made with some, if not all the other Islands of the West Indies and Colonies, previous to the transfer of the Post Offices to the local Governments. We learn from the next notice, taken from *The Gazette* of the 25th April, 1860, that when the Colonial Government took over the control of its own Postal affairs, British stamps were no longer allowed to be used.

NOTICE.

"POST OFFICE, ST. LUCIA,
18*th April*, 1860.

"BRITISH Postage Stamps will not be available for the prepayment of Postage upon letters posted in the West Indies, after the transfer of the Post Office to the Colonial Government on the 1st May next; such pro-payment must thenceforth be made in money, as formerly, unless the Colonial Government shall deem it advisable to issue Postage Stamps for the purposes of its own Post Office.

"(Signed)   O. LAFFITTE,
                    "*Deputy Postmaster General.*"

Immediately on taking over the Post Office, the Local Government authorised the collection of an inland rate of one penny for half ounce letters, as the following notice taken from *The Gazette* of May 9th, 1860, shows :—

NOTICE.

"POST OFFICE, ST. LUCIA.
"9*th May*, 1860.

"By Ordinance No. 1—7th March, 1860—which transfers to the Local Government the control of the Post Office in this Island, from and after the 1st May, 1860, an *inland rate of one penny* on every letter of half an ounce weight or under, and *one penny* additional for every half ounce or part thereof, over and above the first half ounce, is charged on all letters arriving in this Island from any place except from, or coming through, the United Kingdom, and on all letters posted in this Island for transmission to any place, except to or through the United Kingdom. The above rates are chargeable in addition to the postage payable to Her Majesty on every such letter.

"Letters liable to the inland rates above mentioned, which may be posted without payment of the said rates, will not be forwarded, but will be detained at this Office until the payment be made. A list of such letters so detained will be published monthly in the *Official Gazette* of this Island.

"(Signed)   O. LAFFITTE,
                    "*Prov. Col. Postmaster.*"

R

The date of the first issue of postage stamps for St. Lucia is given in the earliest catalogues, and in the most recently published ones also, as 1859. We see from the following notice, taken from *The Gazette* of December 19th, 1860, that the issue did not take place until quite the end of the latter year.

NOTICE.

" Post Office, St. Lucia,
" 18*th December,* 1860.

" Postage Stamps for the prepayment of Letters may be obtained at this office at the following rates, viz. :—

Stamps of a red colour at one penny.
Do. do. Blue at four pence.
Do. do. Green at six pence.

" These Stamps are applicable to St. Lucia only.

" The Inland rate of one penny per half ounce on Letters posted at this office which are subject thereto under the Ordinance, No. 1 of 7th March, 1860, according to a Notice in the *Official Gazette* of 9th May, 1860, *must* be paid in Stamps.

" (Signed) O. Laffitte,
" *Colonial Postmaster.*"

Besides the date of issue the above establishes the postal value of each of the three stamps. These values are correctly given in the catalogues, but as the stamps bore none on their face, it is only by a document of this kind that the true denominations can be determined. All the stamps were printed by Messrs. Perkins Bacon and Co. from one plate, of their own construction, which was of steel, and contained 240 labels in twenty horizontal rows of twelve. The plate was handed over to the Crown agents on the 28th January, 1862, and was afterwards given by them to Messrs. De la Rue and Co., who printed all future supplies of stamps for the Colony. Proof impressions in black, of the engraved die, upon white card are known.

On April 1st, 1863, the packet rate to England was increased from 6d. to 1s., as the following, taken from *The Gazette* of January 28th, 1863, proves :—

" Government Office,
" 28*th January,* 1863.

" The Administrator notifies for general information that on and after the 1st April next the single rate of postage on letters conveyed by Packet between the United Kingdom and the West Indies will be increased from 6d. to 1s. and by private ship will be reduced from 6d. to 3d. It is proposed to introduce an improved ascending scale of Postage simultaneously with these alterations in which half an ounce will be taken as the unit of weight, increasing by single rates for each additional half ounce. Under this system the following will be the charges :—

	By Packets.	By Private Ships.
Letters not exceeding ½ an ounce	1s. ...	3d.
Do. above ½ oz. and not exceeding 1 oz. ...	2s. ...	6d.
Do. above 1 oz. and not exceeding 1½ oz. ...	3s. ...	9d.
Do. above 1½ oz. and not exceeding 2 oz.	4s. ...	1s.
&c. &c.	&c.	&c.

" (Signed) J. M. Grant,
" *Administrator.*"

The postage on all correspondence to the United Kingdom had since April 1st, 1858 (as I have already shown), to be prepaid : and in February, 1863, and at intervals afterwards (as arrangements were made with the various Colonies), prepayment of postal rates was made compulsory to all parts of the Empire.

After the second issue of the three first stamps, with the watermark changed to Crown C.C., of which no notice is naturally taken in *The Gazette*, we find that the third set was issued on November 19th, 1864. The notification of this issue was published in *The Gazette* of November 23rd of that year.

"GOVERNMENT OFFICE,

"*19th November*, 1864.

"NOTICE is hereby given that, on and after this day, Postage Stamps of the colours and denominations undermentioned may be obtained at the Post Office, and that the issue of those hitherto used has been stopped.

Orange-red ...	...	...	...	...	*One Shilling.*
Lilac ...	...	...	...	...	*Six Pence.*
Light yellow ...	...	...	...	...	*Four Pence.*
Black ...	...	...	...	...	*One Penny.*

"Persons, however, who have any of the old stamps in their possession are informed that, for the present they will continue to be received on letters, &c.

' (Signed)   J. M GRANT,

" *Administrator.*"

These stamps were all similar in type to those first issued, and bore no value upon their face. Here, again, the notice is important as fixing the true postal denomination of each colour.

On the admission of St. Lucia into the Postal Union on January 1st, 1881, new stamps of the values of a halfpenny, and two pence halfpenny, with a three halfpenny postcard, were required and should have been issued. The two adhesives were printed in new colours from the old plate used for the previous issues, the former in bright green, the latter in red-vermilion. Both these stamps had the value surcharged in black in a straight line across the lower part. As neither of the two stamps nor the card appear to have been chronicled before October, 1881, it is probable they were not ready for issue at the time the new rates came into force. No mention, so far as I have been able to discover, is made in *The Gazette* as to the date when they were first brought into use. According to the terms of the following notice found in *The Gazette* of December 14th, 1881, the rates to certain places in the Postal Union were reduced at this time.

NOTICE.

"IN future the following rates of Postage will be charged upon letters, &c., to places in the Postal Union within three hundred miles.

"(Signed)   AMELIE RICHARD,

" *Postmistress.*

"POST OFFICE, ST. LUCIA,

"*14th December*, 1881.

Letters ...	...	...	...	...	...	2½d. per ½ oz.
*Post Cards...	...	...	...	...	...	1d. each.
Newspapers	...	...	...	...	...	½d. „
Books, and other printed matter			...	...	½d. per 2 ozs.

Increasing by ½d. for every 2 oz. additional.

Commercial Documents (initial charge)	...	2½d. per 10 ozs.

Increasing ½d. for every 2 oz. additional.

Samples and Patterns (initial charge)	...	1d. per 4 oz.

Increasing ½d. for every 2 oz. additional.

*Pending the arrival of a supply of Post Cards at 1d., the present rate—1½d.—will continue to be charged.

"(Signed)   A. R."

I have found no mention in *The Gazette* of the date when the one penny card was issued, but if we may take the journals as a guide, it was not till nearly two years after the above notice, as the earliest description of it was given in *The Philatelic Record* for November, 1883. The following was published in *The Gazette* of March 29th, 1882 :—

" GOVERNMENT OFFICE,
" 22nd March, 1882.

"WITH reference to the Government Notices dated the 16th November, 1881, and the 3rd February, 1882, and published in *The Gazette* of the 16th November, 1881, and the 8th February, 1882, the Governor-in-Council has resolved that the Postage Stamps therein mentioned to be used as Inland Revenue Stamps may bear either the word 'Stamp' or 'Revenue' overprinted under the value. The Governor-in-Council has further resolved that the Postage Stamps of the following colours and values may be used as Inland Revenue Stamps :—

"Light Blue—Two pence—over-printed in black with the words 'Two Pence Revenue.'

"Dark Blue—Three pence—over-printed in red with the words 'Three Pence Revenue.'

" (Signed)   CHARLES J. M'LEOD,
" Clerk of Councils."

This notice and the two notices referred to in it, authorise postage stamps to be surcharged for fiscal purposes, and in a paper professedly dealing with postal issues alone, there is no object in giving copies of the two former. With the one given, however, the case is different, for it speaks of a postage stamp, which, so far as I know, is to be found in no collection or catalogue, *i.e.*, the two pence. Copies of the three pence are known without the word "Revenue," and the stamp also exists without any surcharge whatever. I have always looked upon these two last varieties as having the overprinted words discharged by some chemical agency, and even in face of the above notice I still adhere to this belief. Stamps of two pence and three pence were not required for the postal service, and my own opinion is that they were only issued bearing the word "Revenue" for fiscal purposes. The notice is couched in similar form to the previous ones dealing with fiscals, and in the case of these two stamps I think it is most probably carelessly worded, and what should have been stated was that the stamps were of the same design as those used for postage. On the other hand, I think it is only right to give a copy of the notice, and I hope by drawing attention to it that some writer will shortly decide this knotty point.

The next notice, which is found in *The Gazette* of March 21st, 1883, gives us the date of issue of the reply three halfpenny post card.

NOTICE.

"REPLY paid Post Cards are now in use between this Island and other Offices of the Postal Union, and may be had at this Office.

" (Signed)   A. RICHARD,
" Postmistress.

" POST OFFICE, 19th March, 1883."

The first issue of adhesives of Messrs. De la Rue and Co.'s design took place on July 6th, 1883. The notice is taken from *The Gazette Extraordinary* of that date.

" GOVERNMENT OFFICE,
" 6th July, 1883.

"NOTICE is hereby given that on and after this day, Postage Stamps of the colours and denominations undermentioned may be obtained at the

Post Office, and that the issue of those of the same values, hitherto used, has been stopped.

LIGHT RED	...	...	...	...	ONE PENNY.
Do. BLUE	...	...	...	...	TWO PENCE HALF PENNY.
Do. GREEN	...	..	...	...	HALF PENNY.

Persons, however, who have any of the old Stamps in their possession, are informed that, for the present, they will continue to be received on letters, &c.

" (Signed)   MACNAMARA DIX,

" *Administering the Government.*"

In April, 1885, Revenue and Postal stamps were allowed to be used indiscriminately for either service. The following is a copy of the Government authorisation, published in *The Gazette* of April 22nd of that year.

" GOVERNMENT OFFICE,

" *14th April*, 1885.

" THE following Rule passed by the Governor-in-Council by virtue and under the authority of the Stamp Duty Ordinance, 1881, and of the Post Office Ordinance, 1881, is published for general information. 'In future Revenue Stamps may be used for Postage Stamps and *vice versa*.'

" By order,

" (Signed)   J. B. CROPPER,

" *Acting Clerk of Councils.*"

The notice, giving the date of issue of the registration envelopes and newspaper wrappers, is found in *The Gazette* for December 23rd, 1887.

POST OFFICE NOTICE.

" NOTICE is hereby given, that on and after the 20th instant the fee chargeable for registering letters, &c., to places in the Postal Union will be TWO PENCE.

"Registered Letter Envelopes bearing a two penny stamp embossed on the flap for the payment of the registration fee are of two sizes, and can be purchased at the following prices, viz. :—

Size.

G.—6 in. by 3¾ in., 2½d. each, or 2s. 6d. per packet of 12.

H.—8 in. by 5 in., 3d. each, or 3s. per packet of 12.

"Newspaper Wrappers with impressed halfpenny and penny postage stamps, are also obtainable.

" (Signed)   F. S. REEVE,

" *Colonial Postmaster.*"

" GENERAL POST OFFICE,

    " 19*th December*, 1887."

REFERENCE LIST OF THE PHILATELIC SOCIETY, LONDON.

Issue I. December 18th, 1860.

Three values. Engraved in *taille-douce*, and printed by Messrs. Perkins Bacon and Co., London, on medium white wove paper, watermarked with a six-rayed star, yellowish gum, machine perforated 13½ to 16 compound. Design : Diademed profile of Queen Victoria to left on an engine-turned background, within a white oval band, inscribed in coloured Roman capitals with the words ST. LUCIA above and POSTAGE below, the two inscriptions being separated by an elongated ornament on each side. The spandrels are filled in with reticulations, and a single outer line encloses the stamp. It is to be observed that it bears no indication of the value. Shape, upright rectangular. (*Illustration* 229.)

> (1d.) brick-red　　(shades).
> (4d.) deep-blue　　(　,,　)
> (6d.) yellow-green (　,,　)

Issue II. 1863.

Three values. The same stamps, printed from the same plate by Messrs. De la Rue and Co., London, on slightly surfaced paper, watermarked Crown C.C., white gum, machine perforated 12½. (*Illustration* 229).

> (1d.) brownish-lake (shades).
> (4d.) indigo-blue　　(　,,　)
> (6d.) emerald-green (　,,　)

Varieties. Imperforate.

> (4d) indigo-blue.
> (6d.) emerald-green.

Remarks. The *blue* and *green* stamps of this issue are known surcharged " Six pence " and " Halfpenny " respectively, in two lines of lower case Roman type, but the authenticity of these surcharges has never been established. (*Illustrations* 230, 231.)

Issue III.　November 19th, 1864.

Four values. Printed from the same plate by Messrs. De la Rue and Co. upon the same paper and with the same watermark as Issue II. (*Illustration* 229.)

> A.—*Perf.* 12½.

> (1d.) black　(shades).
> (4d.) yellow (　,,　), straw.
> (6d.) lilac-mauve (slight shades).
> (1s.) orange-yellow, orange, orange-red (shades).

> B.—*Perf.* 14.

> (1d.) black　　(slight shades).
> (4d.) yellow　　(　,,　　,,　)
> (6d.) lilac-mauve (　,,　　,,　)
> (1s.) orange　　(　,,　　,,　)

Issue IV.　September, 1881.

Two values. Printed from the same plate by Messrs. De la Rue and Co., and surcharged with the value across the stamps in black block letters 3 mm. high— HALFPENNY 14 mm. in length, and 2½ PENCE 15¼ mm. in length. Watermark Crown C.C., machine perforated 14. (*Illustrations* 232, 238.)

> ½d., black surcharge, on green　　(shades).
> 2½d.,　,,　　　,,　on vermilion (　,,　)

Issue V.　April, 1882.

One value. Printed in the same manner as the last, and with value, ONE PENNY surcharged across it in carmine block letters, 3 mm. high, 14 mm. in length. Watermark Crown C.C., perforated 14. (*Illustration* 232.)

> 1d., carmine surcharge, on black.

Remarks.—This value is known divided in half, and the halves employed as halfpenny stamps.

Issue VI.　1883.

One value. In 1883 the black stamp of 1864, perforated 14, was surcharged, by hand, " 1d." in the centre and a numeral " 1 " in the four corners in violet aniline ink, and was used to supply a temporary deficiency of the stamps of Issue V. (*Illustration* 239.)

1d., violet surcharge, on black.

Variety. Without the numeral 1 in the four corners of the stamp.

Remarks.—Various fiscal stamps are known to have been used postally about this time and subsequently.

Issue VII. 1883-1884.

Six values. Similar to the stamps of Issues IV and V. Printed on medium white wove surfaced paper, watermarked Crown C.A., machine perforated. The surcharge on the THREE PENCE measures $15\frac{1}{2}$ mm. by $2\frac{1}{2}$ mm., that on the FOUR PENCE 16 mm. by 3 mm., and that on the ONE SHILLING 16 mm. by $2\frac{1}{2}$ mm. (*Illustrations* 232, 229.)

A.—*Perf.* 14.

(April, 1883) $\frac{1}{2}$d., black surcharge, on green.

(1884)	1d., carmine	,,	on black.
(,,)	3d., ,,	,,	on dark blue.
(,,)	4d., black	,,	on yellow.
(,,)	6d., ,,	,,	on mauve.
(,,)	1s., ,,	,,	on orange.

Varieties. ONEE PENNY, carmine surcharge, on black.

(3d.) no surcharge, deep blue.

(6d.) ,, mauve.

B.—*Perf.* 12.

4d., black surcharge, on yellow.

Remarks.—Halves of the (4d.) yellow stamp, *without* surcharge, are known to have passed the post in December, 1883, apparently doing duty as two penny stamps.

Issue VIII. July 6th, 1883.

Three values. Engraved and surface printed by Messrs. De la Rue and Co., on white wove surfaced paper, watermarked Crown C.A., machine perforated 14. Design : Diademed profile of Queen Victoria to left on a ground of horizontal lines, within a single-lined octagon. Straight white labels at top and bottom inscribed in coloured block letters. The side frames contain rows of white diamonds on a coloured ground, ornaments in triangular frames fill the spandrels, and the design is completed by a single outer line of colour. Shape, upright rectangular. (*Illustrations* 240, 241.)

T. " ST. LUCIA." B. " HALFPENNY." " ONE PENNY." " $2\frac{1}{2}$ PENNY."

$\frac{1}{2}$d., pale sea-green (shades).

1d., rose (,,)

$2\frac{1}{2}$d., ultramarine (,,)

Issue IX. 1885.

Two values. The same design, paper, watermark and perforation as Issue VIII. (*Illustration* 240.)

T. " ST. LUCIA." B. " FOUR PENCE." " ONE SHILLING."

(March) 4d., brown (shades).

(September) 1s., dull orange-red (shades).

Issue X. 1886-1887.

Four values. Design, &c., of the preceding issue; the two new values are inscribed THREE PENCE and SIX PENCE respectively. The name of the Colony and the value on the three pence and one shilling are printed in different colours from the rest of the impression. ((*Illustration* 240.)

(1886) 1d., lilac.

(„) 3d., „ *inscriptions in green.*

(1887) 6d., mauve.

(„) 1s., lilac, *inscriptions in carmine.*

Remarks.—A six pence lilac, with inscription in *blue*, is catalogued by M. Moens, but is not known to the Society.

REGISTRATION ENVELOPES.

Issue I. December 20th, 1887.

One value. Bag-shaped envelopes of white wove linen-lined paper, with flap to right; inscriptions, &c., in blue, as on the Barbados envelopes, Issue II., with large "R" in an upright oval frame. The stamp is embossed in colour on the flap. Design : Diademed profile of Queen Victoria to left, in plain relief on a solid ground of colour, enclosed within a circular band, bearing inscriptions in coloured block letters on a reticulated ground. (*Illustrations* 28, 243.)

T. " SAINT LUCIA REGISTRATION." B. " TWO PENCE."

2d., blue ; size G.

2d., „ „ H.

Remarks.—The inscription under the flap is "THOS. DE LA RUE & CO. PATENT," in *blue.*

WRAPPERS.

Issue I. December 19th, 1887.

Two values. Similar to the wrappers of Barbados, but with stamp of the following design. Diademed profile of Queen Victoria to left in a circle, enclosed within a rectangular frame, with inscriptions in uncoloured block letters on straight labels of solid colour at top and bottom, foliate ornaments in the spandrels, all on a solid ground of colour. Shape, upright rectangular. (*Illustration* 244.)

T. "ST. LUCIA." D. " HALFPENNY." "ONE PENNY."

½d., deep green.

1d., carmine.

POSTCARDS.

Issue I. ' 1881.

One value. Designed and printed by Messrs. De la Rue and Co., upon medium light buff card. Size, 121×87 mm., or 4⅓×3⅔ inches. The design is the same as that of the first issue card of Antigua, except that the second line is altered to ST. LUCIA (STE. LUCIE), and the name of the Colony at the top of the stamp is changed. (*Illustration* 245.)

1½d., light brown (shades).

Issue II. July, 1883.

One value. Designed and printed by Messrs. De la Rue and Co., upon stout straw card. Size, 139×88 mm., or 5½×3½ inches. The design is the same as that of the preceding issue, except for the value at the bottom of the stamp, which is altered to ONE PENNY. (*Illustration* 245.)

1d., rose (shades).

Issue III. 1889.

One value. Precisely similar to the first issue, but the design is printed upon stout straw card, and the size is increased to 139×88 mm., or 5½×3½ inches. (*Illustration* 245.)

1½d., light brown (slight shades).

REPLY PAID CARD.

Issue I. March 19th, 1883.

One value. Designed and printed by Messrs. De la Rue and Co., upon stout straw card. Size, 139×88 mm., or 5½×3½ inches. The design is the same as that for the single card of Issue I., but each half has additional inscriptions similar to the reply paid cards of Antigua. The cards are joined along the top, perforated 4½, and the design is printed upon the first and third pages. (*Illustration* 245.)

1½d.+1½d., light brown (slight shades).

THE ST. LUCIA STEAM CONVEYANCE CO., LIMITED.

Issue 1873.

Three values. Lithographed upon stout white wove surfaced paper. White gum, imperforate. Design : Ship sailing to left, within a white transverse oval band inscribed ST. LUCIA STEAM CONVEYANCE CY. LIMITED. in small coloured block letters. The spandrels are of solid colour, and contain white conventional ornaments. There is a border of a fancy pattern, which is broken at the bottom by a white label, which slightly impinges upon the oval band. The label contains a coloured Arabic numera of value. The design is completed by a plain outer line of colour. Shape, small oblong rectangular. (*Illustration* 242.)

1 (d.) ultramarine.
3 (d.) lilac-rose.
6 (d.) violet.

Remarks.—These stamps are said to have been used by the Company for the conveyance of letters between certain Ports in the Island where the Steamers called. The values are, no doubt, as given above, but, as the illustration shows, the stamps only bear a numeral.

ST. VINCENT.

PRELIMINARY NOTES.

By E. D. BACON.

POSTAGE STAMPS are said to have been first issued in this Island in 1861, but as the *Saint Vincent Government Gazette* only commenced publication in 1868, I am unable to say from that source, whether the date usually given is the correct one. There is but little doubt, however, that the issue took place in the year mentioned, as Messrs. Perkins Bacon and Co. inform me that the first supply of stamps, which consisted of one penny red and six pence dark green, was sent out by them to the Colony on March 27th, 1861. The plates of the one penny and six pence, and that of the half-penny value which was not issued until December, 1881, each contained 60 stamps in six horizontal rows of ten, the four pence and one shilling plates contained 30 labels in three horizontal rows of ten, while the plate of the five shillings only contained 20 specimens, *probably* in four horizontal rows of five. The halfpenny plate was finished in October, 1881, the four pence on July 9th, 1866, and the one shilling on July 5th, 1866. I am unable to give the dates of construction of the plates of the one penny, six pence and five shillings. Proof impressions in black, struck from the plates, upon plain white paper, of all the above values except the five shillings are known; as well as proofs in black upon white card from the engraved dies. The plates were all handed over to the Crown Agents on the 25th February, 1882, and afterwards by them to Messrs. De la Rue and Co., who have since printed all further supplies of stamps required by the Colony. The following dates of printings are taken from one of Messrs. Perkins Bacon and Co.'s books, to which specimens are attached. The stamps are all upon " star " watermarked paper.

> One shilling, dull red. 1872.
>   ,,   ,,   violet-rose. 1873.
> Six pence, pale green ; one shilling, vermilion. December, 1876.
> One penny, pale green ; six pence, bright yellow-green ; five shillings, rose-red. April, 1880.
> Halfpenny, orange ; one penny, grey; four pence, bright ultramarine. October, 1881.

The volumes of *The Gazette* I have searched give no notices of the issue of postage stamps or cards, and I have been unable to find any reference to the various provisional postage stamps issued at different times.

The Island joined the Postal Union on Sept. 1st, 1881, so the first three halfpenny postcard was probably issued on, or soon after, this date. The postal rates to certain Islands were reduced early in March, 1882, according to the following notice taken from *The Gazette* of March 9th of that year.

" GENERAL POST OFFICE,
" SAINT VINCENT, 9*th March*, 1882.
" FROM this date the Rates of Postage to Barbados, Grenada, St. Lucia,
Tobago, and Trinidad will be as follows :—
Letters,—per ½ oz., 2½d.
Postcards,—each, 1d.
Newspapers, Printed Papers, Books, &c.,—½d. per 2 ozs.
Commercial Papers, 2½d. per 2 ozs., and ½d. for each additional 2 ozs.
Patterns,—1d. for each packet not exceeding 2 ozs. and ½d. for each
. additional 2 ozs.
" (Signed) NEWTON BROWNE,
" *Colonial Postmaster.*"

A one penny postcard should therefore have been issued in March, 1882, but
according to the information I have received from Mr. Griffith, late Acting Colonial
Postmaster, no card of this value was available before February, 1884.

The following is found in the *Supplement to the Government Gazette, No. 39, of*
14*th September*, 1882.

" GOVERNMENT OFFICE,
" SAINT VINCENT, 15*th September*, 1882.
" UNDER the provisions of ' The Stamp Ordinance, 1882,' the Governor-
in-Council directs that Postage Stamps of this Colony, over-stamped with
the word ' Revenue,' and none other, shall be used as the ' Stamps' for
carrying out the provisions of this Ordinance.

" As it is expedient to provide one £50 stamp, the Governor-in-Council
directs that one of the existing five shilling Postage Stamps shall be over-
stamped *Fifty Pounds—Revenue*, and be used as a Revenue Stamp of that
value ; the said stamp shall, before being affixed to any document, be
initialled by the Governor and the Treasurer

" There not being a postage stamp of the value of three pence which
can be utilised as a revenue stamp, the Governor-in-Council directs that
the present six penny postage stamp may be cut diagonally in half—each
half to be over-stamped *3d. Revenue*, and be used as a revenue stamp of
of that value.

" By Command,
",(Signed) NEWTON BROWNE,
" *Confidential Clerk.*"

The Ordinance to impose Stamp Duties was proclaimed in Kingstown, the
capital of the Island, on September 15th, 1882, the date of the above communication.

The notice is principally of importance to collectors of fiscal stamps, as it gives
the date of the *first* issue of Revenue Stamps in the Island, and it speaks of a stamp
that has never been previously catalogued, viz., the high value of £50. It is also
interesting to collectors of postage stamps, as it establishes the true use of the five
shilling stamp. It is for this reason I reproduce it in a work dealing exclusively
with postal issues. The stamp, like the other values, does not bear the word
" Postage," and at the time it first appeared in this country, August, 1880, it was
mentioned in *The Philatelic Record* as a fiscal used postally, and it is so described in
M. Moens' *Catalogue*, whereas it is a postage stamp, and was not used for fiscal purposes until two years later, and then only with the surcharge REVENUE struck across
the centre in black Roman capitals. Mr. Frank W. Griffith, late Acting Colonial
Postmaster, informs me the design on the five shilling stamp represents the Arms of
the Government of St. Vincent, and describes it as " Justice pouring out a libation
to Peace." He corroborates the date of the first issue as 1861 ; and adds, the four

pence blue and one shilling slate came into use in August, 1866, the four pence yellow and one shilling brown in 1869, one penny black in 1871, one shilling pink in 1872, the halfpenny yellow in December, 1881, and the one penny carmine and three halfpenny brown postcards in February, 1884. He further states the provisional stamps were issued as follows, and gives the number of each variety.

Date.	Description and former value.	New value.	Number issued.
May, 1880	6d., dark green ...	1d. on each half.	1800.
Sept., 1881	6d., light green ...	½d. „ „ .,	1440.
Nov. & Dec., 1881 ...	1s., red	4d.	630.
„ „ „ ...	6d., light green ...	1d. (ONE PENNY).	1620.
March, 1885	2½d., carmine ...	1d.	12,060.*
Aug., 1890	4d., chocolate ...	2½d.	1500.

* Of these, five sheets (300) were spoiled whilst being printed, and consequently destroyed.

REFERENCE LIST OF THE PHILATELIC SOCIETY, LONDON.
Issue I. May (?), 1861.

Two values. Engraved and printed in *taille-douce* by Messrs. Perkins Bacon and Co., of London, on white wove unwatermarked paper, varying considerably in substance. Yellowish gum. Imperforate and machine punctured perforation, measuring 14, 14½, 15, 15½ compound. Design : Diademed profile of Queen Victoria to left, on engine-turned background, within an oval of open network broken at the top and bottom by labels of solid colour inscribed with white block letters. In each corner is a white ornamented Maltese cross, and the spandrels are filled in with reticulations. A plain outer coloured line completes the design. Shape, upright rectangular. (*Illustration* 248.)

T. "ST. VINCENT." B. "ONE PENNY." "SIX PENCE."

A.—*Imperforate.*
1d., dull rose.
6d., dark green.
B.—*Perforated* 14 to 15½ compound.
1d., dull rose-red (shades).
6d., yellow-green to dark green (shades).

Remarks.—An imperforate pair of the one penny, and also of the six pence, exist in the collection of the late Mr. T. K. Tapling.

Issue II. August, 1866.

Two values. Exactly similar in design to the preceding issue, except for the alteration of the values. The stamps are also printed upon the same paper. The one shilling is found with a machine punctured perforation of 14 to 15½ compound, a clean cut perforation of 11½, and punctured at the sides and clean cut 11½ at the top and bottom. The four pence is only found with the clean cut perforation of 11½. Shape, upright rectangular. (*Illustration* 248.)

T. "ST. VINCENT." B. "FOUR PENCE." "ONE SHILLING."

A.—*Perforated* 11½ clean cut.
4d., blue (shades).
1s., slate („)
B.—*Perforated* 11½ clean cut top and bottom, and punctured 14 to 15½ at sides.
1s., slate (shades).
C.—*Perforated* 14 to 15½ compound.
1s., slate.

Issue III. 1869.

Four values. Similar in design to the previous issues, and printed upon the same paper, the only differences being in the colours and perforations, the latter now being clean cut. (*Illustration* 248.)

A.—*Perforated* $11\frac{1}{2}$.

1d., dull rose-red (shades).
4d., orange-yellow („)
6d., yellow-green („)
1s., indigo („)
1s., brown (,)

B.—*Perforated* $12\frac{1}{2}$.

1s., indigo

Issue IV. 1871-1876.

Four values. Precisely similar in design to the last, but the stamps are printed upon white wove paper varying in thickness, watermarked with a six-rayed star, and the colours are changed. Machine perforated $11\frac{1}{2}$ to $15\frac{1}{2}$ compound. (*Illustration* 248.)

(1871) 1d., black (shades).
(1876) 4d., dark blue („)
(1871) 6d., dark green („)
(1872) 1s., dull rose-red („)
(1873) 1s., lilac-rose („)

Variety. Imperforate vertically.

1d., black.

Issue V. January, 1877.

Two values. Changed in colour, but the design remains as before. The stamps are watermarked with a six-rayed star, and are machine perforated $11\frac{1}{2}$ to 15 compound. (*Illustration* 248.)

6d., pale green (shades).
1s., vermilion („)

Issue VI. 1880.

One value. Engraved and printed in *taille-douce* by Messrs. Perkins Bacon and Co., on white wove star watermarked paper. Yellowish gum. Machine perforated 12. Design: In the centre of the stamp on an engine-turned background, are the arms of the Island, and above them a royal crown with scroll beneath it, with the motto, PAX ET JUSTITIA, in small coloured block letters. The central vignettes are enframed by a white oval band inscribed in coloured block letters, an ornament at either side separating the two inscriptions. The side borders are reticulated and two plain outer coloured lines complete the design. Shape, large upright rectangular. (*Illustration* 250.)

T. "ST. VINCENT." B. "FIVE SHILLINGS."

5s., rose-red (shades).

Issue VII. May, 1880.

One value. In May, 1880, owing to the stock of one penny labels being exhausted, recourse was had to a provisional, which was formed by perforating the six pence dark green of 1871 vertically down the centre, and surcharging each half $\frac{d}{1}$ in vermilion, the numeral being $8\frac{1}{2}$ mm. in height. The central perforation is clean cut and measures 12. (*Illustration* 249.)

1d., vermilion surcharge, on right half of 6d. dark green.
1d., vermilion surcharge, on left half of 6d. dark green.

Issue VIII. June, 1880.

Two values. Of the design of the first issue printed upon star watermarked paper; machine perforated 11½. (*Illustration* 248.)

1d., pale olive-green   (shades).
6d., bright yellow-green („)

Issue IX. September to December, 1881.

Three values. In 1881, St. Vincent joined the Postal Union, and a new value was required, viz.: one halfpenny to make up the Inter-Island rate of two pence halfpenny, whilst the disused four penny value again became necessary. In September, 1881, a provisional halfpenny was made after the same fashion as the one penny of May, 1880, by perforating the six pence of 1880, vertically down the centre, and surcharging each half ½ in vermilion 16½ mm. in height. The central perforation measures 12. Pending the arrival of new four penny stamps from England, a few of the blue labels of this value were used. The small stock of the old four penny stamps having been exhausted before the new ones arrived, a provisional four penny was made in November, 1881, by surcharging the current one shilling vermilion across the centre 4d. in black, both numeral and letter measuring 8½ mm. in height. The original value is obliterated by a thick black bar.

About the same time, the olive-green penny stamps, the colour of which it had been decided to change, were exhausted. Prior to the arrival of the new ones, a provisional stamp of this value was formed by obliterating the original value of the current six pence with a black bar and surcharging it above in black block letters 2 mm. in height ONE PENNY, the surcharge extending 17½ mm. across the stamp. (*Illustrations* 251, 252, 253.)

(Sept., 1881) ½d., vermilion surcharge, on right half of 6d. bright yellow-green.
½d., „   „   „ left „ „ 6d. „   „   „
(Dec., 1881) 1d., black   „   „ 6d. bright yellow-green.
(Nov., 1881) 4d., „   „   „ 1s. vermilion.

Variety. The numeral 1 on the halfpenny is sometimes found with a straight instead of a curved "serif."

Issue X. End of 1881.

Three values. Engraved and printed in *taille-douce* by Messrs. Perkins Bacon and Co., on white wove paper watermarked with the old six-rayed star of the preceding issues. Yellowish gum. Machine perforated 12 for the halfpenny, 11½ for the other two values. Designs: That of the halfpenny comprises a diademed profile of Queen Victoria to left, within an ornamental engine-turned oval, cut at the top and bottom by straight labels of solid colour inscribed in white block letters. The corners contain white square blocks with star-like ornaments, and the remainder of the stamp is filled in with reticulations. Shape, small upright rectangular. The one penny and four pence are of the old design. (*Illustrations* 248, 254.)

T. " ST. VINCENT."   B. " HALFPENNY."   " ONE PENNY."   " FOUR PENCE."
½d., orange (shades).
1d., drab („)
4d., bright ultramarine (shades).

Remarks.—The paper used for the halfpenny was the same as that employed for the other values. The stamp being smaller, the watermarks are found irregularly disposed in respect of some of the stamps.

Issue XI. 1883.

Three values. Printed by Messrs. De la Rue aud Co., of London, from the plates constructed by Messrs. Perkins Bacon and Co. The paper is slightly surfaced white wove, watermarked Crown C.A., and the stamps are machine perforated 14. The new value, the two pence halfpenny, is made by printing a stamp from the old one penny plate in a new colour, obliterating the value by a black bar, and adding a surcharge above of $2\frac{1}{2}$ PENCE in black block letters, $3\frac{1}{2}$ mm. in height and $15\frac{3}{4}$ mm. in length. (*Illustrations* 248, 255.)

> 1d., drab (shades).
> 2½d., black surcharge, on 1d. carmine-lake.
> 4d., bright ultramarine (shades).

Issue XII. End 1883 to 1884.

Four values. Printed by Messrs. De la Rue and Co. from the plates constructed by Messrs. Perkins Bacon and Co. The paper is slightly surfaced white wove, watermarked Crown C.A., and the stamps are machine perforated 12. The Halfpenny was not issued until towards the end of 1884. (*Illustrations* 248, 254.)

> ½d., green.
> 4d., ultramarine, dark blue (shades).
> 6d., bright yellow-green   („)
> 1s., orange-vermilion   („)

Remarks.—The plate of the halfpenny did not fit the "Crown C.A." paper used by Messrs. De la Rue and Co., and on inspecting an entire sheet one row of the stamps will be found watermarked with letters forming the words CROWN AGENTS.

Issue XIII. March, 1885.

One value. Issued provisionally, pending a fresh supply of one penny labels. The required value was obtained by surcharging the 2½ pence of Issue XI. **1d** in black, the numeral measuring $8\frac{1}{2}$ mm. in height, and the surcharge 2½ pence being obliterated by two narrow black bars. (*Illustration* 256.)

> 1d., black surcharge, on 2½d., on 1d., carmine-lake.

Issue XIV. 1885-1886.

Three values. The designs are those of the previous issues. Printed by Messrs. De la Rue and Co., upon slightly surfaced white wove paper, watermarked Crown C.A. Machine perforated 14. (*Illustrations* 248, 254.)

> (1885) ½d., green.
> (1885) 1d., carmine-red.
> (1886) 1d., pink.
> (1885) 4d., reddish-chocolate (shades).
> (1886) 4d., dark puce-brown („)

Remarks.—In 1887, some of the stamps surcharged "Revenue" were chronicled as having done postal duty. Although copies are known purporting to bear postmarks, the obliterations are probably fraudulent, as "Revenue" stamps have never been allowed to prepay postage in this Colony.

Issue XV. 1888-1889.

Three values. Printed by Messrs. De la Rue and Co., upon similar paper to the previous issues, watermarked Crown C.A. Machine perforated 14. The five shillings is printed from the plate constructed by Messrs. Perkins Bacon and Co., and the design of the other values is unchanged. The two pence halfpenny is produced from the one penny die, in the same way as the corresponding value of Issue XI. (*Illustrations* 248, 250, 255.)

(1889) 2½d., black surcharge, on 1d. pale blue.
(1888) 6d., purple.
(1888) 5s., deep crimson.

Issue XVI. August, 1890.

One value. The four pence dark puce brown of Issue XIV., surcharged in the Colony, for provisional use as two pence halfpenny. The surcharge consists of the numerals "2½," a letter "d" in lower case Roman type, and a black bar obliterating the original value of the stamp. (*Illustration* 257.)

2½d., black surcharge, on 4d. dark puce-brown (shades).

Remarks.—The position of the fractional line of the surcharge " ½ " varies on different stamps, and the line is sometimes found omitted altogether.

POSTCARDS.

Issue I. January, 1882.

One value. Designed and printed by Messrs. De la Rue and Co., upon medium light buff card. Size, 121×87 mm., or 4⅘×3⅗ inches. The design is the same as that of the first issue card of Antigua, except that the second line of the inscription reads st. vincent (st. vincent), and the name of the Colony at the top of the stamp is changed. (*Illustration* 246.)

1½d., light brown (shades).

Issue II. February, 1884.

Two values. Designed and printed by Messrs. De la Rue and Co., upon stout straw card. Size, 139×88 mm., or 5½×3½ inches. The design is similar to the second issue cards of Antigua, with the exception of the modification of the name of the Colony, mentioned above. (*Illustration* 247.)

1d., carmine   (slight shades).
1½d., dark brown (,,   ,,   )

TOBAGO.

PRELIMINARY NOTES.

By E. D. BACON.

THE first stamps issued in the Island of Tobago were employed for fiscal purposes, and on reference to *The Tobago Gazette* for June 6th, 1879, we shall see they came into use on the 1st July of that year.

GOVERNMENT NOTICE.

STAMPS.

" NOTICE is hereby given that the 'Stamp Ordinance' will come into operation on the 1st day of July next.

" The attention of the Public is called to the provisions of this Law.

" Under it a number of documents will be invalid unless they are properly stamped.

" By His Excellency's command,

" (Signed)   H. L. BYNG,

" *Col. Secretary.*

" COLONIAL SECRETARY'S OFFICE, 3rd *June*, 1879."

These stamps, which consisted of the values of one penny, three pence, six pence, one shilling, five shillings, and one pound, were shortly afterwards issued provisionally for postal service until a fresh supply, bearing the distinctive mark of " Postage," could be obtained from England. The postal issue took place on the 1st August, 1879, in accordance with the following notice found in *The Gazette* of July 18th.

GOVERNMENT NOTICE.

" POST OFFICE,

" SCARBOROUGH, 2nd *July*, 1879.

" NOTICE is hereby given that from and after the 1st of August next, all letters, newspapers, and other articles transmissible by Post must be prepaid by having Postage Stamps of the proper value affixed thereto.

" Postage Stamps of the various values are now on sale at the Treasury, and a supply will in future be kept at this office.

" (Signed)   ROBT. W. McEACHNIE.

" *Acting Postmaster.*"

These provisional postage stamps continued in use until the end of the year, 1880, the new set with the word " POSTAGE " upon them being issued on the 20th December of that year, as the notice published in *The Gazette* of November 5th, 1880, shows.

NOTICE

" IS HEREBY GIVEN that on and after the 1st January, 1881, the Stamps now in use in this Colony are to be applied solely to the purposes specified in the Schedule of the 'Stamp Ordinance, 1879.'

" On and after the 20th December next Stamps having the word ' Postage' on them may be obtained at the Post Office, Scarborough, for postal purposes; and on and after the 1st January, 1881, no letters,

T

papers, books, or other parcels, will be considered prepaid if stamped with other than the 'Postage Stamps.'

" By His Honor's command,

"(Signed)   L. G. HAY,

" *Treasurer.*

" TREASURER's OFFICE, *5th November,* 1880."

The above notice clearly proves that the five shillings and one pound fiscal stamps, watermarked Crown C.A., which are usually catalogued as having been used for postage, were not available for the latter service. This is further borne out by a letter I have received from the present Postmaster of Tobago, Mr. A. L. Marshall, who writes, " It has rarely happened that some of the peasantry, through ignorance, have applied fiscal stamps to their letters, and this perhaps may account for the belief sometimes that they are used for postal, as well as fiscal purposes, but they are not." In face of these statements, these two stamps have no right whatever to be included in a catalogue of the postage labels, and ought for the future to be expunged from all such lists. Mr. Marshall further informs me that the provisional one penny, formed of half a sixpenny stamp surcharged by hand with pen and ink, issued in 1880, was distinctly made for postal use, but inasmuch as at that date the same stamps were used for fiscal purposes, this provisional was probably employed for both branches of the service. No notice appeared in *The Gazette* of this, or of any of the other provisionals issued in after years. Mr. Marshall tells me the later provisionals were all surcharged at the Government Printing Office in Scarborough, and he thinks that not more than four or five hundred, if so many, were issued of any one variety.

The following list of the *Inland Postal Rates* of the Island is found in *The Gazette* of November 5th, 1880.

LETTERS.

Not exceeding ½ an ounce	One Penny.
Exceeding ½ ounce and not exceeding 1 ounce ...	Two Pence.
And for every additional ½ ounce	One Penny.

BOOK PACKETS.

For every 2 ounces, or part of 2 ounces	Two Pence.
And for every additional 2 ounces or part thereof ...	Two Pence.

NEWSPAPERS.

For every paper	One Penny.

And *The Gazette* for December 10th, 1880, contains the following :—

POST OFFICE NOTICE.

" ARRANGEMENTS having been entered into for the adhesion of this Colony to the International Postal Union on and from the 1st January, 1881 ; Notice is hereby given that the following rates of postage will be payable from that date on all letters, newspapers, and book packets posted to any of the Countries within the Postal Union :—

BY ANY ROUTE.

Letters	4d. per ½ ounce.
Post Cards	1½d. each.
Newspapers	1d. per 4 ounces.
Printed papers and patterns...	1d. per 2 ounces.
Commercial papers—The same as for printed papers, but with minimum charge of 2½d.	

By command,

"(Signed)   S. F. FITZICK,

" *Postmaster.*

" POST OFFICE, *6th December,* 1880."

In accordance with the terms of the latter notice, the haltpenny and four penny adhesives, and the three halfpenny card, should have been issued on January 1st, 1881, but it is, of course, possible they did not arrive in the Island until shortly after that date.

The next notice is taken from *The Gazette* of December 16th, 1881.

POST OFFICE NOTICE.

" THE British Islands of Barbados, Saint Vincent, Grenada, Trinidad, Saint Lucia, and Dominica, and the French Islands of Martinique and Guadeloupe being 300 nautical miles of this Island, the Postage on Correspondence and Mail Matter addressed to those Islands will in accordance with the Postal Union Convention be as under :—

Letters 2½d. per ½ oz.

Postcards, 1d. each.

Newspapers, ½d. each.

" (Signed)   S. F. FITZCK,

" *Postmaster.*

" GENERAL POST OFFICE, 15*th December*, 1881."

And the following appeared in *The Gazette* of March 10th, 1882.

POST OFFICE NOTICE.

" IN accordance with the Postal Union Convention, the Postage on Correspondence addressed to the Island of Dominica is at the rate of 4d. per ½ oz., and not at the rate of 2½d. per ½ oz., as stated in my notice of the 15th December, 1881.

" (Signed)   S. F. FITZCK,

" *Postmaster.*

" GENERAL POST OFFICE, 7*th March*, 1882."

From the first of these two notices, we see that postcards of one penny each should have been issued, but, strange to say, in face of this announcement, no card of this value has ever been brought into use.

The notification of the issue of the reply three halfpenny post card may be found in *The Gazette* of August 10th, 1883.

POST OFFICE NOTICE.

" REPLY POST CARDS available for Countries included in the Postal Union may now be obtained at the Post Office ; the cost of a packet of these cards is 1s. 8d.—each packet contains 6 Reply Post Cards. The price of a packet containing 10 single Post Cards has been reduced to 1s. 4d.

" (Signed)   S. F. FITZCK,

" *Postmaster.*

" GENERAL POST OFFICE, 10*th August*, 1883."

The price of the single three halfpenny cards was still further reduced in 1886, as the following " Order," taken from *The Gazette* of August 20th of that year proves.

ORDER-IN-COUNCIL.

" IT is hereby ordered that the Order-in-Council dated the 10th of August, 1883, fixing the price of Post Cards at one shilling and four pence per packet of 10 cards, be cancelled, and that in future Post Cards be sold singly at the Post Office at one penny halfpenny a piece and to Stamp Vendors at one shilling and three pence per packet of ten.

" (Signed)   G. C. M. SEALY,

" *Acting Clerk to the Councils.*

" 16*th August*, 1886."

REFERENCE LIST OF THE PHILATELIC SOCIETY, LONDON.

Issue I. August 1st, 1879.

Six values. Engraved and surface-printed by Messrs. De la Rue and Co., of London, upon medium white wove surfaced paper, watermarked Crown C.C. White gum, machine perforated 14. Design: Diademed profile of Queen Victoria to left upon ground of horizontal lines, enclosed within a circular band of solid colour, which touches the top, right, and left sides of the stamp. The band is inscribed at the top with the name of the Colony, in white block letters, the lower half being ornamented by a white foliate pattern. Straight white label, the width of the stamp, below the band, inscribed with the value in words in coloured block letters. The spandrels contain conventional ornaments, and a plain outer line of colour completes the design. Shape upright rectangular. (*Illustration* 258.)

T. "TOBAGO."   B. "ONE PENNY."   "THREE PENCE."   "SIX PENCE."   "ONE SHILLING."
           "FIVE SHILLINGS."   "ONE POUND."

     1d., rose   (shades).
     3d., blue   (,,   )
     6d., dull orange (,,   )
     1s., green   (,,   )
     5s., grey-black   (,,   )
     £1, mauve   (,,   )

Remarks.—These stamps were prepared for fiscal purposes, but pending the arrival of distinctive postage labels, were issued by the Post Office for the prepayment of letters.

Issue II. November, 1880.

One value. Being the six pence of Issue I. used provisionally as a one penny value. The stamp was divided vertically down the centre, and each half surcharged " 1d. " with pen and ink. (*Illustration* 259.)

     1d., black surcharge, on right half of 6d., dull orange.
     1d., ,,   ,,   ,, left   ,, ,, 6d., ,,   ,,

Issue III. December 20th, 1880.

Five values. Engraved and surface-printed by Messrs. De la Rue and Co., upon medium white wove paper, watermarked Crown C.C. White gum, machine perforated 14. The design is the same as that of Issue I., but the word POSTAGE is introduced into the lower curve of the circular band in white block letters, replacing the white foliate pattern. A star-shaped ornament at either side separates the word POSTAGE from the name of the Colony. (*Illustration* 260.)

T. "TOBAGO."   B. " POSTAGE, HALFPENNY."   "ONE PENNY."   "FOUR PENCE."
       "SIX PENCE."   "ONE SHILLING."

     ½d., brown-lilac (shades).
     1d., red-brown   (,,   )
     4d., yellow-green (,,   )
     6d., stone-brown (,,   )
     1s., yellow-ochre (,,   )

Variety. Imperforate.

     1s., yellow-ochre.

Issue IV. April, 1883.

One value. The six pence of Issue III. surcharged for provisional use as two pence halfpenny. The surcharge consists of "2½ PENCE " in a straight line across the stamp, measuring 16 mm. in length. The chief numeral "2" is 4 mm., and the letters of the word PENCE, which is in Roman capitals, 2½ mm. in height. (*Illustration* 261.)

2½d., black surcharge, on 6d. stone-brown.

Issue V. 1882-1884.

Five values. Engraved and surfaced-printed by Messrs. De la Rue and Co., upon medium white wove paper, watermarked Crown C.A. Yellowish and white gum, machine perforated 14. The design is the same as that of Issue III., the new value of two pence halfpenny being inscribed "2½ PENNY." (*Illustrations* 260, 262.)

(1883)   ½d., brown-lilac   (shades).
(May, 1882)   1d., red-brown   („   )
(End 1883)   2½d., ultramarine („   )
(1884)   4d., yellow-green („   )
(1884)   6d., stone-brown („   )

Variety. Imperforate.

(1884)   6d., stone-brown.

Remarks.—M. Moens states in the *Timbre-Poste* for November, 1883, that one of his correspondents has the one penny of this issue postmarked, May, 1882.

Issue VI. May 1st, 1885.

One value. The four pence of Issue V. changed in colour. The watermark is Crown C.A., and the perforation 14. (*Illustration* 260.)

4d., pearl-grey (shades)

Issue VII. 1886.

One value. The six pence and two pence halfpenny of Issue V. surcharged for provisional use as halfpenny stamps. The surcharge consists of "½ PENNY" in a straight line across the stamp measuring 13½ mm. in length. The letters of the word PENNY, which is in Roman capitals, are 2½ mm. in height. (*Illustration* 263.)

(January, 1886) ½d., black surcharge, on 6d., stone-brown.
(April, 1886)   ½d., „   „   „ 2½d., ultramarine.

Varieties. a. The surcharge is found inverted on the six pence.

        b. Unsevered vertical pairs of the halfpenny on two pence halfpenny, are found without the surcharge on the lower stamp. It is probable that some if not all the stamps in the bottom row of the sheet accidentally failed to receive the surcharge.

Issue VIII. 1886.

Three values. The same as the stamps of Issue V., but with the colours changed. The watermark is Crown C.A., and the perforation 14. (*Illustration* 260.)

(August, 1886)   ½d., green   (shades).
(January, 1886)   1d., carmine-rose („   )
(November, 1886)   6d., orange   („   )

Issue IX. 1889.

Two values. The two pence halfpenny and six pence of Issues V. and VIII., respectively, surcharged for provisional use. The surcharge on the two pence halfpenny consists of "1 PENNY," in a straight line across the stamp, measuring 13½ mm. in length. The numeral 1 measures 4 mm., and the letters of the word PENNY, which is in Roman capitals 2½ mm. in height. The surcharge on the six pence is the same as that for Issue VII. (*Illustrations* 263, 264.)

(July, 1889) 1d., black surcharge, on 2½d., ultramarine.
(Oct. „) ½d., „   „   „ 6d., orange.

POSTCARD.

Issue I. January 1st (?), 1881.

One value. Designed and printed by Messrs. De la Rue and Co., upon medium light buff card. Size, 121×87 mm., or 4¾×3⅜ inches. The design is the same as that for the first issued card of Antigua, except that the second line of the inscription is replaced by TOBAGO (TABAGO), and the name of the Colony at the top of the stamp is changed. (*Illustration* 290.)

1½d., light brown (shades).

Remarks.—A *one penny* card was chronicled in some of the Magazines early in 1886, and is also mentioned in certain dealers' price lists; but no card of this value is known to members of the Society, and there is but little doubt that it was catalogued in error.

REPLY PAID CARD.

Issue I. August 10th, 1883.

One value. Designed and printed by Messrs. De la Rue and Co., upon stout straw card. Size 139×88 mm., or 5½×3½ inches. The design is the same as that for the single card of Issue I., except that both halves have an additional inscription similar to the reply paid cards of Antigua. The cards are joined along the top, perforated 4, and the design is printed upon the first and third pages. (*Illustration* 290.)

1½d.+1½d., light brown (slight shades).

TRINIDAD.

PRELIMINARY NOTES.

By E. D. BACON.

Some Remarks on the Earlier Stamps of this Colony.

(A Paper read before the Philatelic Society of London, January 17th, 1890, and re-printed from "The Philatelic Record" of February, 1890.)

From the earliest days of collecting the stamps of Trinidad have always presented more difficulties to philatelists than those of any other of the British West Indies. The two most important points in connection with their history that require elucidation are, as you know, the following: (a) What were the franking powers of the labels without expressed values? (b) What was the method of production employed for the native-printed stamps? Both questions have raised much controversy amongst collectors, and many divergent opinions are held upon each; they practically, however, remain unsolved to the present day. The object of this paper is to try and throw some new light upon the general history of these stamps, more particularly with reference to the two questions I have named.

As far back as April last I commenced collecting together what materials I could find, with the view of seeing whether it was possible to offer any reasonable explanation of the difficulties connected with these stamps. It was only when I came to search through the philatelic journals for papers treating on these subjects that I learnt how very little has at any time been written upon the stamps of this Island, and I at once saw I should not get much assistance from that source. I then addressed a letter to Mr. J. A. Bulmer, the present Postmaster-General of Trinidad, asking him for certain particulars relating to the issue of the stamps. In his reply he says: "I have the honour to inform you that my appointment to this Colony as Postmaster-General only dates back to 1883, and that there are absolutely no official records of the postage stamps, &c., issued for any period prior to that time. I have forwarded your letter to the persons long resident in the Colony who have taken an interest in the collection of postage stamps, and I now enclose the reply of Mr. Taylor, one of the best informed persons in Trinidad on such matters." Thanks to Mr. Bulmer's courtesy, his letter put me in correspondence with Mr. Taylor, and he and I have been in constant communication ever since. Mr. James Graham Taylor, the gentleman referred to in Mr. Bulmer's letter, has been a stamp collector for many years, and he at once became interested in the investigation I had begun. He has devoted a great deal of his leisure during the last few months in endeavouring to obtain as full and complete replies as possible to the various questions I addressed to him at different periods, and I am indebted to him for much of the new information I am able to lay before you this evening.

The inland postal service of the island was first commenced in the year 1851 the Ordinance establishing the post being published in *The Trinidad Royal Gazette,* for April 16th of that year. I take the following clauses from that document :—

"TRINIDAD, *4th April,* 1851.

" *An Ordinance for Establishing an Inland Post and Rates of Postage within the Colony.*

" II. And be it enacted, That there shall be one General Post Office in the Town of Port of Spain, where letters may be received from all places within the colony and parts out of the colony, and whence all letters may be despatched to all places within the colony and to all parts out of the colony.

" VIII. And be it enacted, That on every letter arriving in this colony from any place beyond the limits of the colony, if delivered from the General Post Office in Port of Spain, and on every letter posted at the General Post Office in Port of Spain for transmission to any place beyond the limits of the colony, there shall be charged and shall be paid to Her Majesty for the use of the colony one uniform rate of one penny.

" IX. And be it enacted, that the postage payable on all letters arriving in this colony from any place beyond the limits of this colony shall be paid by the person to whom the same may be addressed on the delivery of the same to him.

" X. And be it enacted, That all letters arriving in this colony from any place beyond the limits of this colony, and delivered from any post office except the General Post Office in Port of Spain, and all letters posted at any post office in this colony except the General Post Office in Port of Spain, for transmission to any place beyond the limits of this colony, and all letters transmitted by the post from any one place to any other place within the limits of this colony, shall be charged by weight, according to the following scale, and the several numbers of rates of postage hereinafter set forth shall be charged, and shall be paid to Her Majesty for the use of the colony on all such letters ; that is to say, on every letter not exceeding half an ounce in weight, one rate of postage ; on every letter exceeding half an ounce and not exceeding one ounce in weight, two rates of postage ; on every letter exceeding one ounce and not exceeding two ounces in weight, four rates of postage ; on every letter exceeding two ounces and not exceeding three ounces in weight, six rates of postage ; and on every letter exceeding three ounces and not exceeding four ounces in weight, eight rates of postage ; and for every ounce in weight above the weight of four ounces there shall be charged and taken two additional rates of postage ; and every fraction of an ounce above the weight of four ounces shall be charged as one additional ounce. And on all such letters there shall be paid the following rates of postage ; that is to say, on every letter not exceeding half an ounce in weight, one uniform rate of one penny ; and on every letter exceeding half an ounce in weight, progressive and additional rates of postage (each additional rate being estimated at one penny), according to the scale of weight and number of rates hereinbefore fixed and declared.

" XI. Provided always, and be it enacted, That as regards all letters posted at any post office within this colony, all such letters when posted shall have thereon or affixed thereto a stamp or stamps to the amount of the rates of postage payable on the same under this Ordinance ; and in all cases in which any letter shall be posted at any post office within this colony without having thereon or affixed thereto such stamp or stamps, or having thereon or affixed thereto any stamp or stamps, the value or amount of which shall be less than the rate of postage, to which such letter would be liable under this Ordinance, such letter shall not in any case be forwarded by the post, but shall if posted at any other office than the General Post Office be transmitted to such General Post Office, and shall so far as may be practicable be returned to the sender thereof.

"XII. And be it enacted, That the Governor shall from time to time provide proper and sufficient dies or other implements for expressing and denoting rates or duties of one penny and two pence, or rates or duties of any other value or amount as the Governor shall see fit for the purposes herein mentioned ; and stamps shall be made or impressed from such dies or other implements as the Governor shall from time to time by writing under his hand direct.

"XIII. And be it enacted, That it shall be lawful for the Governor to appoint such persons as he shall see fit to retail the stamps denoting the duties of postage on letters.

"XIV. And be it enacted, That printed newspapers may be sent free of postage, or liable to postage according to the rates and regulations hereinafter set forth ; that is to say :—

"Printed British and Foreign Newspapers brought to this colony by packet boats or private ships... ... } Free.

"Printed British or Foreign Newspapers or Island Newspapers transmitted by post from any one place to any other place within this colony... ... ... } Each One Penny.

"Island Newspapers sent by post from this colony ... } Free.

"Printed Votes and Proceedings of the Imperial Parliament, Periodical Publications, Pamphlets, Magazines, Reviews, and other Publications sent to this colony by packet, if delivered at the General Post Office, in Port of Spain ... ... } One Penny.

"If delivered at any other Post Office, and if not exceeding one ounce ... ... } One Penny.

"If exceeding one ounce, for every ounce beyond that weight ... ... } One Penny.

"Patterns :

"Packets or covers containing patterns or samples, being open at the sides, and not exceeding one ounce, and without any letter or writing in, upon, or within any such packet or cover, other than the name of the sender, his place of abode, the prices of the articles contained therein, and the name and address of the person to whom the packet or cover shall be sent ... ... } One Penny.

"Letters not open at the sides containing patterns or samples, and not exceeding one ounce in weight.. } Two Pence.

"XV. And be it enacted, that it shall not be compulsory to send newspapers by post.

"Passed in Council this Fourth day of April, in the Year of our Lord One Thousand Eight Hundred and Fifty-one.

"(Signed)   RICHARD D. CADIZ,
"*Clerk of Council.*

"The foregoing Ordinance was duly proclaimed by me in Port of Spain, this 11th day of April, in the Year of our Lord One Thousand Eight Hundred and Fifty-one.

"(Signed)   W. B. GOULD,
"*Marshal.*"

Although, as we see, the above Ordinance was proclaimed on the 11th April, 1851, Mr. Taylor informs me the inland postal service was not commenced until August 14th of that year. The latter would, therefore, be the correct date of the first issued stamps, which we know were those without expressed values. There is a somewhat curious incident in connection with the date of this issue, which I am unable to give a satisfactory explanation of. Messrs. Perkins Bacon and Co. tell me they sent the first supply of stamps out to the Island on December 21st, 1848, and a second lot in December, 1850, so the authorities must have had a stock of stamps on hand long before they were needed. Why they should order a second lot before the first were issued will probably remain known to themselves alone. I have searched *The Gazette* for the years 1849 and 1850 in vain for any notice of the issue of stamps prior to 1851.

I have also looked through *The Gazette* for 1847 and 1848 without finding any notice or even reference to the " Lady McLeod " local. As the Inland Postal Service was only started in August, 1851, the stamp was probably employed by the owners of the steamer as a purely private means of franking letters carried by their vessel between the towns of San Fernando and Port of Spain, and had no connection whatever with the Post Office.

Now with regard to the much-disputed question of the postal values of the early stamps. We see from Clauses VIII. and X. of the Ordinance that there was one uniform rate of One Penny for the transmission of half ounce letters within the Island, and a similar charge, irrespective of weight and the foreign rate, for letters forwarded to or despatched from places outside the Colony, when those letters were posted at or delivered from the General Post Office in Port of Spain. Clause XII. states that the Governor shall provide One Penny and Two Penny stamps, or such other stamps as he may find requisite for carrying out the new arrangements. It is quite obvious no other values would be required to defray the new rates; in fact a One Penny stamp was all that was really necessary. Foreign letters, as was usually the case in those days, would mostly be forwarded unpaid, provided they bore a colonial Penny stamp for the local rate, or the postage would be defrayed in money, for it was not until January 1st, 1859, that the prepayment of letters to Great Britain was made compulsory. Now entire letters are known with the red, blue, or lilac stamp upon them which have passed between two towns in the Island ; and I have before me three entire letter-sheets sent from the Colony to Barbadoes. One of the latter bears the brown stamp, and is dated Trinidad, Nov. 27th, 1851 ; the second has a blue stamp of the first issue, and is postmarked Trinidad, October 28th, 1852 ; and the third carries a grey stamp, and the postmark Trinidad, July 10th, 1853. Each letter has also the Barbadoes postmark, dated two days later than the Trinidad one. All three letters have the numeral 4 written in ink on the face, which I take to signify the foreign postage, which being identical in each instance points to the same postal value of One Penny (the local Island rate) for all three stamps. Then we have used pairs and blocks of the blue stamp, the late Mr. Tapling's collection containing an unsevered used strip of five of the native printed grey. It is true the letters with the blue, lilac, and grey stamps may have been heavy ones, but we should remember the former stamp, if it only represented Two Pence, would carry an ounce letter, and I think we may consider this a slight argument against a higher value for this stamp. Let us next see what help Messrs. Perkins Bacon and Co. the printers of the stamps—can render us. I have had one or two interviews with the manager and other members of this firm upon the subject of the different values, and by their kindness I am able to give you the following interesting information. The first supply, which, as I have already stated, was sent out on December 21st, 1848, consisted of blue and lilac stamps, no values being given in their books. These were followed in December, 1850, with blue and brown ; January

1852, blue and brown; September, 1852, One Penny, no colour given; February, 1853, red and blue; September, 1853, red; February, 1854, One Penny, red; July, 1854, One Penny, purple; December, 31st, 1855, and December, 1st, 1856, no colours or values given; June 24th, 1857, One Penny, red; and a further supply of One Penny, red, stamps on each of the following dates : February 17th and October 26th, 1858 ;* April and August 5th, 1859; March 24th, 1860, and so on to 1862. You will notice there were never more than two colours ordered at the same time, and these only for the first few consignments, which is certainly strange if three values were wanted for the service. Taking these particulars into consideration, with what I have previously said, I would suggest that the brown, red, lilac, and purple stamps probably each represented One Penny at different periods, while the blue may have done duty during the first year for Two Pence, but afterwards for only One Penny. I am aware in making this suggestion I am entirely at variance with all former writers upon the subject, but not one of these, so far as I have been able to discover, had any good reason for assigning the values they did—of Six Pence to the blue and One Shilling to the lilac. It would certainly be interesting to know how in the first instance these values came to be given to these two stamps. The earliest work I possess that gives any values to these stamps is the English translation of M. Moens' *Catalogue* by Dr. C. W. Viner, published in 1864. In this book, at page 114, the following remarks will be found : "NOTE.—The value of the red stamp is 1 penny, of the blues 6 pence, of the others 1 shilling." As I have no copy of the French edition from which the translation was made, I am unable to say whether this note is given on M. Moens' authority, or whether it was added by the editor, Dr. C. W. Viner. If on the former's, M. Moens appears to be now more undecided upon the subject, as in the sixth edition of his *Catalogue* he puts a note of interrogation after all except the red stamp, which he calls One Penny. Several writers have even added a fourth value to the first issue—viz., Four Pence—which they say was represented by the reddish-puce stamp on "blued" paper. I think, however, the majority of collectors are now agreed no such value existed at this time, and that the variety of colour was merely an early shade of the One Penny. I feel there is still a good deal to be said upon this difficult question of the values, but I hope you will consider the suggestions I have put forward are worthy of some consideration, should you not think them sufficient to prove my contention. At any rate, the information of Messrs. Perkins Bacon and Co., if they have made no mistake, helps to prove the purple stamp was One Penny, and not One Shilling, although it is still possible this stamp may have been issued as some other value during a portion of its existence.

I may add, Messrs. Perkins Bacon and Co. inform me that the same plate was used for printing all the stamps with unexpressed values. The plate was of steel and contained 110 stamps, arranged in eleven horizontal rows of ten.

We will now pass on to consider the native-printed stamps. These stamps were issued at different periods as provisionals, pending a fresh supply of the stamps then in use from England. According to dated specimens, there appear to have been at least three separate issues of these makeshifts. The first took place apparently in October, 1852; the second at the end of 1856; and the third towards the autumn of 1858. The earliest copy I have seen to which a date can be assigned is one of the first and best impressions of the blue, on a letter-sheet in the late Mr. Tapling's collection, post-marked Trinidad, October 10th, 1852 ; Barbadoes, October 12th, 1852.

---

*A supply of 4d., lilac, 6d., green, and 1s., purple stamps, with values expressed, was also sent out with this and the succeeding consignments.

Then I have seen another blue, not so good an impression, which was taken off a letter dated January 8th, 1857; and lastly, the very poor "blurred" copies are usually found on envelopes postmarked about the autumn of 1858.

Mr. Taylor tells me the stamps were produced by a French artist named Charles Pétit, who was living in the island at that time, and he sends me the following short account of his history, which he has obtained from one of his people. Charles Pétit, who was an engraver and lithographer, was born at Bordeaux, in 1822 or 1823. He left France after the third revolution and the deposition of Louis Philippe, his father having lost most of his property during that eventful period, having been engraver, lithographer, and printer to the Government. The subject of our sketch went from Bordeaux to Surinam, also to Demerara, Cayenne, Barbadoes, and Venezuela. He then went to Trinidad, where he only remained two years. He left in September, 1853, for New York, for the benefit of his health, but died at sea during the voyage there.

Mr. Taylor further informs me, the stones from which the stamps were printed are still preserved in the Colonial Secretary's Department at Government House. They are both ordinary lithographic stones of a light greyish colour. The one I designate A, is in shape an irregular narrow upright rectangle, measuring 9 inches in length, by 3½ inches in width at the top, and 4½ inches at the bottom, and is 1¼ inches in thickness. It has only one design upon it, which is placed about 2½ inches from the bottom of the stone. The other, B, is an oblong, measuring 8¾ inches by 7¼ inches, with a thickness of 1½ inches. It bears fifty-four designs, arranged in six horizontal rows of nine stamps each. The design on the first is drawn reversed, and is engraved— *i.e.,* cut into the stone—while those on B are also reversed, but appear slightly raised. It is evident this was a lithographic transfer made in the usual way from A. Mr. Taylor has kindly sent me over the tracings of the two stones I now hand round for your inspection. He obtained these by placing the face of the stones on the card and drawing his pencil round them. He has also, as you will observe, located the exact position of the designs as they exist upon each. The cut on stone A is quite fresh and very distinct, so that if more than one transfer had been taken we should not get the extremely poor blurred impressions we find among these stamps, and the gradual deterioration I have shown took place, by the postmarked copies I have already drawn attention to. No other stones or plates are to be found in the Colonial Secretary's Office, so there is little doubt, I think, that all the provisional stamps were produced from the two stones I have described. What I am not quite so sure of is, whether stamps were printed from stone A for issue to the public. The stone has blue colouring matter upon it, so impressions have evidently been taken off in this colour, but whether these were merely proof copies or not is, I think, uncertain. The process of printing stamps one at a time would be necessarily so tedious that, if resorted to at all, it would only have been so for a short period—say, during the manufacture of the lithographic transfer. On the other hand, we find some of the earliest of these stamps with such clear impressions that they have somewhat the appearance of engravings, and they have been actually described as such by several philatelic writers, one of whom, the late Captain H. O. Weare, in a paper on "The Stamps of Trinidad," published in *The Philatelical Journal* for April 15th, 1872, went so far as to state the specimens I now refer to were printed from an engraved copper-plate. My own belief is no stamps were printed from stone A for issue, and my opinion is corroborated by a horizontal pair of the earliest impressions in the late Mr. Tapling's collection. These two stamps show the same distance between each other as some of the later issued poor copies do, which certainly belong to stone B, and both stamps have also evidently been printed at one and the same time. I am consequently of opinion that all the native stamps ever issued were printed from stone B, and that the impressions taken from this stone gradually degenerated, partly from wear, and it may be partly from carelessness in the printing of the stamps after Mr. Pétit's death.

All conceivable shades of blue, from indigo to very pale and even blue-green, are known for these provisionals. The stamp is also found printed in shades of grey, which, judging from the impressions, was the last colour employed previous to the change to red. The paper also varies from pelure to thin card, the earliest and best impressions being usually found upon a yellow-toned paper. In some catalogues the grey stamp is put down as representing one shilling, but, like the so-called four pence of the first issue, most collectors now consider this a variety of colour only, and that the stamp had the same postal value as the blue.

Mr. Taylor tells me, in one of his letters, that stone B is very much blurred over with red colouring, thus proving the red stamp was the last printed. I notice M. Moens, in the sixth edition of his *Catalogue*, mentions the red stamp was reprinted in 1882. I do not know on whose authority this statement is made, but I should be more inclined to believe the stamps that turned up in some quantity about that date were remainders, of which there were probably many on hand, as the variety was so little used.

As regards the colour employed for these native stamps. It may be, blue was first selected as being the colour of the One Penny stamp then in use, or that the printer chose it in preference to any other, either on account, as he thought, of its better printing qualities, or because no supply of red "ink" was available. When the last lot of stamps was required in 1858, the colour would naturally be changed to red to conform to that of the One Penny then current, which we see from Messrs. Perkins Bacon and Co.'s list of stamps sent out had been red, without intermission, for sometime previously.

This completes all I have to say upon the native-printed stamps, but before concluding my paper I propose to give you copies of a few further postal notices I have extracted from *The Trinidad Royal Gazette*. The first institutes a postal delivery of correspondence within the towns of Port of Spain and San Fernando, letters, &c., having previously only been delivered when called for at the various post-offices. This notice appeared in *The Gazette* for August 11th, 1852 :—

NOTICE.

" *Postal Delivery within the Towns of Port of Spain and San Fernando.*

"GENERAL POST OFFICE, PORT OF SPAIN, *9th August*, 1852.

" His Excellency the Governor having authorised A DAILY POSTAL DELIVERY (Sunday excepted) within the *Towns of Port of Spain and San Fernando,* commencing this day, the undersigned hereby gives Notice thereof to the Public; and that in order to give greater facility to such delivery, it is necessary that Parties should direct their correspondents to add to the usual address on their Letters, &c., the name of the Street, and also the number of the House in which they reside. In the case of Merchants' Letters, however, these particulars will be unnecessary.

"(Signed)   JAS. H. O'BRIEN, *General Postmaster.*"

Mr. James H. O'Brien was appointed Postmaster of the General Post Office in Port of Spain on August 13th, 1851—the day before the commencement of the Inland Postal Service. The following is a list of the subsequent postmasters who have held office from that date to the present time : Mr. Ellys Layton succeeded Mr

O'Brien as Colonial Postmaster on 1st June, 1853; and Mr. William Eversley was appointed Postmaster-General of the Colony on December 14th, 1860. He was succeeded in 1865 by Mr. Charles Chipchase, who was followed on October 13th, 1866, by his brother, Mr. Henry Chipchase. The latter was succeeded, on January 1st, 1879, by Mr. J. W. O'Brien, who was a son of the Mr. O'Brien appointed in 1851. He remained in office until the year 1883, when the present Postmaster-General, Mr. J. A. Bulmer, who was formerly Postmaster of Cyprus, was appointed.

The next two notices are taken from *The Gazette* for October 20th, 1858, and January 5th, 1859, respectively.

"GENERAL POST OFFICE, *9th October*, 1858.
NOTICE

" Is HEREBY GIVEN, that *from* and *after this date* ALL LETTERS addressed to the UNITED KINGDOM must be PREPAID, in order to obviate the apprehended inconvenience of a large number of letters being detained, owing to the writers being ignorant of the new regulations, and thus posting them *unpaid;* the transmission of such letters for a further limited period, say, until 31st December next, has been sanctioned, but imposing on each a a fine of *Sixpence*, in addition to the Postage due upon them.

"(Signed)   ELLYS LAYTON, *Col. Postmaster.*"

" *Compulsory Prepayment of Letters to the United Kingdom.*

"GENERAL POST OFFICE, *27th December*, 1858.

"FROM FIRST JANUARY NEXT all Letters addressed to the UNITED KINGDOM *must be prepaid.* Any Letters posted *unpaid* will not be forwarded to their destination, but will be opened and returned to the writers. The Colonial Penny Stamps now in use will answer the purpose of prepaying Letters until such time as the requisite description shall have been received from England.

"(Signed)   ELLYS LAYTON, *Colonial Postmaster.*"

The last notice is particularly important, as you will observe it speaks of the postage to England being paid by the Colonial Penny stamps until the arrival of the required values. The rate to England at this period was six pence the ½ oz. ; so it is certain if other values had previously been in use in the island, only one penny stamps were in stock at this time. We see from the following notice, published in *The Gazette* for May 11th, 1859, that the four penny, six penny, and one shilling stamps, with the values expressed, were first issued on May 9th in that year :—

"GOVERNMENT HOUSE, *9th May*, 1859.

" POSTAGE STAMPS, representing 1s., 6d., 4d., and 1d., are now procurable, on application to Mr. EVERSLEY, the Confidential Clerk in the Colonial Secretary's Office, on the terms mentioned in the notice issued on the 24th February last.

"(Signed)   J. SCOTT BUSHE, *Colonial Secretary.*"

We shall find on referring to Messrs. Perkins Bacon and Co.'s list of the stamps sent out to the Island that the colour of the One Penny mentioned in this notice was red.

The above issue completes the list of the imperforate stamps of Trinidad, with the exception of one or two accidental varieties found among some of the later printings. I purpose breaking off my paper to-night at this point, and I have now given you as much of the history of these early imperforate stamps as Mr. J. G. Taylor and I have been able to collect together to this date. In conclusion, let me add, I regret I have been unable to produce sufficient official information to prove conclusively what were the actual postal values of the early stamps, but I hope by drawing fresh attention to the subject we shall not have long to wait for a decisive solution of this philatelic problem.

Since the publication of the preceding paper, I have had some further correspondence with Mr. Taylor, and I have also made a list of the dates, &c., of all the stamps, with unexpressed value I have seen on letter sheets or envelopes. But before giving the results of my subsequent investigations, I propose to make one or two remarks upon the contents of my earlier paper.

1. Mr. Taylor tells me I was wrong in stating that the first issue took place on August 14th, 1851. It was at this date that the *Inland* postal service was commenced, but the stamps had been employed on correspondence forwarded between Port of Spain and San Fernando (the two chief towns of the Island, both of which are on the coast), since April 11th, 1851, the time of the proclamation of the Ordinance I have given extracts from. The latter is therefore the more correct date for the first issue.

In connection with the starting of the Inland Post, I have found the following paragraph in the newspaper, *The Port of Spain Gazette*, in its issue of Friday, August 15th, 1851. "The working of the Inland Postal arrangements commenced on Thursday morning last (Lord Harris' birthday). Two mounted policemen left the General Post Office, in Frederick Street, at 8 o'clock in the morning with the letters for the eastern and western parts of the Colony; and the mails for the southern portion were duly forwarded by the steamer. We sincerely wish this undertaking, which commenced so appropriately on the anniversary of the birth of its noble originator, every sucess; and trust that the advantages, which cannot but result from it, will again and again recall to the minds of the inhabitants of this Colony the deep debt of gratitude they owe to his Excellency, Lord Harris, for his unceasing and energetic efforts for the improvement and prosperity of Trinidad." (Lord Harris was Governor of the Colony at this time.)

2. With regard to what I said about the "Lady McLeod" local, Mr. Taylor writes as follows: "The owners of the steamer used to carry letters at ten cents or five pence each, and as the people were in the habit of sending large pieces of money to pay, the captain used to be at his wits end to scratch up the small change, so the expedient of the stamp was adopted, and I still have the letter where one of the former partners of my business, writing to the other at San Fernando, advises him to buy some of Bryce's stamps." Mr. Taylor has since shown me the letter he refers to. It is dated April 28th, 1847, and has the following paragraph at the end: "You must buy some of Bryce's stamps at $4 per 100, or else we must pay a bit for each of your letters." The letter in question is franked with one of the local stamps.

Since writing the above, I have come across a file of the Trinidad newspaper before alluded to, *The Port of Spain Gazette*, and in the number for April 16th, 1847, I found the following notice, which gives the exact date of issue of the stamp, together with other particulars. The "Notice" is headed with a "cut" of a steamer:—

"THE Subscriber experiencing inconvenience in Collecting the Money for Letters of Non-Subscribers, has procured Labels, which may be had of him or the Agents for the Steamer, at five cents each, or Four Dollars per Hundred.

"No other Letters but those of subscribers who have paid in *advance*, or such as have these labels attached, will be carried, from and after the 24th instant.

"Freight for parcels and small packages as heretofore.

"(Signed)   DAVID BRYCE,
"16*th April*, 1847."   "*Proprietor.*

3. Referring to the "note" on the values of the first issued stamps, given in Dr. C. W. Viner's translation of M. Moen's *Catalogue*, published in ·1864, Mr. W. A. S. Westoby informs me, that the edition of M. Moens, from which the translation was made, only gives the value of one penny for the red stamp. Dr. Viner is therefore alone responsible for the values given for the remainder, and he is now unable to remember how he came to assign sixpence to the blue, and one shilling to the other colours.

4. Mr. Taylor tells me that what I said about the improbability of the "native" red stamps having been reprinted is quite correct. He says in one of his letters, "Moens' statement that the reds were reprinted in 1882 is quite a myth. It was in 1882 that the *remainders* of the reds were found in the Colonial Secretary's office, by Mr. Cunningham, with whom I am most intimate. He was allowed to take them, and he sold some to Mr. Hoffmann, who sold them in Germany and London that same year."

This concludes the list of remarks I have to make upon my first paper, and I now proceed to give particulars of my new researches.

With the object of determining the postal values of the early stamps, I have tabulated from time to time, every specimen I have seen upon a letter-sheet or envelope. The following is a copy of the table as it now stands :—

STAMPS PRINTED BY MESSRS. PERKINS BACON AND Co.

	COLOUR.	WHERE AND WHEN POSTED.	WHERE AND WHEN DELIVERED.	COLLECTION.	REMARKS.
1	Reddish - puce paper blued more or less	Port of Spain, Aug. 21, 1851	San Fernando	J. G. Taylor ..	One stamp, on large double letter-sheet. Contained no enclosure.
2	" "	" 23, "	" "	" "	" " "
3	" "	" "	" "	E. & A. W. Chambers	" " "
4	" "	" Sept. 3, "	" "	I. G. Taylor ...	" " "
5	" "	" 8, "	" "	" "	" " "
6	" "	" 13, "	" "	" "	" " "
7	" "	" " "	" "	" "	" " "
8	" "	" "	" "	E. & A. W. Chambers	" " "
9	" "	" 15, "	" "	I. G. Taylor ...	One stamp. Face of letter-sheet only with letter at back. Enclosed another letter.
10	" "	" 16, "	" "	" "	Two stamps, on large double letter-sheet. Enclosed three notes.
11	" "	" 22, "	" "	" "	One stamp, on large double letter-sheet. Contained no enclosure.
12	" "	" 30, "	" "	" "	" " "
13	" "	" Oct. 1, "	" "	" "	" " "
14	" "	" 2, "	" "	" "	" " "
15	" "	" 4, "	" "	" "	Four stamps, on large double letter-sheet. Enclosed several accounts.
16	" "	" 6, "	" "	" "	Two stamps, on large double letter-sheet. Contained enclosure.
17	" "	" 10, "	" "	" "	One stamp, on large double letter-sheet. Contained no enclosure.
18	" "	" 16, "	" "	" "	" " "
19	" "	" 24, "	" "	" "	" " "
20	" "	Nov. 4, "	" "	" "	" " "
21	" "	" 12, "	" "	" "	" " "
22	" "	" 16, "	" "	" "	One stamp, on small double letter-sheet. Contained no enclosure.
23	" "	" 17, "	" "	" "	One stamp, on large double letter-sheet. Contained no enclosure.
24	" "	" 27, "	Barbadoes, Nov. 29, 1851	C. K. Tapling ...	One stamp. Face of letter-sheet only, with letter at back. "4" in writing on the face.
25	" "	" Dec. 3, "	San Fernando	J. G. Taylor .	Two stamps, on large double letter-sheet. Enclosed two notes.
26	" "	" 8, "	" "	" "	One stamp, on large double letter-sheet. Contained no enclosure.
27	" "	" 10, "	" "	" "	Two stamps, on large double letter-sheet. Enclosed another letter.
28	" "	" 17, "	" "	" "	Two stamps, on large double letter-sheet. Enclosed an invoice.
29	" "	" 18, "	" "	" "	One stamp, on large double letter-paper. Contained no enclosure.

Stamps Printed by Messrs. Perkins Bacon and Co.—*Continued.*

	Colour.	Where and When Posted.	Where and When Delivered.	Collection.	Remarks.
30	Reddish - puce paper blued more or less.	Port of Spain, Dec. 22, 1851	San Fernando ...	J. G. Taylor ...	One stamp; on large double letter-paper. Contained no enclosure.
31	,, ,,	,, 23, ,.			
32	,, ,,	... ...	Barbadoes, Dec. 31, 1851	O. N. Biggs ..	One stamp, on large double letter-sheet. Contained no enclosure. " 4 " in writing on the face.
33	,, ,,	,, Mar. 29, 1852	San Fernando ..	J. G. Taylor ...	One stamp, on small double letter-sheet. (Printed notice from Colonial Bank)
34	Blue, on blued paper.	,, Dec. 29, 1851	,, ,, ...	E. & A. W. Chambers	One stamp, on medium size double letter-sheet. Enclosed a letter and also a delivery order.
35	,, ,,	Trinidad, April 14, 185.	Barbadoes, April 16, 185.	C. N. Biggs	One stamp. Face of letter-sheet only, without letter " 4 " in writing on the face.
36	,, ,,	,, ...	,, June 13, ,,	T. K. Tapling ...	One stamp, only on part of letter-sheet.
37	,, ,,	Trinidad, Sept. 25, 185	,, Sept. 27, ,,	Pemberton Wilson & Co.	One stamp. Face of letter-sheet only, without letter " 3 " in writing on the face.
38	,, ,,	,, Oct. 28, ,,	,, Oct. 30, ,,	T. K. Tapling..	One stamp. Face of letter-sheet only, with letter at back. Contained list of prices current. " 4 " in writing on the face.
39	,, ,,	,, Nov. 9, ,,	,, Nov. 11, ..	Pemberton Wilson & Co.	One stamp. Face of letter-sheet only, with letter at back. Contained an enclosure. " 5 " in writing on the face.
40	,, ,,	San Fernando Sept. 29, 1853	Port of Spain ..	J. G. Taylor ...	Six stamps, on large double letter-sheet. Contained several enclosures.
41	Grey, on blue paper.	Port of Spain, Dec. 26, 1851	San Fernando ...	E. & A. W. Chambers	One stamp, medium size double letter-sheet. Contained no enclosure.
42	,, ,,	San Fernando, Feb. 9, 1852	Port of Spain ...	J. G. Taylor ...	One stamp, on large double letter-sheet. Contained no enclosure.
43	,, ,,	,, 23, ,,	,, ,, ...	,, ,, ...	One stamp, on small double letter-sheet. Contained no enclosure.
44	,, ,,	Trinidad, Mar. 30, ,,	Barbadoes, April 1, 1852	Pemberton Wilson & Co	One stamp. Face of letter-sheet only. " 4 " in writing on the face.
45	,, ,,	,, Dec. 14, ,,	,, Dec. 14, ..	O. N. Biggs ..	One stamp. Face of letter-sheet only, with letter at back. States P/C is annexed. " 4 " in writing on the face.
46	,, ,,	,, June 25, 1852	... ...	T. K. Tapling ...	One stamp, only on part of letter-sheet.
47	,, ,,	,, July 10, ,,	Barbadoes, July 12, 1852	,, ,, ...	One stamp. Face of letter sheet only, with letter at back. States P/C is annexed, " 4 " in writing on the face.
48	Grey, on white paper	San Fernando, Jan. 21, 1855	Port of Spain ...	J. G. Taylor ...	One stamp. Face of letter-sheet only.
49	Purple, on white paper	Cedros, Nov. 17, 1854	,, ,,	E. & A. W. Chambers	One stamp, on small double letter-sheet. Contained no enclosure.
50	Red, on blued paper	Trinidad, Nov. 26, 1853	Barbadoes, Nov. 28, 185:	Pemberton Wilson & Co	One stamp. Face of letter-sheet only. " 4 " in writing on the face.
51	,, ,,	,, Jan. 9, 1854	London	E. & A. W. Chambers	One stamp, on large double letter-sheet.
52	Red-brown, on blued paper	Arima, June 3, ,,	Port of Spain ...	,, ,, ..	One stamp, on large double letter-sheet. Contained no enclosure.
53	,, ,,	Port of Spain, July 24, ,,	San Fernando ...	J. G. Taylor ...	One stamp, on large double letter-sheet. Contained no enclosure.
54	Red, on blued paper	San Fernando, Aug. 23, 1855	Port of Spain ..	,, ,, ..	One stamp, on small envelope.
55	,, ,,	,, 30, ,,	,, ,,	,, ,, ..	One stamp, only on part of letter-sheet.
56	,, ,,	,, Nov. 6, ,,	,, ,,	,, ,, ..	Two stamps, on small envelope.
57	,, ,,	,, Dec. 20, ,,	,, ,,	,, ,, ..	One stamp, on small envelope.
58	,, ,,	,, Jan. 18, 1856	,, ,,	,, ,, ..	One stamp, on letter-sheet. ,,
59	,, ,,	,, Mar. 22, ,,	,, ,,	,, ,, ..	One stamp, on small envelope.
60	,, ,,	,, 24, ,,	,, ,,	,, ,, ..	,, ,, ,,
61	,, ,,	,, July 11, ,,	,, ,,	,, ,, ..	,, ,, ,,
62	,, ,,	,, July 11, ,,	,, ,,	,, ,, ..	Two stamps, on large envelope.
63	,, ,,	,, Oct. 10, ,,	,, ,,	,, ,, ..	Two stamps, on large double letter-sheet. Contained enclosures.
64	Red, on slightly blued paper	,, April 21, 185 7	,, ,,	,, ,, ..	One stamp, on large double letter-sheet. Contained no enclosure.
65	,, ,,	,, Sept. 21, ,,	,, ,,	,, ,, ..	One stamp, on large double letter-sheet. Contained no enclosure.
66	Rose-red, on white paper	Trinidad, Nov. 9, ,,	Barbadoes, Nov. 11, 1857	Pemberton Wilson & Co	One stamp. Face of letter-sheet only, with letter at back. States P/C is annexed " 4 " in writing on face struck out, and " 5 " written in place.
67	,, ,,	,, 25, ,,	,, 27, ,,	,, ,, ,,	,, ,, ,,
68	,, ,,	,, Dec. 10, ,,	,, Dec. 12, ,,	T. K. Tapling ...	,, ,, ,,
69	,, ,,	San Fernando, Dec. 4, ,,	Port of Spain ...	J. G. Taylor ...	One stamp, on small envelope.
70	,, ,,	,, July 3, 1858	,, ,,	,, ,, ..	One stamp, on letter-sheet.
71	,, ,,	Couva, Mar. 23, 1859	,, ,,	,, ,, ..	One stamp, on small envelope.
72	,, ,,	San Fernando, Mar 29. ,,	,, ,, ...	,, ,, ..	One stamp, on letter-sheet.

x

STAMPS PRINTED IN THE ISLAND.

	COLOUR.	WHERE AND WHEN POSTED.	WHERE AND WHEN DELIVERED.	COLLECTION.	REMARKS.
73	Blue, on yellowish paper (1st stage)	Trinidad, Oct. 10, 1852	Barbadoes, Oct. 12, 1852	T. K. Tapling ...	One stamp. Face of letter-sheet only. "8" in writing on it.
74	,, ,,	,, (date indistinct)	,, ,, 30, ,,	C. N. Biggs ...	One stamp. Face of letter-sheet only. "4" in writing on it.
75	Pale blue ,,	San Fernando, Oct. 30, 1852	Port of Spain	J. G. Taylor ..	One stamp, on medium size double letter-sheet. Contained a cheque.
76	Blue	,, Dec. 18, ,,	...	,, ,, ...	One stamp, only on part of letter-sheet.
77	Blue, on thin bluish card	San Fernando, Mar. 8, 1853	...	,, ,, ,,	,, ,, ,,
78	,, ,,	,, May 12, ,,	...	,, ,, ,,	,, ,, ,,
79	Pale blue-green, on thin yellowish paper (2nd Stage)	,, April 4, 1855	...	,, ,, ,,	,, ,, ,,
80	,, ,,	,, 5, ,,	...	,, ,, ...	,, ,, ,,
81	,, ,,	,, 7, ,,	...	,, ,, ...	,, ,, ,,
82	,, ,,	,, 13, ,,	...	,, ,, ...	,, ,, ,,
83	,, ,,	,, 21, ,,	...	,, ,, ...	,, ,, ,,
84	,, ,,	,, May 2, ,,	...	,, ,, ...	,, ,, ,,
85	,, ,,	,, 10, ,,	...	,, ,, ...	,, ,, ,,
86	,, ,,	,, 11, ,,	...	,, ,, ...	,, ,, ,,
87	,, ,,	,, 25, ,,	...	,, ,, ...	,, ,, ,,
88	,, ,,	,, June 5, ,,	...	,, ,, ...	,, ,, ,,
89	,, ,,	Port of Spain, June 8, ,,	San Fernando	,, ,, ...	One stamp, on large double letter-sheet. Contained a receipt.
90	,, ,,	San Fernando, June 9, ,,	...	,, ,, ...	One stamp, only on part of letter-sheet.
91	,, ,,	,, 12, ,,	...	,, ,, ...	
92	Blue-green (3rd stage)	,, Nov. 2, 1856	Port of Spain	,, ,, ...	One stamp, on small envelope.
93	,, ,,	,, Dec. ,,	...	,, ,, ...	
94	Blue	,, Jan. 8, 1857	...	T. K. Tapling ...	One stamp, taken off letter with this date by Mr. M. Burnett.
*95	Dark blue	Trinidad, Nov. 9, 1858	Baltimore, U.S.A. Nov. 30, 1858	Burger & Co. ...	One stamp. Face of letter-sheet only. Figure "8" in red-chalk pencil on face.
96	Slate-blue (4th stage)	San Fernando, Jan. 18, 1879	Port of Spain	J. G. Taylor ...	One stamp, on medium size letter-sheet. Contained two enclosures.
97	,, ,,	Couva, Mar. 12, 1860	,, ,,	,, ,,	One stamp, on small double letter-sheet. Contained no enclosure.
98	,, ,,	,, 24, ,,	,, ,,	,, ,,	One stamp, on large double letter-sheet. Contained no enclosure.
*99	,, ,,	Trinidad, April 7, ,,	Baltimore, U.S.A. April 28, 1860	Burger & Co ...	Four stamps, and one (id.) red punctured perforation. Face of letter-sheet only. Figure "4" in red chalk pencil on the face.
100	,, ,,	Couva, April 12, ,,	Port of Spain	J. G. Taylor ...	One stamp, on small double letter-sheet. Contained no enclosure.
101	,, ,,	,, 20, ,,	,, ,,	,, ,, ...	,, ,, ,,
102	,, ,,	,, 30, ,,	,, ,,	,, ,, ...	One stamp. Face of letter-sheet only : with letter at back. Contained no enclosure.
103	,, (almost grey)	,, May 1, ,,	,, ,	,, ,, ...	One stamp, on large double letter-sheet. Contained no enclosure.
104	Slate-blue	,, 29, ,,	,, ,,	,, ,, ..	One stamp. (Sold Cheveley & Co.'s sale 19/4/90.)
105	,, ,,	,, June 12, ,,	,, ,,	,, ,, ..	One stamp, on small double letter-sheet. Contained no enclosure.

The above lists are, in my opinion, sufficient to prove the suggestion I made in my first paper, that the value of all the various coloured stamps was the same, viz.: one penny, is the correct one.

Numbers 1 to 33 inclusive are franked with the stamp that has sometimes been catalogued as four pence. A large majority of these letter-sheets passed between Towns in the Island, the postal rate for which was one penny per half ounce, so it is perfectly clear that the value of the reddish-puce stamp was one penny. It will be noticed, that when a letter contained an enclosure either half the sheet was torn off as in number 9, or extra stamps were added, where the weight was over the half ounce. The same remarks apply to numbers 35 to 94, & 97 to 105, both inclusive,

---

*These two letters were forwarded viâ St. Thomas. On the former, the St. Thomas postmark is dated November 11th, 1858, and on the latter, April 13th, 1860. Each letter has in addition a large circular postmark with "Steamship" round the inner curve, and in the centre "20" in numerals on the first, and "10" on the second.

and it is equally clear that the blue, grey-lilac, purple, red, and the native printed blue all had the same postal value of one penny. It might possibly be argued from numbers 34 and 96, that the value of the blue stamp was two pence, and it certainly looks as if these two letters must have been over half an ounce in weight, considering they each contained two enclosures. But this is only conjecture, and in face of the other letters, which were under the half ounce, I am inclined to think that *if* these two letters were over that weight, they were insufficiently stamped, and were passed unnoticed through the Post. This certainly must have been the case with No. 96. There is still another alternative as regards number 34, which I alluded to in my first paper, viz.: That the blue stamp might have been issued at first as two pence, and later on the value was reduced to one penny, but as this is the only letter I have come across that supports such an hypothesis, I consider it is untenable. It will be noticed that some of the letters sent to Barbados have a figure " 4 " or " 8 " written upon the face. This was evidently the unpaid foreign postage of four pence per half ounce and eight pence per one ounce which was collected on the delivery. The fact of some of *these* letters being marked " 8," and consequently over half an ounce in weight, does not effect the value of one penny for the Trinidad stamp upon them, as they were all sent from Port of Spain, and we see from Clause VIII. of the Ordinance of April 4th, 1851, that letters posted at the General Post Office of this Town for foreign places only required a one penny stamp, whatever their weight might be. Numbers 66, 67 and 68 are curious. A figure " 4 " has been written upon the face, and has been struck out, a numeral " 5 " being added in its place. I am unable to give the explanation of this, but presume it had reference to some alteration made in the rate on Trinidad letters at Barbados.

The following notice appeared in the newspaper, *The Port of Spain Gazette*, for August 22nd, 1851 :—

NOTICE.

" GENERAL POST OFFICE, PORT OF SPAIN,

" *22nd August*, 1851.

" THE UNDERSIGNED begs to direct the attention of the Public to the Ordinance now in force " for establishing an Inland Post and Rates of Postage within the Colony," by which it is enacted that on all Letters received at this Office from places beyond the limits of the Colony, and on those posted thereat for such places, there shall be paid one uniform rate of one penny—the penny postage stamp being affixed to every such letter when posted, and a penny being paid at the time of delivery at this Office.

" It is also enacted, in the case of all such Letters posted or received at any *Inland* Post Office, that the rates of Postage shall be paid *according to weight*.

" Newspapers are to be received at and dispatched from this Office *from* and *to* places *beyond the limits* of the Colony free of Inland Postage, but are liable to a penny each when transmitted by Post from one place to any other place *within the Colony*, which may either be on posting or on delivery.

" (Signed)   JAMES H. O'BRIEN,

" *Postmaster General.*"

I have given a copy of this notice, as the wording seems to corroborate to some extent the theory that the postage stamps in use were all of one value, as it states " *the* penny postage stamp being affixed," &c. If stamps of other values were on sale, it is surely reasonable to suppose the word " the " would have been replaced by the article " a."

The tables, besides determining the values of the stamps, give some idea of the dates at which the various colours did duty. The so-called reddish-puce seems to have been that first issued, while the blue and grey-lilac first appear towards the end of December, 1851, the purple about the autumn of 1854, and the red from 1853 onwards.

The native-printed blue stamps were in use more frequently than I previously thought was the case. The first issue of them seems to have lasted from October, 1852, to June, 1853, the second from April to July, 1855, the third from November, 1856, to February, 1857, the fourth from the autumn of 1858, to February, 1859, and the fifth from March to July, 1860. The table also shows the different shades of blue for the various printings.

The only piece of new information I can give respecting the production of the native stamps, is a copy of the following interesting and important original document, which Mr. Jas. H. O'Brien, the first Postmaster-General of Trinidad, has found amongst his papers, and which is now in my possession.

" *Memo.*

"Mr. Pétit agrees to make. say, 4,000 or 5,000, Postage Stamps, the same as those now in use, of a different colour if necessary, and to put on the gum, for $5 the thousand.

" He also agrees to allow some person appointed for that purpose to be present and see that that number only is struck off.

" And he further agrees that the Stone from which they are struck off shall be afterwards handed over to the Government, and, when called upon to do so, to deface it in the presence of Witnesses.

" He can have them done by Saturday, and the gum is to be of the necessary preparation for preserving the stamps from vermin.

" (Signed)   JAS. H. O'BRIEN.

" Appd.¹
J. L. W.
" Genl. Post Office,
15th *Sept.*, 1851.

" S. 5,000 to be struck off in the presence of a Police Constable, and the stone left in the Postmaster's hands till required again.

"(Signed)   J. L. W."

" Appd. J. L. W.", and the note at the foot is in the handwriting of Mr. J. Lushington Wildman, at that time the Colonial Secretary.

We see from the memorandum the number of the native stamps first printed was 5,000, and we also learn the price paid Mr. Pétit for his work, which seems little enough considering he had to find the whole of the materials. The curious part about this document is the date, " 1851." The earliest post-marked specimen of these stamps, at present known, is dated October 10th, 1852, just over a year later. It is stated in the last paragraph that the stamps could be ready by the following Saturday, which looks as if they were urgently required, and they would therefore be probably first issued about September 21st, which would coincide sufficiently with the used copies but for the year. Again, if we refer to my table of dated specimens, we find no break in the use of Messrs. Perkins Bacon's stamps in 1851, and it is strange that with all the number of stamps that have been found upon letter-sheets, no specimen of these native productions are known with the date of this year. Once more, if we look at the list of stamps sent out by Messrs. Perkins Bacon and Co., we shall see there were two consignments of blue, one of lilac, and one of brown or reddish-puce, in stock at the commencement of 1851, so there should have been no want of stamps that year, especially as the *Inland* postal service was only started on August 14th. Putting all these circumstances together, it really appears as if the date of the letter was inaccurate, and that it should be 1852. It is certainly an unaccountable mistake, especially for an official to make, but I can see no other way out of the difficulty, unless the stamps were printed off in September, 1851, and kept for a year before being issued.

With regard to the deterioration that took place in the later issues of these stamps, I can add the following explanation, which was given me by a practical lithographer, whose firm has printed large numbers of postage stamps by this method. He told me that for every separate printing of stamps, they took fresh lithographic transfers from the original engraved die, so as to assure satisfactory results. He said, that if a " stone " was put away for future use, after printing off a supply, great care should be taken that it was properly cleaned, so that the ink was not allowed to " cake " on the stone, otherwise after impressions would be smudgy and indistinct. Even if this precaution was taken, the later printings would never equal the earlier ones. Mr. Pétit, as I have said, died in 1853, and it is possible no one else in the Island knew how to make a new transfer, when the fresh supplies of stamps were wanted. Anyhow, no second transfer was ever made, and the gradual degeneration of the stamps is accounted for by the ink being allowed to accumulate and cake on the stone after each separate printing, until, when the last was made in vermilion, the design becomes almost undecipherable.

As every collector knows the early stamps of this Colony were obliterated by a postmark containing a number. This number represented the Office at which the letter was posted, and the following list, furnished by Mr. Bulmer, gives the names of all the first Post Offices in the Island with the corresponding numbers that used to be attached to them :—

1.	Port of Spain.	13.	Diego Martin.	25.	(Vacant.)
2.	San Fernando.	14.	Moruga.	26.	Erin.
3.	St. Joseph.	15.	St. Mary's.	27.	Monos.
4.	St. Juans.	16.	Chaguanas.	28.	Mucurapo.
5.	Santa Cruz.	17.	Couva.	29.	(Vacant.)
6.	Arouca.	18.	Princes Town.	30.	Carapichaima.
7.	Arima.	19.	Oropouche.	31.	Caroni.
8.	Toco.	20.	La Brea.	32.	St. Ann's.
9.	Manzanilla.	21.	Cedros.	33.	Maraval.
10.	Mayaro.	22.	Claxton Bay.	34.	Cunupia.
11.	Tunapuna.	23.	The Cedros Steamer.	35.	California.
12.	Blanchisseuse.	24.	St. Madelaine.	36.	Carenage.

A few other Offices have since been opened, but no number was attached to some of them, as this system was given up some years ago. Each Office now possesses a date stamp with its own name. The list is useful, more especially for determining the values of the early stamps, as one can tell on reference to it what towns an envelope or letter-sheet passed between, when the letter, as is so often the case, is missing.

The four pence, six pence, and one shilling stamps issued on May 9th, 1859, were printed from steel plates constructed by Messrs. Perkins Bacon and Co., each plate containing 240 specimens arranged in twenty horizontal rows of twelve. These plates, together with that employed for the stamps with unexpressed values, were handed over to the Crown Agents on the 28th January, 1862, and afterwards by them to Messrs. De la Rue and Co. The latter firm have since printed all further supplies of stamps required by the Colony, the set with large perforation measuring 11¼, being probably the first lot printed by them. The stamps with this perforation were issued in 1863, as is proved by a letter-sheet in the possession of Mr. Graham Taylor, which is franked with the carmine stamp, and is postmarked November 4th of that year. Proof impressions in black upon white card, struck from the dies of the four pence, six pence, and one shilling are known.

After the notice dated May 9th, 1859, given at the end of my first paper, I have found nothing further in *The Gazette* touching upon stamps, until early in the year 1879, when the Island was admitted into the Postal Union. This notification is found in the number of *The Gazette* for March 26, 1879.

" GENERAL POST OFFICE,

" *24th March*, 1879.

" THE following Notices are published for general information, and the attention of the Public is particularly requested thereto : —

ALTERATION IN RATES OF POSTAGE.

" In consequence of the new Postal Convention signed at Paris on the 1st June, 1878, for the revision of the Treaty of Berne, constituting the General Postal Union, the following alterations in the rates of Postage and conditions of Transmission of correspondence of various kinds between the United Kingdom and the British Colonies mentioned in the margin will be made on 1st April, 1879.

> Bermuda.
> British Guiana.
> British Honduras.
> Jamaica.
> Trinidad.
> Mauritius and its dependencies.
> The Gold Coast.
> Sierra Leone.
> Gambia.
> Lagos.
> Falkland Islands.

" LETTERS.—The rate of postage will be reduced from 6d. to 4d. per fifteen grammes, when prepaid. Unpaid letters will be charged double, viz., 8d. per fifteen grammes. Insufficiently prepaid letters will be charged on delivery with double the amount of the deficiency of the prepaid rate, instead of, as at present, with the unpaid rate less the value of the stamps affixed.

" POST CARDS.—The issue of Post Cards will no longer be optional as heretofore. The postage for each card will be 1½d., instead of 3d. Prepayment is compulsory.

" Post Cards must not exceed the following dimensions :—

Length, 14 centimetres = 5½ inches.

Width, 9   ,,   = 3½   ,,

They must bear the superscription " *Universal Postal Union,*" followed by the name of the Colony (to be repeated in the French language).

" OTHER ARTICLES.—

" REGISTRATION.—

" LIMIT OF WEIGHT AND SIZE.—

" REDIRECTION.—

" PROHIBITED ARTICLES.—

PILLAR LETTER BOXES.

" Postage Stamps may be purchased at the shops immediately opposite the Pillar Boxes on the St. Ann's Road, and at the Police Station, Picton Street.

POST CARDS.

" Post Cards for Countries of the Postal Union will be issued on and after the first April next, from which date it is also intended to issue *Inland* Post Cards at the same rate as for Letters, viz., *one penny each*.

"(Signed)   Jas. W. O'Brien,

" *Postmaster General.*"

The above notices, among other particulars, give the date of issue of the first postcards. A Postal Union three halfpenny card was printed in the Island for provisional use, until a supply could be obtained from England. A card for Inland service was issued, as we see, at the same time. This was also printed in the Island, and was similar in design to the Postal Union card, but for the inscription and the colour, which was black in place of vermilion, the colour of that for the Postal Union card. Both these cards were franked by adhesives. The Inland card could have had but a limited circulation, as specimens of it are very seldom met with, in fact as far as my experience goes I consider it should rank as one of the rarest postcards in existence. The high price asked for the card, one penny, would certainly militate against its use, and as a letter could be sent at the same rate, I cannot see the object of its emission. The use of the card, even as a Government issue, has never been authentically proved to collectors before, but the notice I have reproduced finally disposes of the question. That the card really was issued is proved by used specimens in the hands of one or two collectors, Mr. Taylor possessing a copy postmarked April 28th, 1879.

We see from the next notice, taken from *The Gazette* of March 8th, 1882, that the rates to certain of the adjacent Islands were reduced on April 1st of that year; and the notice also gives the date of issue of the one penny postcard for use to these places.

NOTICE

" Is hereby given that on and after the 1st APRIL next the following rates will be collected on correspondence to Tobago, Grenada, St. Vincent, and Barbados, viz:—

On Letter, per ½ oz.	2½d.
On Post Cards (each)	1d.
On Newspapers, Printed Papers, Books, &c., per 2 oz. ...	½d.
Commercial Papers—Same as Printed Papers, except that the lowest charge for each packet is	2½d.
Patterns—Same as Printed Papers, except that the lowest charge for each Packet is	1d.

" Post Cards on which a penny stamp may be affixed will be ready for issue on the 1st April.

"(Signed)   Jas. W. O'Brien,

" *Postmaster General.*

" *8th March,* 1882."

The card mentioned in the notice was printed in the Island and used provisionally, until a supply of the required value could be obtained from England. Besides the usual inscription, it bore the words " For Countries within 300 miles served by British Packets." The notice gives a list of these places, and from the limited number, it is evident the use of the card was restricted.

The next notice was published in *The Gazette* of March 21st, 1883.

" General Post Office,

"15*th March,* 1883.

" A REGULAR HALFPENNY POSTAGE STAMP being now in circulation, the half of a Penny stamp which has been for some time used will not be recognised after the 1st of April next.

"(Signed)   O'Conl. Fitzgerald,

" *Acting P.M.G.*"

Ever since the issue of the provisional three halfpenny card on April 1st, 1879, which was franked at first with one and half another penny adhesive, the use of half a penny stamp as a halfpenny seems to have been permitted, even after a supply of halfpenny stamps had been received from England. Altogether four varieties of the one penny stamp are found divided, viz. : the stamp without expressed value, the same stamp surcharged in black "one penny," the provisional one penny on six pence, and the one penny carmine of Messrs. De la Rue and Co.'s design. The halfpenny referred to in the notice was the green stamp with the head of Her Majesty, similar in type to the one penny carmine just mentioned. These two adhesives with a two pence halfpenny ultramarine and four pence grey, were issued in January or February, 1883. I have found no mention in *The Gazette* of the issue of the halfpenny mauve of the old "Britannia" type, with the value surcharged in black. The earliest post-marked copy I have seen is dated August 8th, 1879.

The following appeared in *The Gazette* of August 6th, 1884 :—

RATES OF POSTAGE.

On and from 1st July, 1884, the undermentioned Rates of Postage will be collected in Trinidad.

INLAND.

"LETTERS.   Not exceeding ½ oz.   ...   .   1d.
         Every additional ½ oz.   ...   .   1d.

"POSTCARDS.   Official Postcards impressed with a halfpenny stamp may be transmitted between places in Trinidad with Letters printed or written upon the back.   Adhesive Stamps are not accepted in payment of Postage on Post Cards.

"NOTE.—Postage Stamps, Post Cards, Registered Letter Envelopes, and Newspaper Wrappers of the following denominations may now be obtained at the General Post Office, Port-of-Spain, and the Post Offices at San Fernando and Couva. At all other Post Offices in Trinidad all the undermentioned (except 1s. and 5s. Postage Stamps) may be obtained, viz. :—

POSTAGE STAMPS.	POST CARDS.		REGISTERED LETTER ENVELOPES.	NEWSPAPER WRAPPERS.	
	Single	Double or Reply.		½d.	1d.
½d.	½d.		Of two sizes.	Available Inland, and for Grenada, Barbadoes, St. Vincent, and Tobago,	Available outside the Colony. Where the Postage exceeds 1d. the additional sum should be affixed in Postage Stamps.
1d.	1d.	2d.			
2½d.	1½d.	3d.	2d. each.		
4d.	2d.	4d.			
6d.					
1s.					
5s.					

"NOTE.—The Post Cards, Registered Letter Envelopes, and News-paper Wrappers are sold to the Public at their face value.

"(Signed)   J. A. BULMER,
                        "*Postmaster General.*

' GENERAL POST OFFICE,
    "TRINIDAD, *June*, 1884."

The Registration envelopes and newspaper wrappers mentioned in the above were probably issued for the first time at the date of the notice, as they are not described in *The Philatelic Record* or the *Timbre-Poste* previously to August and October, 1884. The postcards, with the exception of the reply two penny, which did not appear in the magazines until February, 1887, were chronicled in the first named Journal, in March, 1884. We may therefore give March 1st of that year as the date of issue of all the cards, with the exception of the reply two penny, which may be put down as June, 1884. The last NOTE of the notice, respecting the price of post-cards, &c., is worthy of the attention of the Officials of Great Britain, who might well follow a similar course.

The set of "unpaid letter" stamps was brought into use on January 1st, 1885, and the following memorandum was sent round by the Postmaster to the chief commercial houses in the Island. A copy was forwarded by Mr. J. Graham Taylor to the Editor of *The Philatelic Record*, and was published in the number of that paper for December, 1884.

" GENERAL POST OFFICE, PORT-OF-SPAIN,
" 17th November, 1884.

MEMORANDUM.

" On and after 1st January, 1885, the sum to be collected in Trinidad from the addressee, on unpaid and insufficiently-paid correspondence, will be represented by a special stamp or stamps similar to the specimen below. These stamps will be affixed to the cover of the letters, &c.

" With a view to expediting the delivery of mails by abolishing the present system of debiting unpaid charges in the books of this department, and also of preventing errors by over-charges, I beg to solicit your co-operation by providing your messenger, on the arrival of each mail, with a sum sufficient to cover the charges on any unpaid or insufficiently-paid correspondence, so that such charges may be collected when the correspondence is delivered.

" From the date mentioned all registered and unpaid correspondence for your firm arriving by the English mail will be delivered in the room set apart for delivery to private box-holders together with the ordinary correspondence.

" I am, gentlemen,
" Your most obedient servant,
" (Signed)   J. A. BOLMER,
" *Postmaster General.*"

The next notice is taken from *The Gazette* of July 22nd, 1885.

NOTICE.

" ON and from the 1st September, 1885, all Postage Stamps (other than those described below) issued in this colony prior to 1st September, 1883, will become obsolete, and will not after that date be accepted in prepayment of postage.

" Anyone having such Postage Stamps may, before the above date, exchange them for their value in the current issue Stamps on application at the General Post Office, Port-of-Spain.

Current issue of Trinidad Postage Stamps.

½d. Green.	Head of Queen Crowned to left on shaded
1d. Pink.	circle. Inscription " TRINIDAD POSTAGE,"
2½d. Blue.	in curved label above. Value in words on
4d. Slate.	lower part: ornamental angles, colour on
6d. Olive.	white.
1s. Brown.	

5s. Rose, large rectangular.

" (Signed)   J. A. BULMER,

" GENERAL POST OFFICE, TRINIDAD,   " *Postmaster General.*
" 20th July, 1885."

Y

The next and concluding notice I have to give, refers to a reduction in the postal rates to the Island of Tobago. It is found in *The Gazette* of January 9th, 1889.

NOTICE.

" On and from this date the Inland rate of Postage will be charged on all Postal matter forwarded from Trinidad to Tobago.

"(Signed)   J. A. BULMER,
" *Postmaster General.*

" GENERAL POST OFFICE, TRINIDAD,
" 1*st January*, 1889."

REFERENCE LIST OF THE PHILATELIC SOCIETY, LONDON.

Issue I. April 11th, 1851.

One Value. Engraved in *taille-douce* and printed by Messrs. Perkins Bacon and Co., of London. Coloured impression on medium wove unwatermarked paper, varying in substance. Yellowish gum, unperforated. Design : Figure of Britannia, on enginc-turned background, seated on bales of merchandise, her right hand holding a spear and her left arm resting on a shield, charged with the Union Jack. In the right background there is a three-masted ship in full sail. A straight coloured label at the bottom of the stamp contains the name of the Colony in white block letters. There are white square blocks in the four corners, each containing an eight-rayed star with a white centre. White reticulated borders at the top and sides. The design is completed by an outer line of colour. The stamps have no expressed value. Shape upright rectangular. (*Illustration* 265.)

n. " TRINIDAD."

A.—On paper blued by chemical action of the ink.
    (1d.) reddish-puce (shades).
    (1d.) blue, dull blue, pale to deep   (shades).
    (1d.) grey, brownish-grey, dark grey (,,)
    (1d.) brick-red, pale to deep   (,,)

B.—On white paper.
    (1d.) blue, dull blue.
    (1d.) dark grey, brownish-grey (shades).
    (1d.) brick-red, brownish-lake (,,)

Remarks.—With the exception of the blue, the shades of each colour are very numerous. Full particulars relating to the values will be found in Mr. E. D. Bacon's Papers, as well as a detailed list showing the dates when the various colours were in use.

Issue II. October, 1852.

One Value. Provisional issue. Engraved on stone by M. Charles Pétit in Trinidad, and printed by means of lithographic transfers. Coloured impression on yellowish, bluish, and white wove unwatermarked paper, varying greatly in substance. Yellowish gum. Unperforated. Design : The design is an imitation of that of the preceding issue, but the fancy reticulated border is replaced by thin parallel lines, and the stars in the four corners have four instead of eight points. The flag of the ship is blowing to the right instead of to the left, and the background is composed of oblique crossed lines. Shape upright rectangular. (*Illustrations* 266, 267, 268, 269.)

B. " TRINIDAD."

(1d.) blue, pale to deep, Prussian blue, indigo   (shades).

(1d.) grey, pale to deep, greenish-grey, brownish-grey (,,)

(1860) (1d.) dull red, pale to deep (shades).

Remarks.—The shades of this stamp are almost endless, and it is not easy to find two alike. There appear to have been several separate editions of these provisionals, for particulars of which, and of the values, see Mr. E. D. Bacon's Papers. The printings took place pending the arrival of fresh supplies of the engraved stamps of Messrs. Perkins Bacon and Co. The stamps may be divided into three sets, distinguishable from each other by the stages of wear of the impressions, but specimens belonging to intermediate stages also exist. Some discussion has taken place as to whether the earliest specimens were printed from an engraved plate, but the information given by Mr. Bacon in his papers seems to prove beyond all doubt that no such plate ever existed. The stamps (to the number of 54 to the sheet) were reproduced by lithographic transfer from one matrix engraved on stone ; but while it is possible that a few of the clearest impressions were printed singly from the matrix, it is far more probable that all were printed from the stone with the 54 designs, which is still in existence in the Colonial Secretary's Department at Government House at Trinidad. If an engraved plate as well as an engraved stone had been employed as matrices, there would have been two varieties of type. None such are known.

Issue III. May 9th, 1859.

Four values. Engraved in *taille-douce* and printed by Messrs. Perkins Bacon and Co. Coloured impression on stout white wove unwatermarked paper. Yellowish gum, unperforated. Designs : That of the one penny is the same as Issue I. The design of the others is similar, but the values are now given in the bottom label, and the name of the Colony is printed in a curve in the upper portion of the stamp. The value is printed in white on colour, and is in block type for the FOUR PENCE and ONE SHILLING, and in Roman capitals for the SIX PENCE. The name of the Colony for all three values is printed in white block letters. Shape, upright rectangular. (*Illustrations* 265, 270.)

B. " TRINIDAD."   T. " TRINIDAD."   D. " FOUR PENCE."   " SIX PENCE."   " ONE SHILLING."

(1d.) rose-red (shades).

4d., dull lilac, dark brown-lilac, grey-lilac (shades).

6d., yellow-green   (shades).

1s., indigo, purple-blue (,,)

Issue IV. End of 1859.

Four values. Same in all respects as the stamps of the preceding issue, but machine perforated. The stamps may be classified according to their perforations as follows, and all four values are found with each. (*Illustrations* 265, 270.)

A.—Roughly punctured, compound, 12½ to 16.

B.—Clean cut perforation, compound, 12½ to 16.

C.—Clean cut perforation, 15½ all round.

(1d.) dull red, brick-red, brownish-red (shades).

4d., dull lilac, dark grey-lilac, dark brownish-lilac (shades).

6d., yellow-green, dark green (shades).

1s., indigo, purple-blue (shades).

Remarks.—The varieties of the compound perforations are, of course, exceedingly numerous. As in other cases, no detailed list of them is given, it being considered that the above classification will prove sufficient for all practical purposes. A copy of the one penny with roughly punctured perforation, has been seen on a letter-sheet postmarked October 25th, 1859, and a specimen of the same stamp with clean cut perforation 15¼ on an envelope dated November 1st, 1861.

Issue V. 1863.

Four values. Same in design, &c., as the stamps of the preceding issue, but the paper is slightly surfaced, and the perforation is regular and clean cut, gauging 11½ all round. The stamps are of slightly smaller dimensions. (*Illustrations* 265, 270.)

    (1d.) deep red   (slight shades).
    4d., deep lilac   (,, ,,)
    6d., deep yellow-green (,, ,,)
    1s., indigo   (,, ,,)

Remarks.—These stamps were printed by Messrs. De la Rue and Co., and the differences in size may probably be accounted for by the shrinkage of a new kind of paper, which seems harder and more glossy than that previously employed.

Issue VI. 1864-1866.

Four values. Printed by Messrs. De la Rue and Co. Coloured impression on white wove paper, varying in substance, watermarked Crown C.C. White gum, machine perforated 12¼. Designs : Same in all respects as those of the preceding issue. (*Illustrations* 265, 270.)

    (1d.) red, brownish-red, red-violet, brownish-lake (shades).
    4d., lilac, grey-lilac, mauve, grey-black   (,,)
    6d., green, dark green, yellow-green, emerald-green (,,)
    1s., mauve, purple (shades).

Varieties. All four values exist unperforated, and were undoubtedly postally used in this condition.

Issue VII. 1869.

One value. Engraved and surface-printed by Messrs. De la Rue and Co. Coloured impression on medium white wove surfaced paper, watermarked Crown C.C. White gum, machine perforated 12¼. Design : Diademed profile of Queen Victoria to left on ground of horizontal lines within a circle of one white and two coloured lines. A circular band, filled in with arabesques, enframes the above, and its outer line touches the sides and the top and bottom labels, which are of solid colour and inscribed with white Roman capitals. The spandrels are filled in with arabesques, and two plain outer lines, one white and the other coloured, complete the design. Shape, large upright rectangular. (*Illustration* 271.)

    T. "TRINIDAD." B. "FIVE SHILLINGS."
    5s., dull lake (shades).

Variety. A specimen exists unperforated and postmarked.

Issue VIII. 1872.

Two values. Same as the stamps of Issue VI., but changed in colour. Paper, watermark, &c., as before. Machine perforated 12½. (*Illustration* 270.)

    4d., neutral grey (shades).
    1s., orange-yellow (,,)

Remarks.—The one shilling is known fraudulently surcharged with a large "4d." in black.

Issue IX. 1876 (?).

Four values. Same as to design, paper, &c., as the stamps of Issues VI. and VIII., but machine perforated 14. (*Illustrations* 265, 270.)

(1d.) red, brownish-red (shades).
4d., neutral grey.
6d., green, emerald-green (shades).
1s., orange-yellow.

Variety. The one penny was allowed to be divided in 1879, and each half used as a halfpenny value. The halves are found cut sometimes vertically, sometimes diagonally.

Issue X. 1879-1882.

One value. The design is precisely the same as that of the one penny of Issue IX., but the stamp is printed in pale mauve, and surcharged HALFPENNY across the lower portion in black block letters 3 mm. in height, the surcharge being 16 mm. in length. Machine perforated 14. (*Illustration* 272.)

A.—Watermarked Crown C.C. placed sideways.
½d., black surcharge on pale mauve.
B.—Watermarked Crown C.A. (1882).
½d., black surcharge on pale mauve.

Remarks.—This stamp is sometimes found *deep brown* in colour. The variety is believed to be due to a change in colour of the mauve stamp, probably from accidental causes.

Issue XI. April, 1882.

One value. The design is precisely the same as that of the one penny of Issue IX., but the stamp is watermarked Crown C.A., and surcharged ONE PENNY across the lower portion in black block letters 3 mm. in height, the surcharge being 16 mm. in length. Machine perforated 14. (*Illustration* 272.)

1d., black surcharge on vermilion-red.

Variety. Cut in half and used as a halfpenny value.
(½d.) black surcharge on vermilion-red.

Issue XII. May, 1882.

One value. Provisional issue. This is the six pence of Issue IX., surcharged "1d." by hand in red or black ink, and the original value obliterated by a thick or thin bar of the same colour. Paper, watermark, &c., as before. (*Illustrations* 273, 274.)

A.—Surcharged in red.

(i.) Thin red bar, 1d., red surcharge on 6d. green, emerald-green (shades).
(ii.) Thick red bar, 1d., „   „   „ 6d. „ (shades).

Varieties.   *a.* Double red bar across value, 1d., red surcharge on 6d. green.
b. Cut in half and used as a halfpenny value.

B.—Surcharged in black.

1d., black surcharge on 6d. green.

Remarks.—The earliest postmarked copy of this surcharged stamp known to the Society is dated May 9th, 1882.

Issue XIII. 1882 (?).

One value. Same in all respects as the four pence of Issue IX., with the exception of the watermark, which is changed to Crown C.A. Paper, perforation, &c., as before. (*Illustration* 270.)

4d., neutral-grey.

Issue XIV. 1883-1884.

Six values. Engraved and surface-printed by Messrs. De la Rue and Co. Coloured impression on medium white wove paper, watermarked Crown C.A. White gum, machine perforated 14. Design: Diademed profile of Queen Victoria to left on background of horizontal lines, within a treble-lined circle, the centre line being coloured, and the outer and inner lines white. Above and following the shape of the circle there is a curved coloured label containing an inscription in white block letters. Below, and extending across the stamp, there is a straight white label containing the value in coloured block letters. The spandrels and corners are filled in with arabesques, and the design is completed by a double outer line of colour. Shape, upright rectangular. (*Illustration* 275.)

T. "TRINIDAD POSTAGE." B. "HALFPENNY." "ONE PENNY." "TWO PENCE HALFPENNY."
"FOUR PENCE." "SIX PENCE." "ONE SHILLING."

(January (?) 1883.) ½d., dull green   (slight shades).
(„   ) 1d., rose-red   („   „   )
(„   ) 2½d., ultramarine   („   „   )
(„   ) 4d., grey   („   „   )
(Early in 1884.) 6d., olive-brown   („   „   )
(„   ) 1s., orange-brown („   „   )

Variety. The one penny is known cut in half and used as a halfpenny value.
(½d.) rose-red.

UNPAID LETTER STAMPS.

Issue I. January 1st, 1885.

Nine values. On the 1st January, 1885, a series of stamps was brought into use to denote the charge on unpaid or insufficiently prepaid letters. Engraved and surface-printed by Messrs De la Rue and Co. Black impression on medium white wove paper, watermarked Crown C.A. White gum, machine perforated 14. Design : A white circular space, enframed with a single black circular line, constitutes the centre of the design, and contains the value in fancy block numerals. Above and below, and following the shape of the circle, are two curved bands of colour, containing the name of the Colony and an inscription in white block letters. A narrow rectangular fancy patterned border enframes the circle and the curved bands, and is impinged upon by both. The spandrels consist of white triangular blocks, and the design is completed by an outer line of colour. Shape, upright rectangular. (*Illustrations,* 276, 277.)

T. "TRINIDAD." B. "SURCHARGE POSTAGE."

½d., grey-black.
1d., „   „
2d., „   „
3d., „   „
4d., „   „
5d., „   „
6d., „   „
8d., „   „
1s., „   „

TOO LATE STAMPS.

Various stamps of certain of the preceding issues are to be met with surcharged "TOO LATE" in black or red block letters, and with the same surcharge double or inverted. No such stamps were ever sold to the public in Trinidad. The varieties are entirely devoid of Philatelic interest, and owe their existence to obliging post office officials, the surcharges being nothing more than *griffes de complaisance*, made for the benefit (?) of collectors.

REGISTRATION ENVELOPES.

Issue I. 1880.

Three sizes. Bag-shaped envelopes of white wove, linen-lined paper, with inscriptions, &c., in *blue*, as on the first issue for Jamaica, but in different type. On the flap is an arched label, bearing the words FOR REGISTRATION ONLY in block letters, in plain relief on a solid *green* ground. (*Illustration* 291.)

Without expressed value, green and blue, size F.
        „   „   „   „ G.
        „   „   „   „ K.

Remarks.—These envelopes have under the flap the inscription : McCORQUODALE & Co. CONTRACTORS, printed in blue block letters, and beneath this in a straight line, in black block letters, McCORQUODALE & Co.'s PATENT REGISTERED ENVELOPE.

Issue II. June, 1884.

One value. Similar to the envelopes of Barbados Issue II., with a large letter " R " in an upright oval frame in the left upper corner, and the flap to the right. The stamp is embossed in colour on the flap. Design : Diademed profile of Queen Victoria to left, in plain relief on a solid ground of colour, enclosed within a circular band bearing inscriptions in coloured block letters on a reticulated ground ; this is surrounded by an outer border of a white and a coloured line with eight scallops, the same design as that of the stamp on the one penny Registration Envelopes of Barbados. (*Illustrations* 28, 305.)

T. "TRINIDAD REGISTRATION." B. "TWO PENCE."

2d., blue, grey-blue, size F.
2d., „   „   „ G.

Remarks—The inscription under the flap in blue, is—

McCORQUODALE & Co.   CONTRACTORS.
LIMITED.

Towards the end of 1890, a modification was made locally to size G of these envelopes. To obviate the difficulty of opening the linen-lined envelope a line of perforations is run across near the right-hand side, through the flap and the two thicknesses of the envelope, and on the flap is printed in *red*, To WITHDRAW CONTENTS, CUT AWAY PER—FORATED PORTION OF ENVELOPE, in thick block letters in two lines. Across the lower part of the back (not the address side) of the envelope is printed, also in *red*, " If any investigation is required to be—made about this letter the envelope must—accompany the complaint," in three lines.

WRAPPERS.

Issue I. June, 1884.

Two values. Similar to the wrappers of Barbados, and with a stamp on the ONE PENNY of the same design as that on the Barbados wrapper of the same value. The stamp on the HALFPENNY wrapper bears the same profile in a circle without the festooned border ; the inscriptions are in similar lettering, on plain curved labels above and below, and the whole is enclosed in a rectangular frame with the corners tapered off, and small white ornaments on a solid ground in the spandrels. (*Illustrations* 292, 293.)

T. "TRINIDAD." B. "HALFPENNY." "ONE PENNY,"

½d., green.
1d., carmine.

Issue II. 1885.

One value. Provisional issue. The one penny wrapper of the previous issue, with the stamp surcharged in black HALFPENNY in block letters across the centre, and with four horizontal lines across the original value. *(Illustration 294.)*

½d., black surcharge, on 1d. carmine.

Variety.—With *five* horizontal lines across the original value.

½d., black surcharge, on 1d. carmine.

POST CARDS.

Issue I. April 1st, 1879.

Two values. Designed and printed in the Island upon stout white card. Size, 134×85 mm., or $5\frac{3}{10}×3\frac{2}{3}$ inches, varying somewhat in dimensions. Design: The cards have a heavy chain pattern border, measuring 119×74 mm., or $4\frac{7}{10}×2\frac{9}{10}$ inches. The upper part of the card is divided by a chain pattern, similar to the border, into an oblong rectangle for the inscription, and a square in the right upper corner for the stamp, the bottom of the square consisting merely of a plain straight line. The chain pattern at the bottom of the rectangle, is interrupted by the insertion of THE ADDRESS ONLY TO BE WRITTEN ON THIS SIDE. in thin block letters, between two straight lines. The square contains in the centre the word STAMP. in slanting capitals reading upwards. The links at the four corners of the card, and at the corners of the rectangle and square, are circular, and are filled in with rosettes. The lower part of the card has four straight dotted lines for the address, the bottom one being shorter than the others. The rectangle on the one penny card contains the following inscription: TRINIDAD. in Roman capitals in the left upper corner, and lower down in the centre INLAND POST CARD. in large fancy capitals in a straight line. The inscription on the three halfpenny card is in three straight lines, 1st. "Postal Union—(Union Postale Universelle.)" in lower case Roman type; 2nd. TRINIDAD to left, in Roman capitals; 3rd. FOREIGN POST CARD. in large fancy capitals. The stamp employed for the Inland card, was the red adhesive, without expressed value, of the "Britannia" type, while the three halfpenny value was made up by the same stamp, and half another divided vertically down the centre, until the issue of the "Britannia" halfpenny adhesive took place, when the latter was used in conjunction with the one penny just mentioned. *(Illustrations 295, 296.)*

A.—For Inland service.

Without expressed value (1d.) black impression: franked by a (1d.) red adhesive.

B.—For Countries in the Postal Union.

Without expressed value (1½d.) vermilion impression: franked by one and half another (1d.) red adhesives.

Without expressed value (1½d.) vermilion impression: franked by one ½d. mauve and one (1d.) red adhesives.

Remarks.—The above cards were issued provisionally pending a supply from England. The three halfpenny was replaced by the card next to be described, while the one penny, to judge from its rarity, seems to have been but little used. This is readily accounted for by the excessive charge made for the card, as a half ounce letter could be sent at the same rate.

Issue II. August (?), 1879.

One value. Designed and printed by Messrs. De la Rue and Co. upon medium light buff card. Size 121×87 mm., or $4\frac{3}{4}×3\frac{2}{5}$ inches. The inscription is the same as that of the first issue card of Antigua, except that the second line is altered to TRINIDAD (TRINITÉ.) The stamp is in the right upper corner. Design: Diademed head of Queen Victoria to left, upon ground of horizontal lines, enclosed within a circular band of solid colour, inscribed TRINIDAD above, POSTAGE below, in plain block letters, the two words being separated at either side by a star-like ornament. Plain straight label below the band inscribed PENNY HALFPENNY in thin block letters. Conventional ornaments in the spandrels and a plain outer line of colour completes the stamp. The card has no frame. (*Illustration* 297.)

1½d., brown (shades).

Issue III. April 1st, 1882.

One Value. Designed and printed in the Colony, as a provisional issue, upon thick cream card. Size 122×88 mm. or 4⅞×3⅜ inches, but varying somewhat in the dimensions. The inscription is in five straight lines at the top of the card, 1st. UNION POSTALE UNIVERSELLE in block letters; 2nd. TRINIDAD (TRINITÉ) in Roman capitals; 3rd. POST CARD in large Roman capitals, the two words being separated by the Arms and Supporters of Great Britain; 4th. FOR COUNTRIES WITHIN 300 MILES SERVED BY BRITISH PACKETS. in small Roman capitals; 5th. THE ADDRESS ONLY TO BE WRITTEN ON THIS SIDE. in tall block letters. In the right upper corner, there is a small upright rectangle for the stamp, composed of four plain straight lines. Outside the frame are the words POSTAGE STAMP. at the top, and ONE PENNY at the bottom in small Roman capitals. The card is without frame. (*Illustration* 298.)

1d., black impression, franked by a 1d. adhesive.

Remarks.—All three varieties of the one penny adhesive, in use during the issue of this card, may be found upon it, viz., the one penny red, without expressed value, the same stamp surcharged ONE PENNY in black, and the provisional one penny surcharged with pen and ink upon the six pence green.

Issue IV. March 1st (?), 1884.

Four values. Designed and printed by Messrs. De la Rue and Co.; the half-penny upon thick white, and the other three values upon stout straw card. Size of the halfpenny 121×75 mm., or 4⅞×2⁹⁄₁₀ inches; that of the one penny, three half-penny, and two pence 139×88 mm., or 5½×3½ inches. The inscription on the half-penny is in four lines—1st. INLAND; 2nd. POST CARD, with the Arms and Supporters of Great Britain between the two words; 3rd. TRINIDAD; 4th. THE ADDRESS ONLY TO BE WRITTEN ON THIS SIDE. The first and third lines are in Roman capitals, the second in large fancy capitals, and the fourth is in small block letters. The inscription on the other three values is like that on the card of Issue II., but the one penny has (FOR COUNTRIES WITHIN 300 MILES) in small Roman capitals added in a straight line beneath THE ADDRESS ONLY, &c., and the two pence has (FOR INDIA AND COUNTRIES IN THE EAST—VIA UNITED KINGDOM), added in two straight lines, in the same type and position as the extra inscription on the one penny, the word VIA being in Italic capitals. The stamp on all four cards is in the right upper corner, and is of the same design as that on the second issue cards of Antigua, but for the change in the name of the Colony. (*Illustrations* 300, 301, 302, 303.)

½d., red-brown   (slight shades).
1d., carmine   („   „   )
1½d., dark brown („   „   )
2d., dark blue   („   „   )

z

REPLY PAID CARDS.

Issue I. March 1st (?), 1884.

Three values. Similar in every way to the single cards of corresponding value of Issue IV., but with the usual additional inscription added to each half, as on the reply cards of Antigua. The cards are joined along the top, perforated 4, and the design is impressed upon the first and third pages. (*Illustrations* 301, 302, 303.)

1d.+1d., carmine   (slight shades).

1½d.+1½d., dark brown (.,   ,,   )

(June, 1884) 2d.+2d., dark blue (,,   ..   )

LOCAL STAMP.

Issue April 16th, 1847.

Without expressed value. Engraved in *taille-douce* and printed upon stout yellowish wove unwatermarked paper, unperforated. Design : A steamer sailing to right, below which is the monogram L.McL. in white fancy letters. The background of the stamp is composed of vertical coloured lines, which are crossed around the steamer and monogram by horizontal coloured lines. The design is completed by a narrow border of reticulations. Shape upright rectangular. (*Illustration* 278.)

Without expressed value (2½d.), dark blue.

Remarks.—This " local " was issued by the owner of the steamer *Lady McLeod*, previous to the introduction of postage stamps, for the pre-payment of letters carried between the ports of San Fernando and Port of Spain, the two chief towns of the Island. The stamps were sold at two pence halfpenny for a single copy, or at the rate of two pence each if one hundred were purchased together. The obliteration usually consisted of a "cross" in pen and black ink. For further information concerning this stamp see Mr. Bacon's papers.

TURKS' ISLANDS.

PRELIMINARY NOTES.

By E. D. BACON.

THESE Islands, Mr. J. C. Crisson, the present postmaster, informs me, take their name from the melon or Turk's head cactus, which was found in abundance on them at the time of their discovery. The Colony has never possessed an *Official Gazette*, but Government notices appear in the newspaper, *The Royal Standard and Gazette of the Turks and Caicos Islands*, published at Grand Turk, Turks' Islands.

The following notice taken from the number of that paper for April 6th, 1867, gives the date of issue of the first set of postage stamps.

NOTICE.

" HIS Honor the President, and Executive Council, having authorised the immediate use of POSTAGE STAMPS in this Colony, the Public are hereby informed that such Stamps can be had at this Office on any day during *Office hours*.

" By Order,

"(Signed)   ROBERT J. DARRELL,

" *Postmaster*.

" POST OFFICE, GRAND TURK,

" *4th April*, 1867."

These stamps, it is known, were three in number, one penny, six pence, and one shilling. They were engraved and printed by Messrs. Perkins Bacon and Co. upon unwatermarked paper, and the plates, which were of steel, each contained 30 specimens, arranged in three horizontal rows of ten. The plate of the one penny was finished on November 6th, 1866, that of the six pence on November 17th, and that of the one shilling on November 20th, the same year. Proof impressions in black, on plain white paper, are known of the three values, taken from the plates, as well as proofs in black on white card, struck from the engraved dies. I have also seen proofs in black of the one penny upon blue, and upon yellow paper. The three plates were handed over to the Crown Agents on the 18th March, 1881, and were afterwards given by them to Messrs. De la Rue and Co., who have since printed all further supplies of stamps required by the Colony.

The following dates of printings are taken from one of Messrs. Perkins Bacon and Co.'s books, to which specimens are attached. These stamps are all upon " star " watermarked paper.

One penny, lake, 1873.

One penny, pale lake, Sept., 1875.

One penny, vermilion, Nov., 1878.

Mr. Crisson informs me that the rates of postage, at the time of the introduction of stamps, were as follows :—

> To England, 1s. per ½ oz.
> „ West Indian Colonies, 6d. per ½ oz.
> Newspapers, 1d. each.

And he says at that time there was no intercolonial postage.

The Islands joined the Universal Postal Union on the 1st January, 1881, the date the first provisional stamps were issued, the new values being required for the reduced rates which then came into operation. A three halfpenny card should also have been issued at the same date, but this was evidently beyond the resources of the Colony to produce, so the inhabitants were compelled to wait until the receipt of one from England, which did not arrive until some months later. Mr. Crisson tells me the following notice was published in July, 1881 :—

POST OFFICE NOTICE.

"THE Turks and Caicos Islands joined the Postal Union on the first of January, 1881, and the following rates of Postage are published for general information :—

> Letters, 4d. per half-ounce.
> Post Cards, 1½d. each.
> Reply do., 3d. „
> Newspapers, 1d each, if under 4 oz.

Books and other printed matter (except newspapers) 1d. per two ounces.

Commercial papers, the same as for printed paper, but a minimum charge of 2½d.

> "(Signed)   J. C. CRISSON,
> "*Postmaster.*

" POST OFFICE, TURKS' ISLANDS,
"*25th July,* 1881."

One would naturally think from the above that single and reply cards were to be had at the Post Office in July, 1881, but I believe the latter was not issued until several years afterwards, as it was not described in the Philatelic journals until 1885.

The file of newspapers I have had access to, is a very incomplete one, and I have found no further notice with reference to postal matters sufficiently interesting to reproduce here, neither can I add any new particulars about the provisional or later issued stamps, beyond those given in the Reference List of the Society.

REFERENCE LIST OF THE PHILATELIC SOCIETY, LONDON.

Issue I. April 4th, 1867.

Three values. Engraved in *taille-douce*, and printed by Messrs. Perkins Bacon and Co., of London, on stout white wove unwatermarked paper. Yellowish gum, machine perforated 11½, 12½. Design : Diademed profile of Queen Victoria to left on reticulated ground, within a narrow white oval band. At the top and bottom of the oval, and following its curves, are plain coloured labels with rounded ends, inscribed in white block letters, with the name of the Colony above and the value below. The remainder of the stamp, which is of upright rectangular shape, having the four corners cut off, is filled in with reticulations, and the design is completed by a single outer line of colour. (*Illustration* 279.)

T. "TURKS' ISLANDS." B. "ONE PENNY." "SIX PENCE." "ONE SHILLING."

> 1d., dull rose (shades).
> 6d., black, brownish-black (shades).,
> 1s., slate-blue (shades).

Remarks.—A specimen of the one shilling in the late Vice-President's collection is of a shade nearly approaching that of the six pence. Whether this is an error or not is not known.

Issue II. 1873.

One value. The one penny of the preceding issue, printed upon stout white wove paper, watermarked with a six-rayed star. Machine perforated $11\frac{1}{2} \times 15$. (*Illustration 279.*)

> 1d., dull rose-lake (shades).

Issue III. 1879.

Two values. The one penny and one shilling of Issue I. changed in colour, and printed upon stout white wove paper, watermarked with a six-rayed star. Machine perforated $11\frac{1}{2} \times 15$. (*Illustration 279.*)

> 1d., vermilion (shades).
> 1s., lilac („)

Remarks.—The six pence is given in the *Catalogue* of M. Moens, as found with star watermark, but no specimen is known to the Society.

Issue IV. January 1st, 1881.

Three values. In consequence of the admission of Turks' Islands into the Universal Postal Union, three new values of a halfpenny, two pence halfpenny and four pence were required, and these were temporarily provided by surcharging the stamps issued in 1867 and 1879 described above, with numerals of value in black. There are a large number of varieties in the surcharges, and illustrations are given of all the more prominent types. The stamps were in use for some months, and more than one arrangement of the types took place. The surcharge $\frac{1}{2}$ (d.) on the one penny (*Illustration 299*), consists of fifteen varieties twice applied on the entire sheet of thirty stamps. The two pence halfpenny was formed of the same varieties with a numeral 2 (with a straight or curved foot) placed before the $\frac{1}{2}$. Only three varieties of the numeral are known of the 4 (d.).

$\frac{1}{2}$ (d.) black surcharge, on 1d., 1879 (*Illustration*	„	- - - - - 299.)
$\frac{1}{2}$ (d.)	„	„ 6d., 1867 (	„	- - - - - 299.)
$\frac{1}{2}$ (d.)	„	„ 1s., 1867 (	„	- - - - - 299.)
$\frac{1}{2}$ (d.)	„	„ 1s., 1879 (	„	- - - - - 299.)
$2\frac{1}{2}$ (d.)	„	„ 1d., 1879 (	„	280, 281, 282, 283.)
$2\frac{1}{2}$ (d.)	„	„ 6d., 1867 (	„	- - - - - 283.)
$2\frac{1}{2}$ (d.)	„	„ 1s., 1867 (	„	- - 280, 281, 282.)
$2\frac{1}{2}$ (d.)	„	„ 1s., 1879 (	„	280, 281, 282, 283.)
4 (d.)	„	„ 1d., 1879 (	„	- - 284, 285, 286.)
4 (d.)	„	„ 6d., 1867 (	„	- - 284, 285, 286.)
4 (d.)	„	„ 1s., 1879 (	„	- - 284, 285, 286.)

Variety. With double surcharge.

> $\frac{1}{2}$ (d.) black surcharge, on 1s., 1867.

Remarks.—Several of the stamps are known with the surcharge inverted, but the authenticity of these varieties requires confirmation.

Issue V. September, 1881.

Four values. Printed by Messrs. De la Rue and Co., on white surfaced paper, watermarked Crown C.C., which is found sideways on the one penny, six pence and one shilling. White gum, machine perforated 14. Designs : Three of the values are the same as those of Issue I., and are printed from the old plates engraved by Messrs. Perkins Bacon and Co. That of the FOUR PENCE is as follows : Diademed profile of Queen Victoria to left on ground of horizontal lines within a single-lined octagon. Straight white labels at top and bottom, inscribed in coloured block letters. The borders at the sides of the stamp contain rows of white diamonds, and the spandrels are filled in with foliate ornaments. As in the case of other stamps of this type the labels are printed separately from the central part of the design. Shape, upright rectangular. (*Illustrations* 279, 287.)

T. " TURKS' ISLANDS." B. " FOUR PENCE."

1d., vermilion-red (shades).
4d., ultramarine („)
6d., black-brown („)
1s., greenish-slate („)

Issue VI. 1882-1884.

Four values. Similar designs to the last issue, the two new values of a half-penny and two pence halfpenny being like the four pence. Printed by Messrs. De la Rue and Co., upon white surfaced paper, watermarked Crown C.A. White and yellowish gum, machine perforated 14. (*Illustrations* 279, 287, 288.)

(Jan., 1882) ½d., sea-green to blue-green.
(1883) 1d., brownish-orange.
(Jan., 1882) 2½d., red-brown.
(End 1884) 4d., grey.

Issue VII. July (?), 1887-89.

Three values. The design is the same as for Issue I., and the stamps are printed from the old plates of Messrs. Perkins Bacon and Co. by Messrs. De la Rue and Co. on medium white wove paper, watermarked Crown C.A., machine perforated. (*Illustration* 279.)

A.—Perforated 12.
(July (?), 1887) 1d., carmine (shades).
B.—Perforated 14.
(July (?), 1889) 1d., carmine (?).
(July (?), 1887) 6d., olive-brown (shades).
(March (?), 1889) 6d., pale chestnut-brown (shades).
(July (?), 1887) 1s , deep brown (shades).

Remarks.—The one penny carmine of this issue is chronicled in *The Philatelic Record* for August, 1889, *perforated* 14, but this variety has not been met with by the Society.

Issue VIII. May (?), 1889.

One value. The two pence halfpenny of Issue VI., surcharged " One Penny " in lower case type, with a capital initial letter to each word. The surcharge measures 16 mm. in length. Watermark Crown C.A. Machine perforated 14. (*Illustration* 289.)

1d., black surcharge, on 2½d . red-brown.

REGISTRATION ENVELOPES.

Issue I. 1881.

Two sizes. Similar in every respect to the registration envelopes issued in Jamaica on the 1st January, 1881. They likewise bear no impressed stamp, and both postage and registration fee are paid by means of adhesives. (*Illustration* 192.)

Without expressed value, blue, size G.
,,   ,,   ,,   ,,   ,,   H.

Issue II. 1885 (?).

Two sizes. These envelopes are the same as those of the second issue of Jamaica, with a large letter " R " in an upright oval frame on the face, in the left upper corner, and the flap on the right instead of on the left, as in the last issue. (*Illustration* 28.)

Without expressed value, blue, size G.
,,   ,,   ,,   ,,   ,,   H.

POSTCARD.

Issue I. 1881.

One value. Designed and printed by Messrs. De la Rue and Co., on medium light buff card. Size 121 × 87 mm., or $4\frac{4}{3} \times 3\frac{3}{3}$ inches. The design is the same as that of the first issue card of Antigua, except that the second line of the inscription is replaced by TURKS' ISLANDS (ILES DE TURC), and the name of the Colony at the top of the stamp is changed. (*Illustration* 304.)

1¼d., light brown (slight shades).

REPLY PAID CARD.

Issue I. 1885.

One value. Designed and printed by Messrs. De la Rue and Co., on stout straw card. Size 139 × 88 mm., or $5\frac{1}{2} \times 3\frac{1}{2}$ inches. The design is a counterpart of that of the single card, with the usual additional inscriptions, similar to those found on the reply paid cards of Antigua. The cards are joined along the top, perforated 4, and the design is impressed upon the first and third pages. (*Illustration* 304.)

1¼d.+1¼d., light brown (slight shades).

VIRGIN ISLANDS.

PRELIMINARY NOTES.

By E. D. BACON.

As in the case of Nevis, I am indebted to Mr. T. Maycock for much of the information I am enabled to give concerning the stamps of these Islands. The stamps, down to the year 1877, were supplied by Messrs. Nissen and Parker, of London. They have usually been described as typographed, but this was not so, for all the Virgin Islands stamps sent out by the firm I have mentioned, were produced by lithography. A single die for each of the four values was engraved on steel, and lithographic transfers taken from these dies were made upon stone. These transfers were cleaned off the stone when the number of stamps required had been printed, and a fresh transfer was taken for each supply ordered. In the one shilling value two printings were necessary, and it appears, from the information Mr. Maycock has received, that the central figure of the Virgin was type printed from a series of "letter press" blocks, and was not printed like the remainder of the design from a lithographic stone.

The following is a list of the various consignments of stamps, with the dates they were sent out from England.

1866.				
November 26	...		20,000	1d.
"	...		2,000	1d.
"	...		10,000	6d.
"	...		1,000	6d.
1867.				
July 12	...		10,000	4d.
"	...		2,000	4d.
"	...		10,000	1s.
"	...		1,000	1s.
1868.				
June 6	...		1,000	1d.
"	...		1,000	4d.
"	...		1,000	6d.
"	...		1,000	1s.
"	...		1,000	1s.
1870.				
October 25			2,000	1d.
1871.				
January 12			2,000	1d.
March 21			3,500	1d.
September 6			4,000	1d.
1872.				
February 7			6,300	1d.

1873.		
March 15	2,000	1d.
1874.		
January 1	4,000	1d.
October 14	7,000	1d.
1876.		
September 2	6,000 ...	1d.

The first two consignments appear to have been split up for some reason, and 2,000 each of the one penny and four pence, and 1,000 each of the six pence and one shilling were forwarded direct to Sir Arthur Rumbold, the President administering the Government; the remainder of each parcel being sent to St. Thomas. The first lot of one penny and six pence forwarded on November 26th, 1866, were perforated 12, whereas all the later stamps supplied by Messrs. Nissen and Parker were perforated 15. We see from the list that only 1,000 of the six pence with the smaller perforation were sent out, which accounts for the scarcity of this variety. The sheets of the one penny, four pence, and six pence first printed contained 25 stamps arranged in five horizontal rows of five. The only sheets of the one shilling I have seen consist of the variety with wide red border, and I am unable to say whether they belong to the first or second printing. These sheets contain only 20 stamps in four horizontal rows of five. As I have already explained, new transfers were made for each subsequent printing, so it is not surprising to find the number of stamps to the sheets sometimes varying. This was the case with the lot of one penny forwarded on October 25th, 1870, for Mr. Maycock possesses an entire sheet of this consignment, showing only 12 stamps in four horizontal rows of three. Whether this latter arrangement was continued in the future printings of the one penny by Messrs. Nissen and Parker, I am unable to say.

One of the most interesting questions connected with the early stamps is the reason why there should have been two varieties for the one shilling, i.e., that with, and that without the coloured border. Mr. Maycock has, unfortunately, been unable to obtain any definite information upon this point. It is quite certain that the 11,000 stamps sent out on July 12th, 1867, embraced the two varieties, as both are described in the Philatelic Journals of that year. Mr. Maycock suggests, and I am inclined to agree with him, that the 10,000 stamps sent to St. Thomas may have been already printed and made up for despatch, and the stone from which they had been printed cleaned; when a request for a supply to be forwarded to Sir Arthur Rumbold was sent in, and a fresh transfer was made without the wide red margin. It would appear that only small proportions, comparatively speaking, of the important quantities sent in the first two consignments were put for a time into circulation, and a considerable stock on hand must have been overlooked, as within twelve months of the parcel of July, 1867, a fresh supply of all four values was ordered from England. In the uncertainty as to which variety of the one shilling was preferred, 1,000 of each kind appear to have been printed, as the book from which the numbers are taken contains two separate entries of 1,000 each for the one shilling, sent in the consignment of June 6th, 1868. No further supply of this value was afterwards printed by Messrs. Nissen and Parker. It will be seen from the above that Mr. Maycock and I both think it probable that there were only 2,000 of the one shilling without the coloured border, i.e., 1,000 of the lot sent on July 12th, 1867, and 1,000 of the parcel forwarded on June 6th, 1868, and that there were 11,000 of the other variety, i.e., 10,000 sent at the same date as the first lot without border, and 1,000 with the second. It is certain from the respective values of the two varieties that there were very many more printed with the wide red border than without, in fact, the other variety has become quite scarce of late years, and sells readily at from four to five times as much as the other. Again, we know there was a comparatively large stock of the stamps with border, on hand, even as late as the year 1888, as this variety was surcharged "4d." for use as a provisional fourpenny stamp, and the Postmaster of the Virgin Islands, Mr. E. J. Cameron, tells me that 2,500 were so surcharged, so part, if not all, of these stamps must belong to the first consignment sent out on July 12th, 1867, as there were only 2,000 one shilling, in all, forwarded after that date. Mr. Cameron further informs me that the surcharge on these one shilling stamps was applied in the Island of Antigua. He also adds that postage stamps were first issued in the Virgin Islands in 1866. If this was so, it must have been quite at the end of that year, as we see from the list that the first consignment only left England on November 26th, 1866.

The dies of all four values were handed to the Crown Agents of the Colony, London, on November 14th, 1876, and afterwards by them to Messrs. De la Rue and Co., who have since supplied all further stamps required by the Islands. As regards the stamps printed by the latter firm from Messrs. Nissen and Parker's dies, I have not seen an entire sheet of the one penny green watermarked Crown C.C., so I am unable to say how many stamps composed the sheet, but in those printed upon paper watermarked Crown C.A., the sheets of the one penny carmine and six pence lilac contain 24 stamps arranged in four horizontal rows of six, while the four pence pale red-brown, and the one shilling brown have likewise 24, but the stamps are arranged in three horizontal rows of eight.

REFERENCE LIST OF THE PHILATELIC SOCIETY, LONDON.

Issue I. December, 1866.

Two values. Lithographed by Messrs. Nissen and Parker, of London, on stoutish white and yellowish wove paper, unwatermarked. Yellowish gum, machine perforated. Designs: ONE PENNY. Allegorical female figure, the head surrounded with a halo, holding in her right hand a lamp, in the left a spray of lily, surrounded by eleven lamps, upon a ground of horizontal lines within a narrow white oval band. A curved label above, and a straight label below, both with rounded ends, contain respectively the name of the Colony and the value in small coloured block letters. White blocks in the top corners contain a rosace. The remainder of the stamp is filled in with reticulations, and two plain outer lines of colour complete the design. SIX PENCE. The central design is the same as that of the one penny in a rectangle on a wavy lined background. Straight shaded labels with fancy ends are at the top and bottom of the stamp, and contain the name of the Colony and value in coloured block letters. Broad side borders are filled in with rosaces and reticulations, and two plain outer lines as before complete the design. Shape, upright rectangular. (*Illustrations* 306, 307.)

T. "VIRGIN ISLANDS." B. "ONE PENNY." "SIX PENCE."

A.—*Perforated* 12.

1d., pale to very deep green and yellow-green (shades).
6d., rose to carmine (shades).

B.—*Perforated* 15. (1868).

1d., yellow-green (shades).
6d., rose   („   )

Remarks.—Proofs upon thin white card are known of both values in the respective colours of the issue, and also of the six pence printed in ultramarine and sage-green.

Issue II. July, 1867.

Two values. Lithographed by Messrs. Nissen and Parker, on stoutish white and tinted wove papers, unwatermarked. Yellowish gum, machine perforated 15. Designs: FOURPENCE. Allegorical full faced female figure with arms folded on breast and aureole of eight stars, standing on a globe surrounded by ocean, upon a plain ground enframed in a beaded circle. Straight coloured labels above, and below, contain the name of the Colony and the value, respectively, in uncoloured block letters. Square blocks in the two lower corners contain rosaces. The design is completed by two outer lines of colour. ONE SHILLING. Central figure in black similar to the preceding value, with rays of light from behind, on a coloured ground with a kind of brick wall pattern. A curved coloured label above, and a straight coloured label below, contain as before the name of the Colony and the value in white block letters. The outside frame of the stamp is 1½ mm. from the inner portion of the design, and presents three varieties :—

A. Two fine coloured lines ; B. A single coloured line ; and C. A coloured border 2 mm. wide. Shape, large upright rectangular.

T. "VIRGIN ISLANDS." D. "FOUR PENCE." "ONE SHILLING."

4d., brownish-red on rose tinted paper. (*Illustration* 308.)
1s., carmine and black, on white paper. Variety A. (*Illustration* 309.)
1s.,   „   „   „   „   „   „   „   B. („   310.)
1s.,   „   „   „   „   „   „   „   C. („   311.)
Variety C. is known without the central black figure.

Remarks.—Variety A., is difficult to find, showing the two lines distinctly apart at all four sides of the stamp, as the lines frequently run into each other and form only one, at some portion of the frame. It is probable that Variety B., is due to a defective transfer, or to wearing of the die, the colour thus running and joining the two lines into one. Proofs, upon thin white card, are known of the four pence, printed in red-vermilion, and also in sea-green ; and of the one shilling (Variety B.) in the colour of the issue, as well as in deep vermilion, including the figure.

Issue III. 1879.

One value. The one penny of Issue I., printed by Messrs. De la Rue and Co., of London, upon medium white wove paper, watermarked Crown C.C. White gum, machine perforated 14. (*Illustration* 306.)

1d., green (shades).

Issue IV. 1880.

Two values. Designed and surface-printed by Messrs. De la Rue and Co., on white surfaced paper, watermarked Crown C.C. White gum, machine perforated 14. Design: Diademed profile of Queen Victoria to left on ground of horizontal lines within a single lined octagon, straight white labels at top and bottom are inscribed with the name of the Colony and the value, respectively, in coloured block letters. The side borders each contain a row of white diamonds, and floriate ornaments fill the spandrels. The labels containing the name and value are, as in the case of other West Indian Colonies, printed separately from the rest of the design. Shape, upright rectangular. (*Illustrations* 312, 313.)

T. "VIRGIN ISLANDS." B. "ONE PENNY." "2½ PENNY."
(Sept., 1880) 1d., green   (shades).
(March, 1880) 2½d., red-brown („)

Issue V. 1883.

One value. A halfpenny value of the same De la Rue type, as the preceding issue, came into use about June, 1883. Watermark Crown C.A. Machine perforated 14. (*Illustration* 312.)

T. "VIRGIN ISLANDS."   D. "HALFPENNY."

½d., buff-yellow (shades).

Issue VI. 1883-84.

Three values. The stamps of Issues IV. and V., changed in colour. Watermark Crown C.A. Machine perforated 14. (*Illustrations* 312, 313.)

(Nov., 1883) ½d., green   (shades).
(15th Sept., 1883) 1d., bright rose („)
(Sept., 1884) 2½d., ultramarine („)

Issue VII. End of 1887.

Two values. The four pence and six pence of Issues I. and II., printed in new colours by Messrs. De la Rue and Co., upon white wove paper, watermarked Crown C.A. Machine perforated 14. (*Illustrations* 307, 308.)

4d., orange-red (shades).
6d., violet-slate („)

Issue VIII. July, 1888.

One value. The one shilling of Issue II., *Variety C.*, Surcharged " 4d." in violet aniline ink, as a provisional issue. The numeral measures 6½ mm. and the letter " D " 4 mm. in height. Unwatermarked white wove paper. Machine perforated 15. (*Illustration* 314.)

4d., violet surcharge, on 1s. carmine and black.

Issue IX. 1889.

Two values. The one penny of Issue I., and the one shilling of Issue II., *Variety B.*, printed by Messrs. De la Rue and Co., upon white wove paper, watermarked Crown C.A. Machine perforated 14. (*Illustrations* 306, 310.)

(June, 1889) 1d., crimson (shades).
(Feb., 1889) 1s., brown („)

POSTCARDS.

Issue I. 1880.

One value. Designed and printed by Messrs. De la Rue and Co., upon medium light buff card. Size 121×87 mm., or 4⅘×3¾ inches. The design is the same as that of the first issue card of Antigua, except that the second line of the inscription is replaced by VIRGIN ISLANDS (ILES VIERGES). and the name of the Colony at the top of the stamp is changed. (*Illustration* 315.)

1½d., light brown (shades).

Issue VI. End of 1887.

Two values. Designed and printed by Messrs. De la Rue and Co., upon stout straw card. Size 139×88 mm., or 5½×3½ inches. The design is similar to the second issue cards of Antigua, with the exception of the modification of the name of the Colony mentioned above. (*Illustration* 316.)

1d., carmine   (slight shades).
1½d., red-brown („   „   )

Remarks.—The postal emissions of this Colony became obsolete at the end of October, 1890, when a uniform set for all the various Islands composing the Leeward Group, took their place.

ADDENDA.

Page 102. JAMAICA. POST CARDS.

Issue II.

It should be stated that a later printing of the one penny value, is found upon *straw* card.

Issue V. October, 1890.

One value. Provisional issue. The one penny value of Issue II., printed upon straw card, having the stamp surcharged across the lower part HALF-PENNY in block letters, in a straight line, measuring $21\frac{1}{2}$ mm. in length, the letters being 3 mm. in height. (*Illustration.*)

½d., black surcharge, on 1d. blue.

Remarks.—At the time when the list of Jamaica postcards was drawn up, it was not known whether the above card constituted a genuine variety, and it was therefore omitted from the list. It has since been ascertained that the card was undoubtedly issued as a provisional halfpenny value.

NOTE BY E. D. BACON.

With reference to what I said on *page* 121, about the probability of British Postage Stamps having been employed in other Colonies besides Jamaica, St. Lucia, and British Guiana, before the transfer of the Post Offices to Local Governments : I find in the *Fifth Report of the Postmaster General of Great Britain*, dated April 7th, 1859, the following paragraph, which leaves no doubt that the same course *was* pursued in other instances. "It having been found that the use of English postage stamps at Malta, Gibraltar, and Constantinople led to no forgery, the privilege has been extended to the British West Indies, and to the Foreign ports touched at by the Mail Packets on the Western Coast of Africa. It is obvious that such an arrangement is applicable only when the whole of the postage belongs to the British Post Office."

1   *2*   *3*   *8*   *9*

10   *11*   *12*   *4*   *13*   *14*

UNION POSTALE UNIVERSELLE

ANTIGUA (ANTIGOA)

POST CARD

THE ADDRESS ONLY TO BE WRITTEN ON THIS SIDE.

5

UNION POSTALE UNIVERSELLE

ANTIGUA (ANTIGOA)

POST CARD

THE ADDRESS ONLY TO BE WRITTEN ON THIS SIDE.

6

UNION POSTALE UNIVERSELLE

ANTIGUA (ANTIGOA)

POST CARD

THE ADDRESS ONLY TO BE WRITTEN ON THIS SIDE.

7

15

UNION POSTALE UNIVERSELLE

BAHAMAS

THE ADDRESS ONLY TO BE WRITTEN ON THIS SIDE.

16

UNION POSTALE UNIVERSELLE

BAHAMAS

THE ADDRESS ONLY TO BE WRITTEN ON THIS SIDE.

17

THE ANNEXED CARD IS INTENDED
FOR THE ANSWER
LA CARTE CI-JOINTE EST DESTINÉE
A LA REPONSE.

■

BARBADOS
5 SHILLINGS
18

19

BARBADOS
20

BARBADOS
ONE SHILLING
21

BARBADOS
THREE PENCE
22

BARBADOS
23

BARBADOS
2½ PENNY
24

BARBADOS
ONE SHILLING
25

29

BARBADOS REGISTRATION FEE
FOUR PENCE
30

BARBADOS REGISTRATION
31

26

R REGISTERED LETTER.
THIS LETTER MUST BE GIVEN TO | AN OFFICER OF THE POST
OFFICE TO BE REGISTERED AND A | RECEIPT OBTAINED FOR IT.

THE STAMP
TO PAY THE
POSTAGE
MUST BE
PLACED HERE

27

R REGISTERED LETTER.
THIS LETTER MUST BE GIVEN TO | AN OFFICER OF THE POST OFFICE
TO BE REGISTERED AND A | RECEIPT OBTAINED FOR IT.

THE STAMP
TO PAY THE
POSTAGE
MUST BE
PLACED HERE

28

This Wrapper may only be used for Newspapers, or for
such documents as are allowed to be sent at the Book-rate
of postage, and must not enclose any letter or communication
of the nature of a letter (whether separate or otherwise).
If this rule be infringed, the packet will be charged as a letter.

32

This Wrapper may only be used for Newspapers, or for
such documents as are allowed to be sent at the Book-rate
of postage, and must not enclose any letter or communication
of the nature of a letter (whether separate or otherwise).
If this rule be infringed, the packet will be charged as a letter.

33

34

UNION POSTALE UNIVERSELLE

BARBADOS—(BARBADE)

THE ADDRESS ONLY TO BE WRITTEN ON THIS SIDE.

UNION POSTALE UNIVERSELLE

BARBADOS (BARBADE)

POST CARD

THE ADDRESS ONLY TO BE WRITTEN ON THIS SIDE.

35

UNION POSTALE UNIVERSELLE.

BARBADOS.—(BARBADE.)

THE ADDRESS ONLY TO BE WRITTEN ON THIS SIDE

36

UNION POSTALE UNIVERSELLE.

BARBADOS--[BARBADE.]

THE ADDRESS ONLY TO BE WRITTEN ON THIS SIDE.

37

UNION POSTALE UNIVERSELLE.

BARBADOS.—(BARBADE)

THE ADDRESS ONLY TO BE WRITTEN ON THIS SIDE

38

POST ✠ CARD

BARBADOS

THE ADDRESS ONLY TO BE WRITTEN ON THIS SIDE.

39

UNION POSTALE UNIVERSELLE

BARBADOS (BARBADE)

POST ✠ CARD

THE ADDRESS ONLY TO BE WRITTEN ON THIS SIDE

40

UNIVERSAL POSTAL UNION.

BERMUDA, *BERMUDA POST OFFICE* LES. ISLES BERMUDES.

Post Card.

Only the address to be written on this side.

41

42 43 44 45 46 47

48 49 50 51 52 53

UNIVERSAL POSTAL UNION.

BERMUDA,  LES ISLES

BERMUDES.

54

Post Card.

Only the address to be written on this side.

POST ✦ CARD

BERMUDA

THE ADDRESS ONLY TO BE WRITTEN ON THIS SIDE.

55

UNIVERSAL POSTAL UNION.

BRITISH GUIANA   GUYANE BRITANNIQUE

56

Post Card.

Only the address to be written on this side.

ADDRESS

·

57 58 59 60

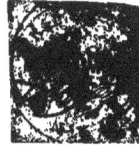

61 62 63

64 65 66 67

68 69

70 71 72 73 74 75

76 77 78 79 80 81

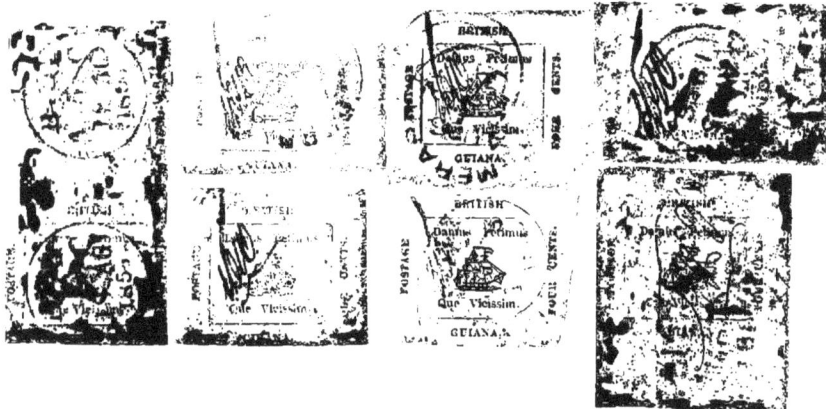

82

83

84

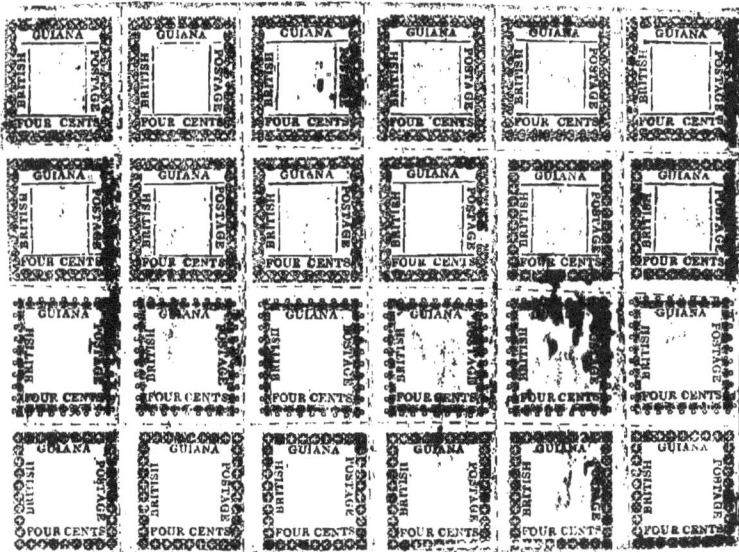

85

86   87   88   89   90   91

92   93   94   95   96   97

98   99   100   101   102   103

104   105   106   107   108   109

112

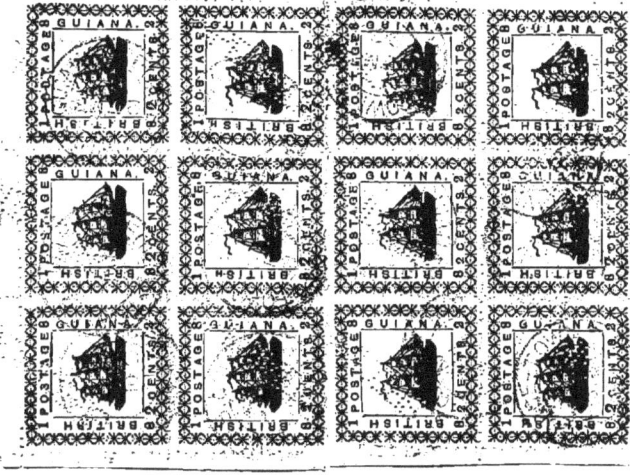

113

114

115   *116*   *117*   *118*   *119*   *120*

This Wrapper may only be used for Newspapers, or for
such documents as are allowed to be sent at the Book-rate
of postage, and must not enclose any letter or communication
of the nature of a letter (whether separate or otherwise).
If this rule be infringed, the packet will be charged as a letter.

 *121*

UNIVERSAL POSTAL UNION.

BRITISH GUIANA   GUYANE BRITANNIQUE    *122*

Post Card.

Only the address to be written on this side.

ADDRESS

BRITISH GUIANA REGISTERED LETTER.

THIS LETTER MUST BE GIVEN TO AN OFFICER OF THE POST OFFICE
TO BE REGISTERED, AND A RECEIPT BE OBTAINED FOR IT.

STAMP
FOR
POSTAGE
TO BE
PLACED
HERE

NAME AND ADDRESS
OF SENDER.

123

124   *125*   *126*   *127*   *128*   *129*

130   *131*   *132*   *133*   *134*   *135*

INLAND POST CARD

BRITISH  GUIANA

THE ADDRESS ONLY TO BE WRITTEN ON THIS SIDE.

 *136*

UNION POSTALE UNIVERSELLE

BRITISH GUIANA—GUYANE BRITANNIQUE

POST CARD

THE ADDRESS ONLY TO BE WRITTEN ON THIS SIDE.

 *137*

UNION POSTALE UNIVERSELLE

BRITISH HONDURAS (HONDURAS BRITANNIQUE)

POST CARD.

THE ADDRESS ONLY TO BE WRITTEN ON THIS SIDE.

 *138*

UNION POSTALE UNIVERSELLE

BRITISH HONDURAS (HONDURAS BRITANNIQUE)

POST CARD.

THE ADDRESS ONLY TO BE WRITTEN ON THIS SIDE.

 *139*

FALKLAND
PAID.
ISLANDS.

140 141 142 143 144 145

UNION POSTALE UNIVERSELLE

BRITISH HONDURAS (HONDURAS BRITANNIQUE)

POST CARD.

THE ADDRESS ONLY TO BE WRITTEN ON THIS SIDE.

146

UNION POSTALE UNIVERSELLE

DOMINICA (DOMINIQUE)

POST CARD

THE ADDRESS ONLY TO BE WRITTEN ON THIS SIDE.

147

UNION POSTALE UNIVERSELLE

DOMINICA (DOMINIQUE)

POST CARD

THE ADDRESS ONLY TO BE WRITTEN ON THIS SIDE

FOR COUNTRIES WITHIN 300 MILES SERVED BY BRITISH PACKETS.

148

UNION POSTALE UNIVERSELLE

DOMINICA (DOMINIQUE)

POST CARD

THE ADDRESS ONLY TO BE WRITTEN ON THIS SIDE.

149

UNION POSTALE UNIVERSELLE

FALKLAND ISLANDS (ILES FALKLAND)

POST CARD

THE ADDRESS ONLY TO BE WRITTEN ON THIS SIDE.

150

151   152   153   154   155   156

157   158   159   160   161   162

163   164   165   166   167   168

This Wrapper may only be used for Newspapers, or for
such documents as are allowed to be sent at the Book-rate
of postage, and must not enclose any letter or communication
of the nature of a letter (whether separate or otherwise).
If this rule be infringed, the packet will be charged as a letter.

169

UNION POSTALE UNIVERSELLE.

GRENADA. (DE GRENADA.)

THE ADDRESS ONLY TO BE WRITTEN ON THIS SIDE.

170

·

171   172   173   174   175   176

177   178   179   180   181   182

183   184   185   186   187

UNION POSTALE UNIVERSELLE

GRENADA (LA GRENADE)

POST CARD

THE ADDRESS ONLY TO BE WRITTEN ON THIS SIDE.

188

POST CARD

GRENADA

THE ADDRESS ONLY TO BE WRITTEN ON THIS SIDE.

189

UNION POSTALE UNIVERSELLE

GRENADA (LA GRENADE)

POST CARD

THE ADDRESS ONLY TO BE WRITTEN ON THIS SIDE.

190

This Wrapper may only be used for Newspapers, or for
such documents as are allowed to be sent at the Book-rate
of postage, and must not enclose any letter or communication
of the nature of a letter (whether separate or otherwise).
If this rule be infringed, the packet will be charged as a letter.

JAMAICA
HALFPENNY

*1*1

of the Post Office
obtained for it.

THE STAMP
TO PAY THE
POSTAGE
MUST BE
PLACED HERE

192

POST CARD.
JAMAICA

THE ADDRESS ONLY TO BE WRITTEN ON THIS SIDE.

JAMAICA
18 77
PAID
THREEPENCE

193

POST CARD.

JAMAICA.

THE ADDRESS ONLY TO BE WRITTEN ON THIS SIDE.

JAMAICA
18 77
PAID
THREEPENCE

POST CARD.

JAMAICA.

THE ADDRESS ONLY TO BE WRITTEN ON THIS...

JAMAICA
18 77
PAID
PENNY

Dr. B. Stevens Esq
Gov Medicie Offir.
Manchester

POST CARD.

JAMAICA.

THE ADDRESS ONLY TO BE WRITTEN ON THIS SIDE.

JAMAICA
18 77
PAID
HALFPENNY

POST CARD.

JAMAICA.

THE ADDRESS ONLY TO BE WRITTEN ON THIS SIDE.

JAMAICA
18 77
PAID
ONE PENNY

J. G. Vaughan Esqr
Superintendent Lunatic Home

POST CARD. JAMAICA. THE ADDRESS ONLY TO BE WRITTEN ON THIS SIDE.

UNIVERSAL POSTAL UNION. POST CARD. JAMAICA. THE ADDRESS ONLY TO BE WRITTEN ON THIS SIDE.

POST CARD. JAMAICA. THE ADDRESS ONLY TO BE WRITTEN ON THIS SIDE.

POST CARD. JAMAICA. THE ADDRESS ONLY TO BE WRITTEN ON THIS SIDE.

```
┌─────────────────────────────────────────────────┐
│ UNIVERSAL POSTAL UNION                            │
│ POST  [crest]  CARD.                              │
│         JAMAICA                                   │
│ THE ADDRESS ONLY TO BE WRITTEN ON THIS SIDE.      │
└─────────────────────────────────────────────────┘
```

202

UNION POSTALE UNIVERSELLE

JAMAICA (JAMAÏQUE)

POST [crest] CARD

THE ADDRESS ONLY TO BE WRITTEN ON THIS SIDE.

203

This Wrapper may only be used for Newspapers, or for
such documents as are allowed to be sent at the Book-rate
of postage, and must not enclose any letter or communication
of the nature of a letter (whether separate or otherwise).
If this rule be infringed, the packet will be charged as a letter.

204

UNION POSTALE UNIVERSELLE

LEEWARD ISLANDS (ILES SOUS LE VENT)

POST [crest] CARD

THE ADDRESS ONLY TO BE WRITTEN ON THIS SIDE.

205

UNION POSTALE UNIVERSELLE

MONTSERRAT (MONSERRAT)

POST [crest] CARD

THE ADDRESS ONLY TO BE WRITTEN ON THIS SIDE.

206

207 208 209 210 211 212 213

214 215 216 217 218

220

219

223

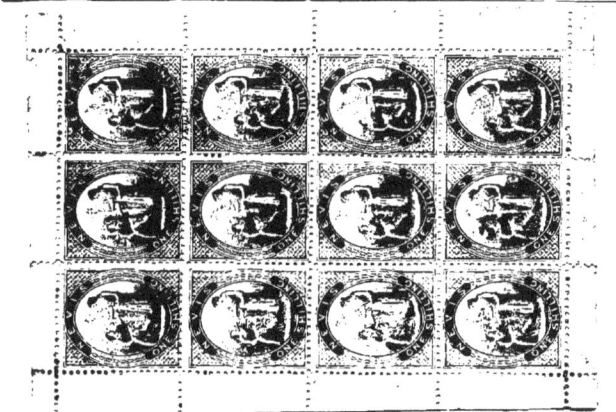

222

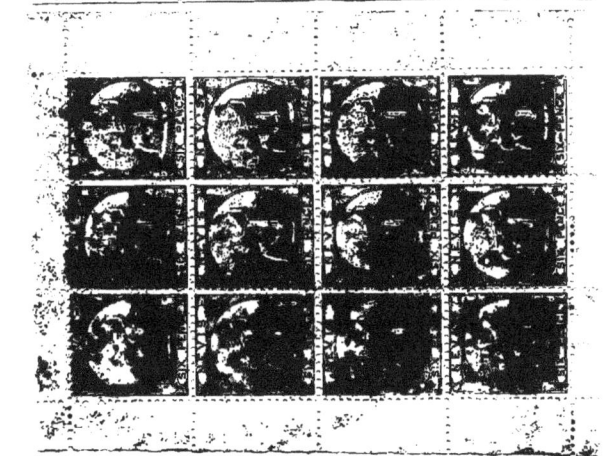

221

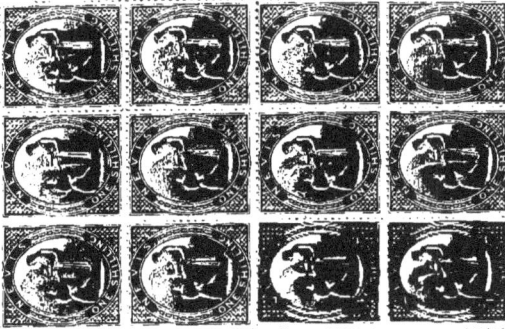

226

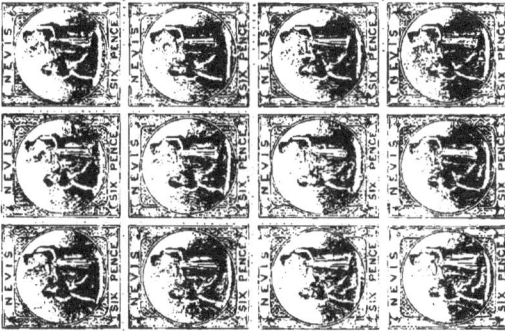

225

224

227

228

229

230

231

232

UNION POSTALE UNIVERSELLE

MONTSERRAT (MONSERRAT)

POST CARD

THE ADDRESS ONLY TO BE WRITTEN ON THIS SIDE.

233

UNION POSTALE UNIVERSELLE

NEVIS

POST CARD

THE ADDRESS ONLY TO BE WRITTEN ON THIS SIDE.

234

UNION POSTALE UNIVERSELLE

NEVIS

POST CARD

THE ADDRESS ONLY TO BE WRITTEN ON THIS SIDE.

235

UNION POSTALE UNIVERSELLE

St. CHRISTOPHER (St. CHRISTOPHE)

POST CARD

THE ADDRESS ONLY TO BE WRITTEN ON THIS SIDE.

236

UNION POSTALE UNIVERSELLE

St. CHRISTOPHER (St. CHRISTOPHE)

POST CARD

THE ADDRESS ONLY TO BE WRITTEN ON THIS SIDE.

237

238   239   240   241   242   243

This Wrapper may only be used for Newspapers, or for
such documents as are allowed to be sent at the Book-rate
of postage, and must not enclose any letter or communication
of the nature of a letter (whether separate or otherwise).
If this rule be infringed, the packet will be charged as a letter.

244

UNION POSTALE UNIVERSELLE
Sᴛ. LUCIA (Sᴛᴇ. LUCIE)

POST   CARD

THE ADDRESS ONLY TO BE WRITTEN ON THIS SIDE.

245

UNION POSTALE UNIVERSELLE
ST. VINCENT (ST. VINCENT)

POST   CARD

THE ADDRESS ONLY TO BE WRITTEN ON THIS SIDE.

246

UNION POSTALE UNIVERSELLE
ST. VINCENT (ST. VINCENT)

POST   CARD

THE ADDRESS ONLY TO BE WRITTEN ON THIS SIDE.

247

248   249   250   251   252   253

254   265   256   257   258   259

260   261   262   263   264   266

266   267   268   269   270   271

272   273   274   275   276   277

278   279   280   281   282   283

284   285   286   287   288   289

UNION POSTALE UNIVERSELLE

TOBAGO (TABAGO)

POST CARD

THE ADDRESS ONLY TO BE WRITTEN ON THIS SIDE.

TOBACO
PENNY HALFPENNY

290

TRINIDAD ONE PENNY

293

TRINIDAD HALFPENNY

292

This Wrapper may only be used for Newspapers, or for such documents as are allowed to be sent at the Book-rate of postage, and must not enclose any letter or communication of the nature of a letter (whether separate or otherwise). If this rule be infringed, the packet will be charged as a letter.

This Wrapper may only be used for Newspapers, or for such documents as are allowed to be sent at the Book-rate of postage, and must not enclose any letter or communication of the nature of a letter (whether separate or otherwise). If this rule be infringed, the packet will be charged as a letter.

FOR REGISTRATION ONLY

291

This Wrapper may only be used for Newspapers, or for such documents as are allowed to be sent at the Book-rate of postage, and must not enclose any letter or communication of the nature of a letter (whether separate or otherwise). If this rule be infringed, the packet will be charged as a letter.

294

TRINIDAD.

INLAND POST CARD.

STAMP.

THE ADDRESS ONLY TO BE WRITTEN ON THIS SIDE.

295

Postal Union—(Union Postale Universelle.)

TRINIDAD.

FOREIGN POST CARD.

THE ADDRESS ONLY TO BE WRITTEN ON THIS SIDE.

296

POSTAGE STAMP.

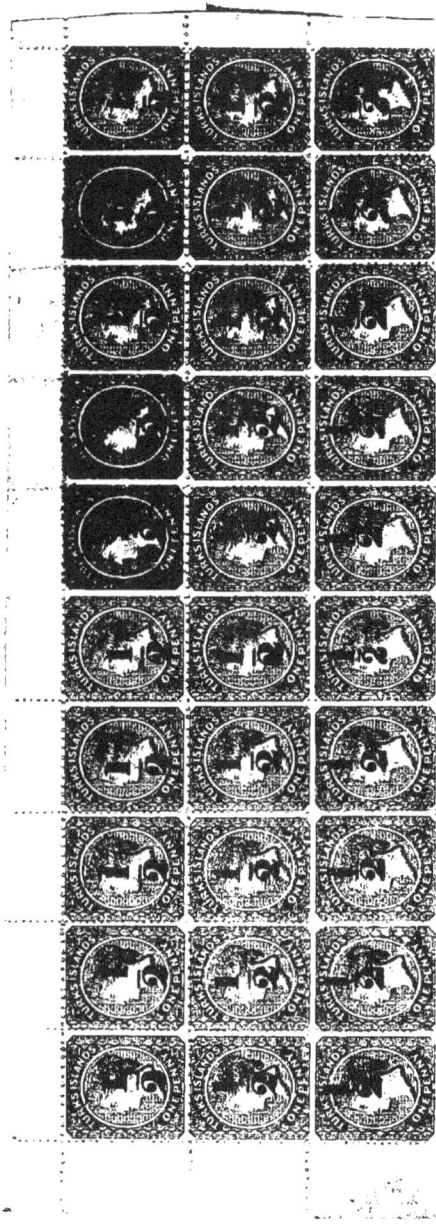

ONE PENNY.

UNION POSTALE UNIVERSELLE
TRINIDAD (TRINITÉ)

POST CARD

FOR COUNTRIES WITHIN 300 MILES SERVED BY BRITISH PACKETS,
THE ADDRESS ONLY TO BE WRITTEN ON THIS SIDE.

PENNY HALFPENNY

UNION POSTALE UNIVERSELLE
TRINIDAD (TRINITÉ)

POST CARD

THE ADDRESS ONLY TO BE WRITTEN ON THIS SIDE.

217

.

INLAND

POST  CARD

TRINIDAD

THE ADDRESS ONLY TO BE WRITTEN ON THIS SIDE.

300

UNION POSTALE UNIVERSELLE

TRINIDAD (TRINITÉ)

POST  CARD

THE ADDRESS ONLY TO BE WRITTEN ON THIS SIDE.

(FOR COUNTRIES WITHIN 300 MILES)

301.

UNION POSTALE UNIVERSELLE

TRINIDAD (TRINITÉ)

POST  CARD

THE ADDRESS ONLY TO BE WRITTEN ON THIS SIDE.

302.

UNION POSTALE UNIVERSELLE

TRINIDAD (TRINITÉ)

POST  CARD

THE ADDRESS ONLY TO BE WRITTEN ON THIS SIDE.

(FOR INDIA AND COUNTRIES IN THE EAST
VIA UNITED KINGDOM)

303.

UNION POSTALE UNIVERSELLE

TURKS ISLANDS (ILES DE TURC)

POST  CARD

THE ADDRESS ONLY TO BE WRITTEN ON THIS SIDE.

304.

305 306 307 308 309

310 311 312 313 314

UNION POSTALE UNIVERSELLE

VIRGIN ISLANDS (ÎLES VIERGES)

POST 🛡 CARD

THE ADDRESS ONLY TO BE WRITTEN ON THIS SIDE.

315

UNION POSTALE UNIVERSELLE

VIRGIN ISLANDS (ÎLES VIERGES)

POST 🛡 CARD

THE ADDRESS ONLY TO BE WRITTEN ON THIS SIDE.

316

www.ingramcontent.com/pod-product-compliance
Lightning Source LLC
Chambersburg PA
CBHW030400270326
41926CB00009B/1190